SUMMER IN
SCOTLAND

Jashinghorn

Also by
JOHN R. ALLAN
Farmer's Boy
Down on the Farm (a book for children)

SUMMER IN SCOTLAND

by

JOHN R. ALLAN

*With 5 decorated maps
and endpapers by*
C. W. BACON
And 8 plates

METHUEN & CO. LTD. LONDON
36 Essex Street, Strand, W.C.2

First published in 1938

PRINTED IN GREAT BRITAIN

CHAPTERS

ILLUSTRATIONS

DECORATED MAPS

SUMMER IN
SCOTLAND

CHAPTER ONE : INTRODUCTION—NOTES
FOR THE ROAD

THIS is a personal book written for those who may wish to know something about life in our curious country.

Now I know there have been several books written on this subject during the last ten years and you may think enough has been said about it. But while a great deal has been said about the scenery of the more picturesque parts and about the habits of the more picturesque inhabitants, some districts have been overlooked, and those contain more than half of the people. So one may guess that the books have been a little incomplete. Besides, many of them have been written in a convention that Scotland is wholly beautiful and everything, except Glasgow, has received the gloss of glamour. While those books may bring tears of longing to exiled Scotsmen and romantical strangers, they are something less than satisfactory to those of us who remain at home. They show us a picture of Scotland rather like those of the Landseer school in which some woolly Highland cattle are posed knee-deep in a bog under birch trees with hazy mountains in the background. Now we can't deny that much of our country is bog and that there are many tedious mountains, but we do think it a little unfair to imply that the chief inhabitants are Highland cattle.

We get equally impatient with books in which we are presented as a comic race wholly taken up with religion, whisky and small change. We are indeed comic, being human; but not more comic than, say, the English from whom we have borrowed a number of absurdities. So we

3

dare to be dissatisfied with some of the books that have been written about us, not because they misrepresent us but because they do not present us at all. Neither their country nor their people are recognizable as Scotland or the Scots at the present time. They deal in the stock figures of a journalistic convention.

Now I wouldn't dare claim that this book will contain the absolute truth. Writing is a personal business and everything the writer sees is subtly distorted by his own personality. So I can't claim to do more than offer a convention of my own in place of the others. But I do hope it will be a different one.

I have not tried to write another guide-book. There are plenty good ones already that tell you about distances and gradients and hotels and places of historical interest. I have tried to make a running commentary that may supplement a guide-book, thinking of my own needs when I have been a traveller. I have spent many days and weeks loitering about in rural England and have got fine pleasure thereby; but I have often wished that I had some companion, a native of the place, who could tell me the implications of the things I saw, and make the agreeable sort of conversation that grows out of the ground you stand on. That is the service I would like to do for the visitor to Scotland.

Therefore this is not a detailed picture of Scottish life. It is written to a plan in so far as the itinerary begins at Berwick-upon-Tweed, follows the East Coast to Dingwall, goes west to Ullapool, down through the Highlands to Glasgow, then along the south-west and the Borders to Carter Bar. But that plan is quite casual. I have followed the road, remembering the times I have passed that way, and whenever something came back to me with such force that I wished to speak about it, I wrote it down in this book. Thus the sight of Loch Leven recalled Mary Stewart and the memory of Kinross brought a disquisition on the building of pleasant towns. In that way I have tried to get the effect of conversation along the road by a person who lives in the country, to be the native who adds a personal flavour to the traveller's delight.

My job, as I have seen it, is not to show you Scotland but to add to your understanding and pleasure after you have seen. So I have not laboured to be unduly superlative. It is one of the best pleasures of travel to sharpen the wits, not to dull the senses; and there is nothing more dulling than to travel in a mood of determined enthusiasm. One often meets a company of travellers who have spent a fortnight in the Highlands and are so reduced that they can only repeat 'lovely, lovely, lovely', being exhausted with trying to appreciate all the beauty they were taught to expect. They are the victims of the kind of guide-book written with an ecstasy proper to advertising but alien to the responsibility of literature. It is unfair so to delude the stranger by leading him to expect more than we have and then exhaust himself in a determination to get his money's worth. Therefore I have tried not to overstate the good, hoping that you may find the reality better than you expected.

I have also exercised what survives in me of an old Scots virtue-criticism, now condemned as 'greetin' (continually wailing about the state of affairs at home, with the implication that things are done better abroad). This is a curious development of modern times. The Scots have had some note for their narking wit, for applying a destructive intelligence to any state of affairs, public and private. But nowadays we are more known for a determined complacency and it is the fashion to say everything is for the best in Scotland. That complacency is significant because it is so desperately maintained that it must really be protection against a fear that many things are not so good. The results are often comic. I have been denounced, very effectively, by an old gentleman in a public meeting because I dared to write that January in Scotland is usually wet and cold. That was, he said, just greetin; although there was a lively gale that night and rain had left many fine pools on the carse around my home. If I must write (which he seemed to think deplorable) then I should point out only the beautiful things in Scotland. That is a very common attitude now.

It is one that I, being young, find intolerable. There are two things comely about a man—a fine scorn in youth and a deep humility in age. Any country needs both at any time and Scotland needs them badly now. If I could think of myself always as an agent for a travel company I might write of Scotland as a tartan paradise. But I have to live in Scotland and it becomes a little dishonest always to praise the bright side when one is increasingly conscious of the amount of truth that lies on the other. That is not confined to Scotland. In all countries and at all times there have been some annoyed by the difference between what is and what might be. They have never been slow in pointing out that difference. Fortunately there are still a few constitutional narkers left in Scotland.

Let me not obtrude those family matters. I'm not an effective narker myself, being of an easy nature, but I have thought it only fair to tell you, as near as I could, what I do think and feel about the country I live in. If I have annoyed any others who live in that country, I am sorry; but not repenting, for it is possible that this book may influence some one to come to Scotland and I have a responsibility to raise no hopes that the country cannot satisfy. I have no obligation to overpraise, because I am not selling Scotland—I am only trying to hire myself.

Just one word about preparations for visiting us. The venture is not comparable to a trek through Central Africa. There are many quite good hotels, excellent shops, passable roads, A.A. Scouts and fast trains. The natives understand English, and some can even converse in French, German or Spanish. Therefore you do not need to bring stocks of food, or clothing or phrase-books.

Speaking of clothes, you may, if you please, wear a kilt of any tartan you fancy; and, should any Scotsman question your right to wear it, you should tell him, politely, to mind his own business. The only right to wear a kilt of any tartan is the receipt from the tailor, or his willingness to give you credit for it. Do not, however, wear a kilt if you need gallowses to hold it up; for the kilt demands a fine manly pair of hips and well-turned legs beneath it. On the other hand, too much generosity of nature is even more disastrous than too little.

And here, in case I forget, I might just mention something you may find useful. Our licensing laws are, like those of England, peculiar; but they give you one privilege that the English laws do not. A bona-fide traveller can have a limited quantity of excisable liquors at any hotel at any time in the twenty-four hours of a Sunday, so if you keep moving you can drink the whole round of the Scottish Sabbath. There are many bona-fide travellers in Scotland on that day.

One other thing. Perhaps you like to read a few books about the country you are visiting. May I suggest three that will maybe give you pleasure and also tell you about Scotland. Two are *Cloud Howe* and *Sunset Song* by Lewis Grassic Gibbon. The third is *Return to Scotland* by Moray Maclaren. The first two are novels about the Lowlands, written in a grand passion: the third, which ends in the remote beauty of the western islands, is the best account of any journey in Scotland that I have read.

Now come to Scotland and see how the Scots live when they stay at home.

Acknowledgment

For the story about the Irishman on page 31, I am very greatly indebted to Mr. Ian Macpherson, the author of *Shepherds Calendar* and *Land of our Fathers.*

2

CHAPTER TWO: GEORDIE AND THE LION

M<small>EN</small> think in images; therefore when they speak about their country by name they have some image of it in their minds. Germany is a Nordic god armed with thunder-bolts against Israel; France a militant young woman with a sword in one hand and the franc in the other; England a stout bourgeois conscious of an imperial destiny. Now who shall stand beside them for Scotland? Some people would say William Wallace, some Robert Burns, some Charles Edward Stewart. A few may still worship the lion so nobly rampant in the Scottish flag; but others see that fiery beast grown old, a shameful trouper in the English circus. So different men have different ideas of Scotland and express their ideas in diverse language. The image that comes oftenest to my mind, when people speak about the Scottish nation, is the face of a ploughman I knew in Aberdeenshire many years ago.

Geordie was a broad man. His face was broad. His shoulders were broad and his bottom completely filled his ample trousers. He had been a man of inexhaustible strength and pleasure in his youth. He had got drunk on Saturday nights; he had fought at fairs and markets; he had wakened up in jail without knowing how he had got there. He had been a great man for the girls. No road was too long, no roof too steep, for his enterprise when he was twenty if there was a girl to be cozened out of modesty before the morning. He thought little of a long day's work and a long night's play; and, like a force of nature, he was feared throughout the country-side.

But he would have been about fifty when I knew him

8

first. The fire and the fury had gone out of him. He was still a splendid hind. He could still work his ten hours stooking or forking or building ricks through the long windless day. Other men grew tired or lost their tempers or had strange moods born of the sultry sun. Geordie's humour never changed. He worked at a steady pace that never varied between morning and night, a pace that required no effort of will but was as easy and as regular as a quiet tide. So with his moods. He was always ready for amusement. He could go on talking all day long about his pleasures at fair and market. He would tease the other men about the ludicrous adventures they met among the girls and, whenever a victim was driven out of patience by that teasing, he would produce some yet more ludicrous adventure of his own. Then the men would lean on their forks, with their mouths open, as if to catch the full savour of the romance; and when Geordie reached the climax of his tale, a climax with a shot-gun or a broken bed in it, there would be a sound of godless laughter in the hay-field. He was a splendid gossip. There was malice in his talk of course and the cruelty that is indigenous to the East of Scotland; but there was also something that gave it a touch of art, for it sprang from an endless curiosity. That curiosity was shared in some degree by all the men. They had a tireless interest in the vagaries of human kind; and if that interest was usually expressed in bawdy terms it was surely another proof that the people of the north-east were much given to an over-fruitful passion.

Now to my mind Geordie was the perfect figure of the man who went adventuring beneath the moon. I was very young then, and in my ignorance I thought the pursuit of women must be the greatest of all earthly pleasures. So Geordie was a kind of god to me—a man who pursued and captured women and loved them and went his way. He was completely above all moral laws. He was a glorious pagan. He was free.

Then one night I saw him in other circumstances and I began to wonder. I was taking a walk across the pastures about the time when the rooks were flying home to their nests in the high woods. It was the kind of night that softens the austerities of an East Coast summer day. The sun had gone down and its frequent companion the east wind had gone down with it. An hour of enchanting beatitude attended the coming of dark. The rooks went flighting home in threes and fours across the west. An owl called gently from the wood. A little dew on the grass filled the air with sweetness. There was, I remember, a field of tares and the smell of the bean flowers was strangely disturbing. To make an end of this matter it wasn't a night for a young man to be alone in: though, heaven knows, perhaps more dangerous if the young man had had company. I thought of Geordie, of what he would have done when he was my age and the beans were in flower, then ' Oh Heavens ' I said to myself, ' how much more splendid a man he is than I will ever dare to be.'

While that idea was still in my head I passed the cottage where Geordie spent the hours that were not devoted to the work of the farm. There at his cottage door was the pagan himself. Ten hours in the turnip field had brought a little weariness into his once unwearied limbs. But there was small rest for Geordie. He was lying on a grassy bank beside his cottage surrounded by his children. Surrounded is hardly the word. The children flowed over him. They rolled on him, pounded him, tormented him with questions and complaints. If ever a man had been drowned by an excess of his own fertility he was the too happy man. They were not only his own children, but his children's children. Following the tradition of the country the elder daughters came home to have bairns as soon as they were of the age. Sons and grandsons, uncles and nieces, played happily together and as happily took what little Geordie had to give them. So he lay on the grassy bank trying to get a moment's peace and sometimes stirring himself to smack a bare brown bottom too impudently raised in the face of the sunset. That was the only protest he could make against such an excess of nature; and that was the harvest his old adventurings had brought him. It was a terrible warning to wantons.

' Gang hame, laddie, gang hame,' he said to me, ' and ye'll never come tae this.'

There had been a dreadful waste of sovereign virtues in his life. It was, at the very least, a pity that so much enterprise should have brought him only a cottage in a turnip field when he was fifty, that the begetting of children, once a glorious adventure, should have become an act of God to be attended with humorous resignation. Geordie, at fifty, had discovered the vanity of the things he had spent his youth on, but there were two things he never doubted —that it was better to be alive than dead; and that human life was sacred. Through all the miseries and humiliations of his life he retained his interest in the curious ways of human nature; in spite of his constant poverty he and his wife could always provide means to celebrate the rather hasty marriages of his children with a night of furious dancing; and in spite of the weariness that was creeping into his bones he not only tolerated all children, but loved them. In his old age he had none of the comforts that sweeten the loss of youth and passion. His life ended as it began, in the barest kind of poverty. Yet, although I have often heard him say that the world's gear is ill divided and that if some masters had to fend for themselves, they would starve in a twelvemonth, I seldom knew him bitter at the manifest injustice of the world. That was not due to stupidity; he had moments when he thought of splendid things beyond his power—of knowledge and wealth and the courts of kings. There were times when he knew that his life might have had a different end if he had been more careful in its beginning. He had had in him qualities that had not been fully realized in action, and it was too late before he came to the knowledge of what was in him. Then he could only make the best of a bad job. When that became too great a burden he died. I often think of him when people mention Scotland.

There is a lot of damned nonsense talked about Scotland, on both sides of the Border. Like most popular beliefs the various parts of this nonsense cancel each other, so that the intelligent observer might think there was no reality at all, that Scotland was only a kind of mirage, a trick of the infrequent sun upon the constant mists that hang beyond the Cheviot Hills. I have met Englishmen who did believe that all Scots were hardly civilized—that they wore the kilt and lived on oatmeal and indulged themselves in Highland dancing on every possible occasion. On the very same day other Englishmen have told me that of course the Scots are marvellously educated people, that even the poorest go to Universities, and that country roadmen can tell you the distance to the nearest public-house in excellent Latin. There is the kind of woman that looks at you with moist shining eyes and says that ' Scotland must be frightfully romantic '. There is the kind of old gentleman who believes that the gangsters of Glasgow are fully worse than the public enemies of Chicago. There are many good people who think that the Scots are a godly race who know the Bible, the Catechism and the Metrical Psalms by heart; and a few are convinced that every person beyond the Tweed is born debauched.

As with the people, so with the face of the country. The ' Land of brown heath and shaggy wood ' idea has gone round the world. I once met a quite intelligent Englishman who showed me a field of very indifferent wheat in Worcestershire and expected me to be uplifted by the sight of it, because, he said, there was so little cultivation in Scotland. The romantic novelists and the railway posters have created a fabulous Scotland composed of mountains, glens, moors, impoverished gentlemen, bare-kneed peasants, and the ghost of Bonnie Prince Charlie. That has little relation to the land that Geordie laboured in; nor has the popular idea of a Scotsman any relation to the kind of man that Geordie was. Yet, how many people have come to Scotland for a summer tour, have spent their fortnight among the Highlands, and have gone home again, sure that the romantic idea is the right one. Because the Highlands are deceiving. They have a fantastic beauty in the height of summer. The beauty is so complete and the larger works of nature so overwhelm the folk who live among them, that the traveller need never think of the natives except as incidentals to the scenery. The Highlands then are a breeding ground for illusion about Scotland.

Our picturesque ruins are another. Scotland is well supplied with castles, keeps, ruined abbeys, and desolate cloisters. Each of them has a custodian and a guide-book for the perpetuation of legends and the resources of both can be tapped for sixpence. A traveller who spends a week among those memorials of the past will go away with a fine illusion that the Scottish people spent a thousand years in endless killings, that fire and sword were our harrow and plough. These, then, are the images that many people see when they think of Scotland—a moor with deer on it and a line of sharp blue peaks against the horizon; a ruined keep perilously built on a rock above the water's edge; an abbey sacked by the English three, four hundred years ago; and Edinburgh Castle standing over the Capital like a memorial to all the country's illusions. There may be other parts of the country; in fact the travellers have seen them as they hurried from ruined abbey to desolate moor; but they have known to neglect them as dull, flat, uninteresting lands with no past and no romantic present.

That is just a little unfortunate, for the most interesting

part of the nation live in those neglected places. There they are neither overawed by the magnificent anarchy of nature nor lost in the glories of the remote past. They live and breed there and do their business, as men live in other parts of the world, but with this one difference that they are Scottish. It is in those neglected parts that the traveller may hope to find the real, the living Scotland—the Scotland where the native traditions have still some real vitality, the Scotland where the future will be born. Life in the ruins is dead: life in the Highlands is slowly dying: but in the Lothians, in Fife and Angus and Aberdeenshire, in Dumfries and the Stewartry of Kirkcudbright and in Ayrshire there is a native and enduring vitality that retains an enduring Scottish quality—Glasgow, Edinburgh, Dundee and Aberdeen, however standardized, have each some quality that cannot be found in any other place. And these—the farming counties, the manufacturing towns, the places where people are living in the present, not in the past—are the real Scotland. For me at least they are the only places worth writing about. There you will find Geordie and his children. And without Geordie Scotland can have no meaning, more than a picture postcard.

We are as our childhood made us, and I am a child of the industrious lowlands. Therefore I cannot be happy for long when I am away from the sight of growing crops, and dairy herds, and towns out of which strange inventions may come. Some years ago I had the rare fortune to live in an old house among the Ochil Hills, in the southern district of Perthshire. The house had been a fortified place in the wilder days of Scottish history: it was traditionally associated with the Douglases; and one could imagine that desperate events had shaped within the secret places of its walls. Its later years were peace. Though it was just a little grim, as it stood on the lower slopes of the hill, where the brackens met the meadow pasture, the feeling inside was quiet and domestic. It was also deliciously romantic. The main part of the house was a square tower with a winding circular staircase in the north-west corner. When you climbed the worn steps you found just one room on each floor of the tower—a square room, with a low roof and small square windows on the east and south and west. The walls were three feet thick. On the east side of the castle there was a low walled garden showing a few fine plum trees and some rabbit burrows as the extremes of its glory: and on the west side a steep bank ran swiftly down to a brown hill burn. A belt of fir trees sheltered the castle from the north, like the high collar of a cloak. The south was open to the sun and the western hills.

It was a quiet place, inside and out, except when the January winds came roaring down out of the north-east or the sheep were being clipped at the fank near-by. We could pass weeks there, seeing only the postman and the local tradesmen and the shepherd that walked the hills above us. Time passed as it were insensibly, with only the slow change of seasons to mark its passing. There never was such a place for quietness, in the heat of the noon when even the cuckoo was silent and in the evening when a curious glimmering half-light brought the hills like vast and friendly presences around our ancient tower. It was a place for quietness and freedom. From our back door we could walk for fifteen miles straight into the hills and no one questioned us, for there was no one but an occasional shepherd to see us. Yet it was not a lonely life. Although there were only thirty other houses in the six miles of the glen, the people were friendly, and there was always enough gossip to keep us wondering through the long winter. It was a good life in a setting of unspoiled beauty; intimate and charming when the river bank was gay with roses, magnificent when the morning sun gleamed on the snow-covered hills. But it was not enough. The sheep is neither an engaging nor beautiful companion.

At the end of two years I was sick of the empty wastes of bracken and sour thin pasture. I wanted crops, and herds of cattle, and the sight of earth turned over by the plough in spring.

The glen was beautiful in one kind of way, but after two years of it I saw more heartening beauty in a plough-man spreading dung and in a fine big field of turnips. The glen was beautiful; but you could see marks on the hills where houses had fallen into ruin a long time ago and you could suspect that others would follow; for the life of the glen seems to be ebbing away. How could those stony hills and all that weary pasture maintain a flourishing life ? I could not see the answer. I left the glen. I was sorry to part from the old house and the dignity of living in a castle; but I had been reared in the industrious farm lands and I could not be happy away from them. Up in the glen, looking across the hills from the small deep windows, I could have imagined myself a Highland gentleman, and even aspired to a tartan of my own, but I have little taste for gentility and I dislike the tartan. I returned to the Lowlands, to a house whence I could look across an orchard to a field of wheat and herds of dairy cows, and a colliery rising, as you might think, out of the very corn. Because that, to me, is the vital Scotland.

As Geordie stands, to me, for all Scotsmen, so the view from my window may be called a miniature of the face of Scotland. I live in a small village on the warm side of the Ochil Hills, three miles from Stirling. This is the centre of Scotland, and the view from my window contains something of all extremes. These are the elements that make up the view. First the orchard where my neigh-bour's cows lie under the apple trees with their long tails folded under their placid bodies, ecstatically ruminant in the heat of the July day. Then fields of level carse land, clay country, a heavy soil that is the devil to work in a wet year; but now it is wearing a crop of hay that would fall down under its own weight if it were not supported by its own luxuriance, like a crowd of drunken men who stand only because they are packed so tightly. Beyond the hay-fields there are patches of wheat, close ranks that bear themselves as stiff and unyielding as their native clay. There is a pasture in between the hay and the wheat where the store cattle graze, up to their bellies in the meadow grasses. All that middle distance is covered with shades of ripening green, all except a brick-red field of summer fallow, where a team of Clydesdale mares in the cultivator are raising a fine red dust upon the wind. Here and there farm-houses stand among trees, and a picturesque cottage with a tangled garden completes a delightful country scene.

An eighteenth-century poet could have made a pastoral about this country-side, by the addition of a few young ladies in elegant sun-bonnets. Those graces are absent. The winding gear and the refuse bing of a colliery rise immediately beyond the corn. A large number of those works in a small space is a total abomination, but this one has a singular appropriateness. Telephone wires and pylons can give a touch of civilized wonder to the desolate Highlands: so the one colliery brings a new wonder into the pastoral scene. All day long a series of dull noises come over the hay-field, the voice of labouring machinery become almost articulate through distance, a strange contrast to the lowing of the cows in the orchard or the whistle of the ploughman over in the summer fallow. And all day long trucks, made tiny by the distance, climb to the top of the bing and empty their load and descend again, each helping to build a little mountain that apes the ever-lasting hills around. Trains run by the colliery, expresses roaring down to Stirling and interminable lines of trucks that squeak along as if they had all eternity before them. The Forth sweeps round beyond the railway. Though the river is far from the sea it is near sea level, so it moves slowly, winding in many links, through the flat carse.

You can just see, through the afternoon haze, the bings of collieries along its banks and, far away, the chimneys of the industrial belt that runs by Falkirk into Lanarkshire.

So there is a kind of unity—the miners digging the coal from the foundations of the land where the corn grows so bravely—an interlocking of town and country, of modern craft and ancient husbandry. Though the unity has not always been achieved with the greatest possible regard for taste; and though it has often been inspired by the greediest possible regard for profit; still it is the basis of life as we know it. But there is one thing more. A small hill, the last outpost of the Ochils at the western end rises out of the carse about a mile from the colliery. The hill is not remarkable in itself, but it is crowned by an antique-looking tower, of great historical interest. For the field of Bannock-burn lies a little to the west, and the tower was erected as a memorial to Sir William Wallace, whose work for the liberation of Scotland was consummated by Robert Bruce upon that field. Some people may regret that Scotland was not also liberated from builders in imitation antique styles, but the victory of Bannockburn may excuse every-thing that has happened since. That is by the way. The hill with its memorial adds a little more of significance to those parts of the scene already described. For the hill redeems the carse, as Scotland is always redeemed from the dullness of a plain too far prolonged; and the Wallace Monument is a reminder of the vast amount of history that lies everywhere about us. The hill that looks on Bannock-burn and the Monument that stands to Wallace make a third part in the unity of coal and corn, and if you have a philosophic turn of mind you may see in them a con-tinuing purpose that runs through the centuries, even though it may sometimes run without any particular sense of direction.

Perhaps it is better to leave Wallace and his Monument to the past. We are concerned with the present. With

the farms and the colliery and the hinterland of industrial
Scotland as I can see them from my window. But there
is one more thing, the line of hills along each horizon.
Wherever you are in Scotland you see the hills—seldom
great mountains, but always a sheltering line up against all
the airts that the winds blow from. There is the real and
sudden contrast—the carses with rich farms, the plains with
rich manufactories; then the sweep of the hills with the
desolate moors behind them. On the hills perhaps a dying
life: down in the carses and the plain a richly diversified,
inveterately persevering life. The past is in the one: the
present is in the other. Let us see then the life of the
Lowlands—the brains and the passions behind the face of
Scotland.

CHAPTER THREE. THE ROAD TO EDINBURGH

THERE are four main ways into Scotland—by Carlisle; by the hill road over the Carter Bar; by Coldstream; or through the ancient town of Berwick-upon-Tweed. The first two must be avoided as highly dangerous and deceiving, for they pass sooner or later through the romantic Border hills and will deliver the traveller to all the popular illusions about Scotland—the brown heath, the shaggy wood, the ruined tower, Sir Walter Scott and the old nobility. Let him therefore travel by Berwick-upon-Tweed and keep his reason for the final assault of the Ross-shire hills that stand against the Western Sea.

I think Berwick-upon-Tweed is an excellent introduction to Scotland, and I say that knowing it is an English town. You see Berwick-upon-Tweed is very old. It was fought for by Scotland and England through many centuries and it is full of that mortal weakness called historical interest. But as far as I have ever been able to see, the people take a lively interest in the present. So you have a walled town that is medieval or older, enclosed by a wall, yet essentially modern in its way of life. The Coronation expresses go steaming past it across the high Border Bridge, sports cars roar through its medieval gate and the town girls are expert in all the latest scandals of Hollywood. Take away the wall and Berwick is only another modern little town built all anyhow upon an ancient foundation. Now that seems to me very true about Scotland. We have our city walls

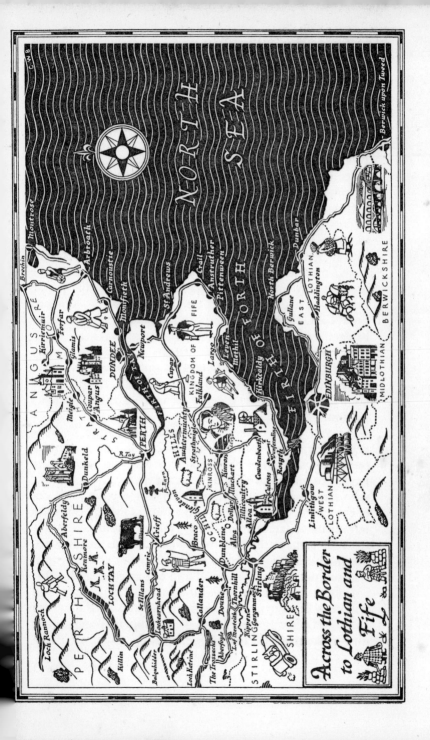

Across the Border to Lothian and Fife

—not stone and lime, but course after course of legend and history, all testifying to a past that made up in vitality what it lacked in peace. The vitality has continued to the present day, but design has been the grace so lacking in later years. Present-day Scotland had been built up all anyhow on the rubble of old foundations—her towns upon the ruins of older burghs, her customs upon the ruins of pagan and catholic morality. The people are living without a plan : Geneva and Hollywood and Heaven are of only relative importance to them as their confusions change from day to day : but they are determined to stay alive and would like to get some pleasure out of living. Therefore the traveller might take a look at Berwick-upon-Tweed—at the modern little town enclosed in its wall, having the sea on one side and the farm land on the other three. With its great background of history and legend; with its three bridges showing as it were the three stages of transport; with its shops and markets and public-houses; with its fields and farm-houses in the country beyond, it is typical of the Lowland part of Scotland. If it is a farewell to England it is a foretaste of much that lies beyond.

As you travel further up the coast road from Berwick you will come to the town of Dunbar and the castle that stands upon a grim headland affronting the sea. There have been many acts played out in the dark castle, and those who like that sort of thing may try to recapture the clink of the swords and the sway of the torches there. But there is something far more exciting around Dunbar—the fine red soil, perhaps the best in Scotland. This soil has unimaginable fertility. If you hold it between your fingers it will run out in grains as small and fine as gold, and that is apt, for it has a sovereign virtue in it. The Dunbar soil will grow anything. If there is any land on earth in which you could plant your seed and then sit down to smoke your pipe in the shade till harvest, which is the townsman's idea

of a farmer's life, it is the land around Dunbar, at the eastern
end of the Lothian plain.

For centuries it has been a grand country to farm in, and
life has been easier than in most other parts of Scotland.
You can see that in the people. The Lothian farmer is a
gentleman. He has a big farm and a fine house. He does
not work in the fields himself: he is not a dirty boot like
the smaller men of the poorer north. Just as this has
always been the most English part of Scotland, so the
Lothian farmer has an English air about him. He has a
taste for sport and contract bridge and may even hunt the
fox. That is not true of all the Lothian farmers; not by
any means; but, unlike most people in Scotland, the
farmers in this plain have had money in their pockets for
generations. Of course they have not passed on to their
servants any more of that money than was their due.
Though the Lothian servant may have a higher standard of
living than a ploughman in Aberdeenshire, it is not in
proportion to the excessive goodness of the soil. Thus the
traveller will notice that the farm cottages are hardly as well
found as the farm-houses and that the farm servants lack the
ease that goes with inheritance. But of course he will know
that is just the natural order of things, though he may be
surprised to find it in a country where one man is said to
be as good as another. However, one is continually meeting little paradoxes of that kind wherever one goes and the
traveller should be advised not to question any that he may
find in Scotland.

People have written books about the Lothians—the
West, the Mid and the East—romantic books full of feast-
ings and killings and the unhappy transits of the Scottish
Kings. All roads in this part lead to England or back
again, and for a thousand years there has been a steady
traffic in both directions. The southward journey has
always been favoured by the Scots, for plunder's sake in
the medieval time; for religion's sake in the time of the

Civil Wars; and now for plunder become a second-rate religion. The reverse journey has never been so popular. True, it brought ambassadors from the court of England with money to stop the itching in the Scottish nobles' palms. But other times it brought armies under Cromwell and the anointed Kings. So there are battlefields in the Lothian plain, at Dunbar and Pinkie, and tales of streams that ran down red with blood. Though the traveller is warned against the seductions of too much history he may indulge himself in a little in passing through the Lothians. He may cast an eye on castles and ecclesiastical houses, listen to legends and rude ballads, for inevitably he must come to Edinburgh, where ghosts are so many that the living walk the pavements by their leave, and the face of Mary Stewart shines like a mirage between the castle and the sky.

You may indeed think of the past when you are in the Lothian plain, because men and women have lived there through immemorial time, and they have left their traces everywhere. That is part of the spirit of the Lothians, a spirit that you will not often find again in Scotland, that there has been a very long tradition of ease and a fair degree of culture. Wealth has come out of that plain for generations, and when the traveller reaches Edinburgh he will find it in the carving of a doorway in wynds of the Old Town and in the gracious squares of the New. Edinburgh has grown out of the Lothians; and in Edinburgh you may still find some of the grace that has flowered out of such a generous earth.

CHAPTER FOUR : EDINBURGH: THE
CAPITAL WITHOUT A CROWN

PERHAPS the best way to approach Edinburgh is in the
dead of night. Though the town contains much that is
old and beautiful, the lovelier heart is so ringed round with
the speculative building of a later time that you might think
you were approaching any common town instead of a
capital city. If you are the sort that does not like exertion
I would advise you to pass the evening in Haddington or
Gullane or North Berwick, making a good meal, so that
the sunset may be warmed by an ampler glow within.
Then, about the time when the town takes on its curious
green and the land is filled with shadows, steal swiftly into
the heart of the town and go to bed. At eight or nine
in the morning you can look from your bedroom window
over the gardens of Princes Street to the cliffs of the Old
Town rising up with a confusion of gables to the Castle
riding on its monstrous rock.

But there is another way. You should leave your carriage
at the eastern border of the town and climb to the top of
Arthur's Seat, the steep hill that rises abruptly from the
Lothian Plain. You should keep to the east side all the
way up and when you have reached the top you should
close your eyes for a moment while you get back your
breath. Then you may open them again and see all Edinburgh below you.

You will see the Palace of Holyroodhouse at your feet,
then the houses of the Royal Mile rising up the slope of the
hill to the gates of the Castle on the summit of the rock away
to the west. Parallel to the Royal Mile and a little to the

right you will see Princes Street, a jumble of more modern styles, as the Royal Mile is a jumble of the old. The ridge on which the Royal Mile is built is, you might say, the spine of the town; you might call Princes Street the spinal cord. The town has grown up along the first and its life is organized about the second. When you have realized those two facts you will have no difficulty in understanding Edinburgh.

You will see the various parts of the town well defined. The oldest part lies immediately at the foot of Arthur's Seat, between Holyroodhouse and the Castle. Its chief characteristic is the lofty tenements called lands. Those were once fine houses adorned with every art, but they have declined into the most degrading of slums. That is the Old Town.

The New Town lies on the north side of Princes Street. It is one of the greater glories of these islands, a magnificent exercise in town planning and building in the Georgian style.

All round these lie the evidences of later expansion—the streets of grey nineteenth-century tenements, the acres of twentieth-century bungalows.

The Braid Hills and the Pentland Hills stand up against the south. The Port of Leith lies over to the north with the deep blue water of the Forth beyond it.

I wish you the good fortune that I have had—to climb to the top of Arthur's Seat on a July morning just on sunrise. There was a light mist over the town as I walked through the quiet streets, but a fresh wind came up from the Firth and cleared it away. When I reached the top, the whole land had been swept and garnished and lay waiting a mystery. Then the sun came up out of the North Sea—first a brilliant shaft of light that raked the meridian, then wave upon wave of brilliance flooding over the sea. Then I saw a strange thing. The sun, being still low in the heaven, struck against the side of Arthur's Seat and thus cast a pointed shadow like the gnomon of a dial over the town. The sun rose higher, warming the houses, touching windows with fire and gilding the gilded towers; but, projected by that rising sun, the shadow of the hill moved round across the town. I must have sat on the top of the hill for a long time watching that shadow; held, as you are held in a theatre, by the play of inhuman forces. But, as the sun rose over the hill, the mystery passed away till the moment when the sun had conquered the hill and Edinburgh lay all open to the light. By that time the kitchen fires were sending up their smoke and Edinburgh had become a busy industrial town again.

I will say nothing at all about the historical monuments of Edinburgh—Holyroodhouse, the Royal Mile, the Castle, Parliament House, and that most Gothic of all romances, the Scott Monument. They are in every guide-book and there, as far as I am concerned, they may remain.

But I would like you to visit the Outlook Tower, where you will get intimate views of the town complementary to the general view from Arthur's Seat. The tower is a curious building standing a little way below the Castle. It was inspired by Sir Patrick Geddes, one of those universal geniuses that nations produce once in a hundred years and completely fail to understand. As Sir Patrick hoped, without much success, to convince people that knowledge is a sovereign art, the tower is a centre of improving works, a sort of world museum, an encyclopædia of knowledge to show a man's relation to the world he lives in. It is also capped by a camera obscura. There, in a little dark room, you may see Edinburgh laid out before you in a magic show, and by means of it you can find your way near the heart of the town. You can see the dignified part—the statues, memorials, offices, hotels and the rest that make up a capital city. And you can also look into the courts that lie behind the Royal Mile. You will see fat old women leaning out of their windows to catch a breath of the August air off the Firth; and, if it is Tuesday, you will also see the family washing spread out on a frame from that same window. There is something uncanny about the camera obscura, for you are in darkness and the rest of the world are in light, so you may look privily into their affairs. And as you spy on them from the camera obscura you may suspect that the affairs behind the Royal Mile have considerable enterprise and moment on a Saturday night.

Compared with the backcourts the rest of the town may seem either too cold and dignified or, in the suburban parts, too self-consciously domestic. You may be inclined to put that down to the camera obscura; but you will be fortunate if your later experiences do not confirm that first impression.

Edinburgh is the capital of Scotland and it has the outward aspect of a capital city. It is, I think, one of the marks of a capital that it draws to itself all the strangest elements in the country. So if you walk down Princes Street at four o'clock in the afternoon you will see many strange sights between the West End and the Register House. Sometimes a young man with red hair and a kilt swings by as if he had come out of a story told a long time ago in a castle among the hills. At another time you will meet a plain Scots girl, the daughter of some country grocer, dressed in the latest fashion, blood-red nails and all, like a juju dancer. Old gentlemen of undeniable birth walk stiffly away to their clubs with sixty years of port and brandy creaking in their joints. Lawyers in tile hats progress sedately on cautious feet, as if every step were a legal opinion. A Lord of Session goes home with hanging matters on his mind. And, specially in the wintertime when the mirk draws in at four, weird creatures come out of the secret places—lonely women under ancient hats and men in fantastic capes carrying tattered books beneath their arms. Nobody knows whence they come: nobody knows whither they go. They are part of the secret life of a capital city, an essential part of the Edinburgh that draws to itself something of all that is curious in Scotland.

A poet once said that Edinburgh was built for empery; so it is, but it is a capital without a crown. It has all the attributes of a capital except the power to lead and direct the affairs of the rest of the country. It has Government offices—but policy is decided in Westminster. It has banks —but policy is decided in the City of London. It has businesses—but the pace is set by the English. Only the Court of Session and the General Assembly of the Church retain their independence; but the first, though it interprets, neither inspires nor directs; and there are ill-conditioned persons who would say that, though the Assembly directs and interprets, it no longer inspires. Edinburgh does not lack important industry; it has breweries that supply the English with beer and printing offices that supply them with books. But, nevertheless, you can't help feeling that initiative has left the town. The Civil Servants and the rest must work with one eye on London. So although it looks like the capital of a country, by its people you know it is really capital of another province in the Empire of London.

There is something invincibly middle class about Edinburgh society, something very correct and cautious and siccar. The ideal Edinburgh man is not a person who makes adventurous decisions in business. He is the lawyer working by Statute, the Civil Servant working by precedent, the manager interpreting his employers' orders. A thousand a year, a good house in a good street, and everything just right are sound Edinburgh ideals. To have a nice little income from Government Bonds is a mark of unassailable gentility. To have come of a good county or legal family, however poor you may be, is to have inherited a sure position. The West End of the town is full of old ladies that exist miraculously on tiny incomes and have never more than one good dress but must be invited on all the best occasions. Edinburgh society is middle class with all the middle class virtues—the stability, the correctness, the discipline and the sound morality in little things. But although the middle class is the backbone of a nation it is neither the brains nor the inspiration. Brains and inspiration together can make a capital city; Edinburgh that once had them now has them no longer. Her kingdom is in the past.

It is easy to find the reason. For some generations now the cleverest young men and women in Scotland have been going to London or abroad. Those who remain at home do so only until they have made something of a name. Then they too follow south to the better money and the society of like minds. Every year, as certain as the harvest comes, Scotland loses those very people that should be the leaders of her communities. It is inevitable they should leave just a little dullness behind them. The trouble has been diagnosed and at least one remedy has been proposed. That remedy is Nationalism.

You may have heard and may wish to know something about the Nationalists, hoping they will have the spirit of Bannockburn and the '45. But I'm afraid you will be disappointed. Scottish Nationalism is not violent, not even in words. It does not send round the fiery cross nor shoot English financiers from behind the drystone dykes. It remains very respectable and law-abiding.

That may be due in part to the fact that people agree about it in a general kind of way. Though they get angry at mention of the National Party, they admit the foolishness of Aberdeen Corporation having to legislate in Westminster before they can build a sewer. They think it would be a good thing if there were some body in Edinburgh that could deal with Scottish affairs as quickly as possible. Many Tories would confess themselves Home Rulers in everything but name. Thus you will find members of all parties vaguely favourable to some kind of Home Rule, or devolution as they prefer to call it. All of them realize, however, that the affairs of Scotland must be subordinated to the greater affairs of their respective parties and they have no intention of reversing that natural order of affairs.

The National Party alone works for the immediate autonomy of Scotland. It contains, or has contained, some of the old Liberal and Radical Home Rulers that were active in politics thirty years ago and a small number of men and women from the post-war generation. Mr. Cunninghame Graham was incomparably its finest showman and most inspiring leader, for he was a man of romantic presence, an aristocrat who has sat in Parliament as a Radical and fought injustice in many parts of the world. But Cunninghame Graham is dead and buried on Inchmahome in the Lake of Menteith and who can take his place ? Sir Alexander MacEwen, once Provost of Inverness, has been the party's ablest propagandist, and Mr. Compton Mackenzie won its only success when he was elected Lord Rector of Glasgow University. The party has made little progress in the last few years and one may doubt its power to inspire the nation.

Why should that be ?

Perhaps its flirtation with Social Credit may have something to do with its failure. Perhaps the dissensions within the party. Or it may be that an Irishman summed up the trouble in four words. Being an Irishman he knew something about the furies of Nationalism and wished to see what the Scottish kind was like, so he was taken to a Nationalist Bazaar in Edinburgh. He walked through the crowd of good respectable Edinburgh people, looked at the stalls of home-made scarves and socks, examined the tartans and tasted the cooking. It was noticed that his curiosity turned into bewilderment and his bewilderment grew so apparent that his companion asked what was the matter.

' Matter ? ' the Irishman said. He waved his hand at the good citizens, the knitting and the scones.

' Matter,' he said. ' I see all this, but—where are the gunmen ? '

Circumstances are against the National Party. There is
no general hatred of the English to be made the emotional
driving force of a political movement. The Scots do not
hate the English; at the best they like, and at the worst they
despise, them. When the Nationalists speak about the
domination of England they are not believed; or, if they
are believed, conviction does not rouse any powerful
emotion. So they cannot make progress by raising a kind
of patriotism that is better dead. If they attack the real
trouble, which is the power of the City of London, they find
the Socialists have attacked it for years in a way that is more
intelligible to the people readiest to listen—the working
class. So the National Party does not yet stand for or appeal
to any powerful body of national feeling. It does work for
the crofters and the fishermen of the west but they are too
few to make a strong party and too little regarded to make a
national cause. Though the National Party works for the
redress of many evils, its time has not yet come; and one
must doubt its chances now when the issues between the
Right and the Left take up so much of our thoughts.
Unless it can find a middle way.

It is beyond all question that we need a body of men and
women devoted to the best interests of Scotland, determined
to see that we make the best use of our resources for the good
of our own people. There is an opportunity for such a
party. Question any intelligent business man or any intelligent workman long enough and he will tell you of some
way in which the centralizing influence of London makes
things difficult for his trade in Scotland. Even Sir Steven
Bilsland, a very orthodox Glasgow business man, giving
evidence for the Scottish Economic Committee before the
Royal Commission on the Distribution of Industrial
Population this year favoured the idea that there should be
some body that would ensure Scotland a fair share of new
industries. At the same time you may hear of Labour
people who complain that provincial interests are too often

lost in the mysteries of Transport House. There are others who feel that London, having some pretensions to be a centre for the world, cannot at the same time be the best centre for those local interests on which their living depends. So, while there does not seem to be any great desire for independence, for a state such as Mr. de Valera is creating in Ireland, there does seem to be a feeling that our interests are overlooked. The National Party have not yet been able to make that feeling into an active political force ; for those of us who have inherited the old radical ideas are suspicious of nationalisms and the business men would put up with their present disabilities rather than risk a change. What is to happen ? We could of course let things go their present way and allow the pull of London to work unchecked till the whole population of these islands is collected in the South Midlands and the Home Counties. That would be a little foolish, from both the economic and the spiritual points of view. It is a good thing for the life of a nation that it should have a healthy provincial society and that it should make the best use of all its resources. How are we to ensure that Scotland shall be developed to the utmost and society kept here in a state of lively develop-ment ? Quite a few people are beginning to wonder. Can the National Party give them the answer ? Is it a matter that must be ground out between Right and Left ? Or can the National Party discover some regional com-promise ? These are questions of some small interest in Scotland to-day.

The Nationalists are not gunmen, yet. In fact you could hardly have a more delightful experience than attending one of their social evenings. They sing the traditional Gaelic songs in the prettiest way and the women play on the clarsach, a kind of harp that is unequalled for showing off a comely arm. You would hear much from them about the glories and the miseries of the west and you should listen, for they know what they speak of ; but when they turn to small-holdings as the salvation of the Highlands you should ask for another song because the small-holding is a dream that ends in a horrid awakening for the holder. Listen to the singing and the melancholy music of the clarsach and the old traditional stories and you will find the magic that is one of the best rewards of travel in foreign parts. It may even make you a Nationalist, till the morning.

I would not say anything to keep you away from Edinburgh. I love it and I have never stepped into Princes Street after being some time away without feeling a rise in my spirits, as if I had snuffed up delight upon the air. Of course the city is often staid and cold; when you see the good citizens stepping down to church at twenty past eleven on Sunday morning, you may think you have found the home of the Scottish Sabbath; but there is another kind of life—if you know where to find it—among the commons of Scotland. I set the commons in the front of this book in the person of Geordie, and I will return to them again and again, for they are the lively ones, creatures of resource and humour. They are the warmth of the cold town and the fruitful life of the capital. On Sunday morning you will see the middle class on the way to church; on Sunday afternoon you will see the commons at Portobello Beach. If you go out along the coast road to Port Seton you may see, as I have seen, thousands of them bathing on the shore. There are few dressing-rooms about and little cover in the way of whins. So a man must undress in the shade of his own modesty. I cannot guarantee you such amusement, but I have seen as much and I may see it again. It would be nothing if one did not remember the stately Church procession; it would be nothing, if it were not the saving grace of Edinburgh life.

You should see the High Street on Saturday night when the commons have a bit of money in their pockets and a bottle of wine costs one-and-ten. Then the Royal Mile is indeed filled with a royal company. That sort of careless

life is not confined to the poorest streets.   Round behind the
genteel establishments of Princes Street and parallel to that
arid highway, there is a narrow lane where public-houses
are so many that no man has ever been able to count them,
after opening time; and in behind the dignified façades
of the New Town there are many quiet little howffs where
you can be sure of a game of dominoes in the backshop.

Not so long ago I dropped into a public-house that I
would call the Open Arms because of the friendliness you
are always sure to find there.   Hoping to meet somebody I
knew, I opened the door of the back room and there found
a delightful thing.   The room was filled with a mixed
company—respectable old married men, large comfortable
women, a few young men and a couple of young ladies who
had done their best to reach the heights of fashion.   All
had their fancy convenient to their hands—a nip and a
chaser, or a pint of beer, or the ladylike port and lemon.
Seeing it was a private sort of occasion, I made to with-
draw; but a large blue-nosed gentleman with a bowler
hat on the back of his head, who seemed to be the chairman,
said good evening to me and invited me to join them.   I
replied that I was honoured, so I was given a seat between
a little man who must have worked in the gasworks and
a vast old woman who told me she washed-down stairs.

We all became very friendly under the leadership of the
blue-nosed chairman.   After he had given us a minute to
settle down, he rose, lifted his bowler hat, gave me a few
well-chosen words of welcome, called on a young man to
sing, replaced the bowler on the back of his head and sat
down again.   The youth obliged with ' The Isle of Capri '.
Then one of the almost fashionable young women gave us
a piece about a girl whose lover had died by the lonesome
pine, and it was such a sad piece that I had to offer her a
port and lemon which she accepted, without obligation.
So each member of the company made some contribution
to the entertainment, not very musically perhaps, but with

feeling, and we became mighty friendly about closing time. It was a good, a memorable evening, conducted with decorum.

And as we were leaving the old charwoman threw her arms round my neck.

'Eh what a bonnie laddie ye are,' she said.

Then she kissed me.

I'm sorry to take leave of Edinburgh, for it has many delightful moods. Best of all I like the windy autumn days. The hills grow red brown : the trees wear the richest colours of the fall and the firth is a startling blue. It is a time of brilliant skies and clear keen airs. There is wonder left in the town, especially when the Castle is flood-lit in the evening. Perhaps you have spent an hour in good company at a public-house and are walking home down one of the dark wynds from the Lawn-market or the High Street. Suddenly fairyland shines before you. Away down below the tramcars move along Princes Street like fairy coaches. You may laugh at them and say they are like a pantomime. Then you turn to your left and you laugh no longer. For there is the dark rock and high above it the Castle shines in a ring of light, like a vision let down out of Heaven.

CHAPTER FIVE : PLEASANT SMALL TOWNS—EDINBURGH TO DOLLAR

From Edinburgh now you must step westward to the town of Sirling.

It is another and an important characteristic of this land that you must always be making a long detour round some intrusive arm of the sea, for it flies away from the head of England like a ragged hood and many a flash of bright blue water has bitten deep across its pastures. Just by Edinburgh the Firth of Forth runs near to Stirling at the very navel of the land. Farther north the Firth of Tay runs near to the old grey town of Perth. Up in the north-east the Moray Firth runs down to Inverness. And all around the west coast the deep sea lochs lie far up in the secret places of the hills. Thus there is hardly a part of the inhabited land that lies so far in the deep country that the sea winds cannot reach it, or the sounds of the greater world disturb their green solitudes. That has had its effect on the people. I do not know of any part in our Lowlands where you can find villages so overgrown with time, as may still be found between Ludlow and the Marches. Wherever you go in Scotland you find that the people have a touch of the wind from the sea—the ruder winds from the German Ocean or the gentler winds from the Atlantic; and they have too an awareness like the quality that gives an edge to the ocean winds—the sense of great distance and of strange lands beyond. That they sometimes don't know what to do with their awareness is no disproof of its reality.

Well, from Edinburgh you must travel along the shore of the Firth of Forth until you reach the town of Stirling.

This is West Lothian as far as Linlithgow but a Lothian growing dour. There are still farms and many of them are good enough, but you soon become aware of the stiff clay. And very aware of the struggle for existence. There has been a fine heap of money taken out of West Lothian in the last hundred years. This is shale country and it will not be long before you realize it, for the plain is broken with refuse bings from the mines. Millions of gallons of oil have been wrung from the shale and the waste products have been heaped up in the great dreary hills that industry loves to raise as memorials to its own disorder. The dull villages and the small depressing towns also look like waste products of the shale. Great wealth has been taken out of West Lothian, but it has not been allowed to fertilize the country-side; though the paraffin oil has cast light over many parts of Scotland, the workings have cast darkness over the country round them. But that is an old story in that ill-guided business, the development of Scotland. Yet, you will notice that corn still grows to the feet of the refuse bings, and that the miners' villages, however dismal, have still green shaws beyond them. People know about the struggle for existence in those parts, but the struggle has still some small amenities to sweeten it.

This is the border of industrial Scotland. When you leave the shale you find the coal. And so, passing alternately farm land and mine and pit, you come to Stirling.

If a man were to come to me and say 'I have only an hour to spend in Scotland, show me something most typical of your country,' I would take him up to the highest part of Stirling Castle and ask him to look around. I do not know any place where he would find the Highlands and the Lowlands more serenely married. Down below him he would see the houses of the town—the old and new and the imitation, then the river winding interminably among its woods and meadows; then the stiff carse land patterned out on little fields; and the whole protected by the many enfolding mountain ranges. Eastward down the river he might imagine the light on the great waters and smell the tang of the sea upon the wind. Southward the colliery bings and chimney stacks would remind him of the smoke that hangs upon industrial Scotland. And westward, if it were evening, he would see the light come flooding out of the tattered blue line of hills. That is a recognizable miniature of the face of Scotland.

But if the traveller had an afternoon to spare I would take him east from Stirling, along the northern shores of the Firth of Forth, into the Kingdom of Fife. The direct road lies through the low country, by Alloa to Dunfermline, but we would take another and kindlier one by the green Ochils and the Hillfoot towns. There, in the course of one afternoon, he could see almost every kind of Scottish life.

This is a curious part of the country, and the Ochils are curious hills, for they rise straight out of the carse land as the mountains of the west rise straight from the sea. Thus you have a rare thing, the rich fertility of the farm lands and the barren beauty of the hills, with no poor grudging fields between them. You might almost think there was a design in it, as if the hills had been set there to shelter the carse against the winter gales, like a wall that is built around a garden. It's a delightful place upon a July morning when the sun seems to be reflected with a double warmth upon the plain below giving, what you so seldom get in Scotland, warmth in which there is no slightest premonition of a colder air. The carse land wears its richness on its face. Growth has come up like a tide that laps against the hills. Every field has its fine crop of hay or corn and the pastures are a jungle of green grasses, where dairy cows chew the cud of a delightful dinner and little pigs go rooting in the tufts of clover.

And, once again, there is the industrial counterpart. Small towns lie along the hills, so close to their rounded flanks that you might fear they would be overlaid in the

4

night-time. These are the older manufacturing parts of Scotland, that tell us a great deal about the past and may even show us one way towards a more gracious future.

Blairlogie, in the warmest corner of the hills, is only a hamlet, now half lost in an orchard of pears and plums and apples, a place that time seems to have forgotten and left behind to ripen into a warm domestic beauty very rare this side of the Tweed. For the sake of the little peace that is left in the modern world, the traveller is invited to look and pass, as quietly as he may.

But in passing he may think for a little of the Soutars of Blairlogie. There were many of them in the good time of a hundred years ago, who made boots in their own homes, for a factory at Blackford at the other side of the hills. On a set day, perhaps once a fortnight or oftener, each made a pack of his finished work and carried it to the factory. There they were paid for what they had done and were given out more leather. Now here is a curious thing. The journey to Blackford could be walked in a single day, but the long road home took two. There must have been some brave nights at the inn that stands at Sheriffmuir, and the ghosts of the Jacobites who fell in battle there must have sighed happily in their graves, knowing that one old custom was still honoured in their land.

We may not envy the Soutars of Blairlogie the sore heads they brought home from Sheriffmuir; but we may indeed envy them the life of that happier time when the craftsman worked in his own home as the spirit willed him. There were many evils in the old system, for the provident merchant could always exploit the improvident craftsman, but a man could at least work in a natural rhythm according to the seasons. If it pleased him, he could shut up his shop on a fine day and go walking over the hills : or he could go after the trout and the salmon when the water was right. Then, come bad weather, he could work a double stent. That wasn't all. Farmers cut their corn with the scythe

Dollar Academy

The Carse : Looking over the Forth to Stirling

in those days, so they needed many extra hands in harvest. It was the rule then that the craftsmen put by their tools and worked in the fields, even contracting with the farmer for the labour of all their family. Now that must have been a saner way of living, not shut up in a trade like a pig in a pen, but keeping a man in touch with the enlivening earth and the spiritual refreshment of the seasons. We may have gained some comforts in the years between, but who can deny that we have lost our freedom ? Are we richer or poorer ? It's not me that can say. But all our improvements will have little value until we recapture that freedom and that casual living. For a man isn't a gelded ox to be doing his eight hours a day at the mill. He is a creature of changing will and various desires. He has a dangerous mind that must be leaping over hedges and to hell with caution. He must have time to waste on error and time to waste in lying on his back. He must have time to get drunk in the daemonic seasons of the year and time to sit on the hills speculating about the mysteries of Heaven. If he is the Lord of Creation he must live like a Lord, get children in a magnificent passion, plan his world as if he were immortal and dying go proudly to his heaven. If our machines and the wealth they make us cannot give us a life like that, then they are less than nothing and their wealth is a burden of vanity.

The echoes in Blairlogie speak of the olden time. The other Hillfoot towns speak with a modern accent. Menstrie lives by a furniture workshop and a distillery that now makes yeast. Alva and Tillicoultry have a coalpit and weaving sheds and a paper mill. Those little towns are not beautiful though they are set in a beautiful country, but they can point the way to better things. They have their past : you will notice they are placed at the ends of precipitous glens whence they drew the water-power for their mills. They have their present, for they have adapted themselves to modern industrial ways. And they will have a future

that can be what we make it. When you see Alva from the
west on a summer evening—the little town set on a slope
rising from the Devon valley up the green Ochils to the
square grey mill that catches the light of the sun in a hundred
windows, you realize that industrial life need not be devoid
of grace. Instead of factories jammed into little room to
the ruin of health and the death of beauty, we might have a
hundred little towns, each with a healthy civic life, a local
character and intimate contact with the fruitful ways of the
country-side. Meanwhile we have the Hillfoots and we
have Dollar.

As you pass through Alva and Tillicoultry you will
notice that the plain has grown narrower till it is no more
than the valley of the Devon. You will realize that you
are leaving the true Lowlands, climbing into poverty of
soil and an austerer air. When you come to the main
street of Dollar and see the grim ruin of Castle Campbell
dominate the glen above you, you may think you have
done with ease and are back among the sternest realities
again.

But Dollar can surprise you.

More than a hundred years ago there lived a man called
John McNabb, a native of the little town. Though born
thus far from the sea, he became a merchant sailor and owned
his ship and made a fortune. When he was grown rich
and old he returned to Dollar and there forgathered with
the minister of the town. Now if one can find a good word
to say about the Scottish clergy, one should not leave that
word unsaid. The minister of Dollar suggested to John
McNabb that he should endow the town with a school.
John McNabb was persuaded and the school now stands
there to his glory.

The meeting between John McNabb and the minister
was a fortunate chance for Dollar: the building of the
school gave Scotland one of her finer pieces of architecture.
The trustees chose Playfair as their architect and he built

them a gracious house in the classical style. Not only that; he built a row of houses for the masters and he also built, or inspired the building of, several others in the town. The result is surprising and delightful; for we become so accustomed to the quaint native style of building, with its turrets and curious angles, or the latter-day exercises in curdled Gothic, that Playfair's classical houses remind us with sudden pleasure of the time when Scotland did enjoy an Augustan age with an harmonious and ample imagination.

If you have an eye for the quiet graces you might spend an hour in Dollar. The Academy belongs to the people of the town, by deed of John McNabb, and the people of the town have a right of entry to it. So pretend for an hour to be a native and walk across the lawn to the school. There you will find great trees casting their shadows on the grass and the chaste lines of Playfair's building set cunningly against the wayward masses of the hills beyond them. That is a double harmony, between the parts of the building, and between the building and its background. Playfair had an eye for the decencies of the picturesque. He had more than that, for I am told by them that are learned in architecture that the library has solved a problem in a daring way. I do not understand these things, but I know the library is very beautiful. If you speak the janitor fair, you may see it for yourself.

In Dollar, too, you can have the pleasure of an exquisite contrast. If you may climb the hill to the oldest part of the town where you will find the douce old houses in the plainer style of native building. There is nothing notable about such houses; nothing at all of the picturesque. They are plain, built of local stone. Their windows are small; the roofs of the rooms are low; when they do conform to the modern standards of public health, they have little to spare. I feel almost apologetic at inviting any one to have a look at them, they have so little to charm you with. But there are some who do not love antiquity for its own sake and would not go ten yards to see a hole that an ancient Pict had lived in, yet have a strange affection for those plain grey houses. They have, I think, a kind of harmony in their plainness. I would even dare to say they have a touch of Playfair not yet gone to town, a touch of classical or pagan simplicity. Perhaps not; maybe we love them because we were born in such houses and were tended there with kindness in our small years, and now we in turn would give them some of the love that we took in so great measure. These are too difficult matters for us alone to decide. We know only that the sight of those old houses gives us a kind of satisfaction, the contentment that a tree might feel if it were conscious of its roots deep in its own earth. If you look with kindness on those houses and try to understand how we could ever love them, then you may learn something worth knowing about Scotland.

I'm afraid I'm a leisurely traveller, but, you see, I haven't a motor-car. Nor would I go in a motor-car to find out the truth about a country. Not that I dislike motor-cars. I have a number of very good friends who drive me about and I find the awful propinquity of death at 80 miles an hour can be a very exhilarating sensation. But I would as soon experience it on a racing track as on the open roads. The motor-car is useless for seeing the country-side, owing to the curious fact that once started it can be stopped only at predetermined places, such as hotels and possible sites for picnics. That may be due either to the nature of the machinery, or some idiosyncrasy of the driver; but if any habitual passenger has ever tried to get an owner-driver to stop for admiration of some sudden beauty, he will know what I mean. It is one of the curiosities of modern life.

Fortunately I was brought up by an old gentleman who drove about the country-side with a pony and trap. There was nothing he liked better than stopping for conversation with a neighbour, or with strangers on the road; and every mile or two he would draw up and look back because, he said, the country looked different that way.   Now the habits we acquire as children stay with us the rest of our lives, so I must always be stopping and looking back, like my grandfather before me.   Therefore we may climb to the top of the hill above the old town of Dollar and look down along the Hillfoot country through which we have come. We will see the grey houses of old Dollar, the Academy among the trees, the little winding Devon flowing down its valley; fields and farms and woods, the smoke from the mills, the workings of a colliery—another bit of Lowland Scots.   As the Hillfoots has been a weaving country for generations, I may be forgiven if I say that the view from Dollar has a homespun air.   It may lack magnificence, but it is full of life, a radical and enduring life that, no matter what Hollywood and the B.B.C. can do, retains something that is truly Scottish.

CHAPTER SIX: GLENDEVON: PORTRAIT OF A LOWLAND GLEN

ON beyond Dollar there is poorer country. The stiff carse land is far away; the eternal rock is nearer the surface. So there is more pasture, less corn, more sheep and fewer cows. But this country is worth looking at, for it is typical of a great part of agricultural Scotland. You will find it at its best in Aberdeenshire and I will have a lot to say about it when we get there, for I was born on that kind of land. Meantime you may care to notice its sparse fertility. The labourer's back does not break under the weight of harvest; he is more likely to break his heart trying to raise enough to fill his girnal. But this sort of country has a virtue in its sparseness—though the farmer may not appreciate that virtue. It has been tamed; oats have disciplined its savage heart; it is tidy and in order. You can see that men have put the pattern of their will on it and maintained their mastery over it for generations. But you can also see by how small a margin they hold that mastery. Thus you find in such country a sense of exquisite balance, of opposing forces nicely poised at a point of equilibrium. There is nothing excessive, no irresistible tides of greenery, just enough to make pleasant the earth without blurring the austerity of its lines. It is a classical sort of landscape, perhaps more satisfying to the observer than to the people who get their living by it.

But we have not far to go before we find a country-side where the balance is increasingly on the side of the wilderness, a place, once civilized, that is slowly returning to the wild.

I cannot pass this way without a detour into the green Ochils, surely the most amenable hills in Scotland. If a country must have mountains, then they should be like the Ochils. These run from Stirling into Fife for over thirty miles, and though they are guilty of an occasional rocky indisposition such as Dunmyat and Ben Cleuch, there are rolling green slopes all the way. You can walk across their shoulders for days without meeting the impassable or slithering down fields of scree in an undignified fashion. They are hills that a man can truly love, as he might love a comfortable wife who offers him quiet domestic joys without the agonies and ardours of pursuit. Most amiable hills, they are so charming to live with. Every hour of the day throws new shadows across their little glens; and even in the dead season of the year, when the glens are filled with mists and rain all day, the hills keep changing as the rain mists rise and fall. If you are content to sit and watch them you will never want for company, for they are so round and kindly that they become personal to you and you can live with them as with good friends.

They offer you other entertainment, many small hill burns run down out of the side-glens: there are many excellent small trout in those burns, and quite a few of them may be caught with the aid of an intelligent worm. I lived among those hills for two years, and of all pleasures I like best to remember the trout. I was no fisherman when I went there; I am no fisherman yet; but I hope I will never be so old or so tired that I will forget the days I spent trying to lure the wily fishes from the burns. There were calm evenings of utter beatitude when the stars in the east grew brighter as the sun fell away beneath the west. Then the hills seemed to grow vast, like great beasts invested with the mystery of the night. It would be dark, or almost, down by the water's edge. Then I felt infinitesimally small as if I were deep in the well of the night. Such, indeed, might have been the place I stood in, for I could see nothing but a pale light, a glimmering shadow of light, on the face of the pool, like the reflection of a dark sky seen in the depths of an old well. I would stand there, patiently, for a long time in a kind of trance, wondering what fish was being tempted by my lure, and what contest between caution and desire was troubling the depths of the waters. Caution almost always won, and I could go home through the dewy bracken guiltless of all but the drowning of a worm. There are no words that I could use to tell you of the still nights, with the sound of the little falling waters, and the small owls chirping in the trees, and the bright stars so far away in the heaven, while the hills drew in around me like friendly presences. But if you will go into the Ochils about midnight and go in quietness you will be, as I, enchanted.

It is perhaps the best thing about the Ochils that they are useful. They feed an excellent type of sheep of the Blackface breed, or the Leicester and Blackface cross. The sheep is not an edifying animal. There is no inspiration in its face, and the constant reiteration of its song can be utterly maddening. But it has been the one animal, and its management has been the one kind of husbandry, that has made money consistently during the last twenty years (with the exception of one year's sudden and inexplicable collapse). The creature's depressing qualities may therefore be forgiven.

Well, if you should care to turn north from the Yetts of Muckart along Glendevon, you will find the third type of farming in this region. The first was the carse land farming round Stirling; the second was the thoroughly mixed farming of the poorer land up Dollar way; the third is the hill sheep farming where there is hardly a single acre under the plough. It is here in hill pasture like the Ochils, in spite of the kindliness of the green slopes, that you can see the slow encroachment of the wild.

You will see a number of farms on either side of the road

along Glendevon. Each has a few small pieces of meadow-land down by the river-side, land that may be cropped with corn or roots. Then there is a great stretch of hill grazing right up to the tops of the Ochils, a thousand acres or more enclosed in a dry stone dyke. That land carries a stock of one ewe to every two acres or more. The ewes lamb in April month and the lambs are sold off in the autumn. In most cases the best ewe lambs are kept to maintain the stock. The farmer may also keep a score of young cattle that do good to the pasture and leave a bit of money behind them.

You should try to meet some of the shepherds, for they are about the best class of men in rural Scotland.

Their life is arduous enough; the money is ridiculously small for the man's responsibility; and yet, taking working lives both by and large, it is a better life than many. There is a certain amount of responsibility and freedom. The farmer does not often go to the hill himself so the shepherd is not being constantly overlooked. If he can give an account of all his sheep at the clipping time, and show good drafts of lambs for the sales, he is his own master up on the hills. So he is usually a more intelligent type of man than the ordinary Lowland ploughman. He has to do a lot of walking. His stretch of a hill may be five miles long, and he will need to walk the most of it, to see what is happening to his sheep. A bad winter of sudden storms is therefore a time of great anxiety and sometimes physical danger. The lambing, too, is a yearly nightmare to a conscientious man. The ewes must be seen to at all hours, even in the best of seasons. But if the winter has been late or severe, or if the lambing begins in difficult weather, troubles increase a hundred times. The lambs may be born dead, or be so weak that they cannot survive; or, if they are born safely, the ewes may have no milk. The shepherd has then to be wet-nurse and midwife both. The weak lambs and ewes are revived with whisky and foster mothers must be found for the lambs of the milkless ewes, all that in the whistling winds and the biting rains of an April night. There never was a shepherd who did not bless the day when the lambing was over, and a thousand little creatures were learning to dance in the first May sunshine.

So far the shepherd's life must seem to be a very lonely one; and indeed he does get blessed relief from chattering fools when he is upon the hill. But his life becomes pleasantly social in the summer time. The sheep are clipped then. In some places the clipping is done by bands of shearers who move from farm to farm. In other places there is still a good custom of neighbouring. In Glendevon, for instance, most of the shepherds help each other. The farms are taken according to a strict rotation and all the shepherds meet to clip the sheep according to that rotation.

If I were a farmer there, all the shepherds would come to clip my sheep on a certain day. When all mine had been clipped, all the shepherds, including mine, would move off to clip my neighbour's flock; and so on. The clipping is hard steady work on a hot summer's day, but the farmer provides a barrel of beer and there is plenty of conversation towards evening. Those social occasions must compensate for a lot of lonely walks across the hills.

The odd times of summer are taken up with what I suspect to be less a work than a ritual—the winning of the meadow hay. Those small patches of meadow land by the river-side grow a superior kind of grass and even a little clover, which make a valuable feed in the winter-time if cut for hay. So they are cut; and thereafter if you see a few men moving across the meadowland almost as slowly as the shadows of the trees, you will know that they are making the hay. This operation lasts till the end of summer, and if a few coles of hay seem to be a poor reward for so long labour you should remember that it isn't sense for a man to be always riving the guts out of himself with work.

Besides, a shepherd must keep himself in trim for the sales. These are the major occasions, the test of the long year's work. The prices gained by the best lots from every farm are reported in the newspapers, and are discussed with authority by every shepherd in the district. Therefore, to do well is a point of honour, something infinitely desired. Bad prices will send the shepherd home even gloomier than his master: excellent prices have been known to send both of them home in a state that can only be described as exaltation ; but there is nothing in that, for it's an old and much-honoured rural custom.

This is only an outline of the shepherd's life, but it may be enough to show you how one part of our farm people live in the Glens that run up from the Lowlands.

So far life in the glen must seem very charming, but it has another aspect. If you like to look at Glendevon you will see another part of the history of Scotland written small in lines on the lower shoulders of the hills, as if the waste had been enclosed in little fields. It was. Once upon a time there must have been many crofts in Glendevon where men won a bare living by an intolerable amount of labour. But that was long ago. Now the decline and disappearance of the crofters in the poorer lands of Scotland is a problem of long standing and present concern. If you talk to old people you will hear a great deal about the crofting communities that filled the glens in the olden time and you may even begin to believe that the days when crofting flourished were a Golden Age in Scotland. Some of us have our doubts about that Golden Age. Of course we have no exact information as to the state of the glens three hundred years ago, for reliable un-biased observers did not venture so far away from the protection of the law. We can only make inferences from the condition of the land to-day.

There is a beautiful idea that the glens were full of peace and plenty in the olden time. Where a dozen families live to-day there would have been a hundred three centuries ago. The little fields grew fine crops of corn giving meal for the

girnal and malt for the ale.   Good young cows grazed on
the lower slopes of the hills, so that the crofter had always
milk and butter and cheese on his table.   A flock of sheep
pastured on the high ground, to give their flesh for mutton
and their wool for weaving.   There was plenty of fish in
the river and fowl on the moors.   Since there was no
thought of an export trade—except, perhaps, in cattle—no
one needed to work for the sake of money alone.   So, when
a man had done enough to fill his belly, he could spend the
rest of his time on the arts.   Therefore the glens were full
of music and singing and dancing and the telling of stories.
It must have been a wise kind of life.   There were no
luxuries, of course, but many of our luxuries are hardly
worth the labour they cost us.   The Calvinist heresy of
work for its own sake and justification by money had not
poisoned the springs of life.   Men worked no more than
they needed to and spent the rest of their time on pleasure.

I like to think of Glendevon as it might have been three
or four hundred years ago.   There would have been many
houses along the river-side.   Not perhaps fine houses with
parlours, yet enough to shelter a man from the wind and the
snow.   There would have been many houses and many
people, for women bore innumerable children then.   How
delightful it must have been on a summer's day when they
were all out working on the hill-sides—cutting the peats,
weeding the corn, herding the cattle, or driving the margins
of their little fields deeper and deeper into the waste-land.
Even more delightful in the evening when the peat smoke
from a hundred chimneys was hanging a most delicate blue
across the glen, shot with the dyes of sunset.   You can
imagine the older people sitting at their doors, in the shade,
perhaps, of an apple tree; the young women spinning to
the lilt of an old song; the young men leaping and running
against each other on a level meadow; and some patient
anglers luring the trout in the river; while the sound of the
bagpipes came with the infinite melancholy of great art

across the hills. Glendevon is still beautiful at all the seasons of the year, but there are times when we get weary of its emptiness, of its silent hills given over to the sheep and bracken; then we may be forgiven if our thoughts turn back with longing to the olden time and the singing and the piping and the sweet society of human kind.

That is a lovely picture of an Arcadian life but I have my doubts that it ever existed. We cannot say for sure, but all possible inferences from the condition of the land to-day point to a very different and very harsh reality.

We know that there were many houses and many people in the glen. Even a hundred years ago, when depopulation was well advanced in similar glens, there were 192 persons in Glendevon, according to the statistical account of 1845. To-day there are about half that number. How could 192 have got a living from the soil of the glen? It is beyond all question that the poor little fields so faintly outlined on the hill-sides could never have carried enough corn to feed them. But there were the sheep and the cattle. Enough of those might have been sold off to buy the meal and firing needed in the glen. Then there was a spinning mill that employed half a dozen families a hundred years ago and was extended later. That would have meant a certain amount of ready money for trade with the Lowlands. So it is possible that the standard of living in Glendevon, though low enough, may have been adequate to the times. And there is one very important fact to be considered. This glen is on the edge of the Lowlands: in fact, it might be said to be right inside the Lowlands, for it is well south of the Highland line. Therefore it was near good markets, and could exchange its beef, mutton and wool for the corn that it could not grow. It was really a very favoured position compared with the glens in the true Highlands.

But there was a sudden rise of population in the first half of the last century: the people, if not the land, seemed to discover the secret of inexhaustible fertility. The poor land could not support them, so they had to migrate either to the manufacturing towns of the south, or to the prairies of America. More than that, the standard of living began to rise all over Scotland. But the crofts could not give that higher standard of living to those who remained on them. The little fields on the hill-side could have been kept in good heart only by unrelenting labour; and even that labour could not have brought a decent return. My wife's great-grandfather, giving an account of land that he reclaimed from waste about 1827, notes that $3\frac{1}{2}$ qrs. of corn was considered an excellent crop in Aberdeenshire then. East Aberdeenshire has never been quite as rich as the Garden of Eden, but it could always yield a lot more than the poor shoulders of the Highland hills. If the farmers harvested $2\frac{1}{2}$ qrs. an acre off those miserable patches it would have been a bountiful harvest, if not a miracle. Some years, of course, there would be no harvest at all, when the corn was lying dead under the snow at Candlemass. That happened oftener then, when winters came early and the corn ripened later. It is a reasonable inference that there must often have been little meal in the girnal; it is an even surer inference that there were many to feed. Could those little patches have fed all those mouths? I doubt it.

But there were the sheep, would they have brought in enough to make up the balance? Perhaps; but it is unlikely.

The husbandry of the olden time has all the marks of subsistence farming. Now, as its name implies, that is a hand-to-mouth business. It gives the farmer and his family just enough to live on by their continuous labour. It gives them subsistence and nothing more. That means that there is no delicious surplus: the surplus that is the very life-blood of good husbandry. If there is none the farmer cannot buy in new animals to improve his stock. Now unless the stock is thus revived it is almost inevitable that its quality will go down, for, whatever nature may think of a vacuum, it does not like a state of equilibrium. So it is another reasonable inference that the sheep would have been below the general standard of the time and tending to fall still lower. If that were so, they could not have done so much to eke out the harvests of the little fields.

You may think that this is an intolerable maze of suppositions, and I will almost agree with you. But I do think that they do something to justify my inference that the husbandry of the Glen was subsistence farming at the best of times, and gave a very low level of subsistence even in the best of times. Any district that has a low standard of living will lose its people to a district that has a better. The depopulation of the Highlands went on. Nothing on earth can stop it until the glens can offer as high a standard of living as any other place in Scotland. You can't fill your belly with sentiment.

Why has Glendevon lost half its population in one hundred years? There are, I think, two causes. The spinning mill, being too far from the railway, could not maintain itself against more conveniently situated competitors. When it was burned down about the turn of the century there was no incentive to rebuild it. That was the end of the Glen's industrial life. By that time all the cultivated patches on the shoulders of the hills would have gone back into pasture, and there would have been only the sheep farms as we know them to-day. Now, even before the war those farms supported more people than they do now. Each would have had one or more married shepherds, and so there were still bands of children walking down the paths to school. Now, however, the farmers are preferring to employ single men as herds. The spinners have gone; the herds grow fewer; the school has been closed for want of children. The last time I passed through the Glen two of the houses were empty, or let for a month in summer; three houses were rented by business people from town who lived in them at the week-ends; six were

5

lived in by retired people; and three attached to the
reservoirs up in the side-glens.

What about the rest ?   The sheep-farms still give a decent
return for good management, but they too show a like
deterioration.   The bracken is spreading across the hills
like plague.   There are other plagues too that attack the
sheep.   That is only to be expected.   The hills which were
never very rich have been robbed for generations.   Thousands of sheep have been raised on them : thousands of
tons of mutton and wool have gone off them ; and nothing
has been given back.   The mineral salts have been depleted ;
the finer grasses have been weakened and the coarser grasses
have taken their place, to be followed by the bracken that
kills all and yet is completely useless.   It is inevitable that
the sheep, fed on those exhausted pastures, should themselves be affected.   The high mortality of ewes and lambs
at lambing time, in spite of all increase of veterinary knowledge, is a sign that the stock have been weakened.   This
problem is not confined to Glendevon.   It is a problem
common to all rough grazings in Scotland ; one more factor
that should be noticed by any one who wants to understand
Scotland to-day.

There is one more thing to be noticed ; one more reason
why the bracken comes creeping down the hills ; the prime
cause of so much of Scotland's rural desolation.   I said
before that a surplus is the life-blood of good husbandry.
All too often any surplus that remained after the most urgent
demands of subsistence had been satisfied were taken by the
lairds.   Now a race of landlords was always a luxury that
Scotland was too poor to afford, except perhaps those
specially fertile parts like the Lothians, that were less burd-
ened with natural weeds.   Though we must not forget
that many of them did very good work by encouraging
improvement in the late eighteenth century, their importance
even then can be overvalued, for the improvements were
paid for out of rents, and the farmers themselves might have

done the improving if they had retained those rents in their own pockets. The landlords were a heavy enough charge when they lived on their estates and spent their rents in the district where the money was earned. They were a fatal burden when they took to living away from home. Then the money that was so urgently needed for improving the farms was spent in Edinburgh and London. The standard of life in capital cities demanded always bigger incomes. Rents had to be raised. The landlords took an always bigger share of the farmer's increase; and on the average, gave less in return, either by way of local spending or improvements on the farms. The poorer lands could not stand such a burden. The small fields went back into pasture, and a dozen crofts became one sheep farm, because, of course, the sheep-farmer, having smaller overhead charges, could pay a bigger rent than the twelve crofters put together. The sheep-farmer paid that rent by robbing the hills; and now the bracken is the end of the story. The landlords have had their tithes for centuries; too many of them have been proud and foolish for generations; and now their fine state is falling in ruins. Soon there will be nothing left but the bracken.

We are not yet finished with Glendevon and all the other glens, for the story is not all a tale of gradual decay. I have been told there were nine inns along the Glen in the olden time, which may support the Arcadian dream. But most of them may be discounted, for almost any house was an inn a hundred years ago. In later times there was only one. Now there is also an hotel in the modern style. This is a sign of the times. As the possibilities of the soil are exhausted we fall back on the scenery. As agriculture fails we begin to think of the tourist. And the tourist is not to be laughed at. He may even be the economic salvation of all the glens. For the glens have inexhaustible resources of the picturesque and the tourist is prepared to pay for it. Besides, he needs to be fed, and the small fields along the river banks might be excellent market gardens. The tourist has money for small luxuries; he loves the indigenous arts and crafts; and he will buy their products if he is offered them. So the Highlands, discovered by Dr. Johnson and developed by Queen Victoria, may yet rival the Alps, and the glens be filled by an industrious population of craftsmen and market gardeners, gaining enough in a short summer to give them a long winter's ease. It is difficult to see any other future for such poor land.

CHAPTER SEVEN : KINROSS AND MARY STEWART

LET us now go down into the Lowlands again and resume our journey to Kinross. This is typical Scots country of the more domestic kind. It is a narrow trough sheltered on three sides by the hills—the Ochils to the north, the Cleish to the south, and the Lomond to the east. Agriculture, which is the only industry you will find hereabout, is a combination of arable and pastoral. Some farms along the foothills have an arable part on the lower ground and a range of grazing on the hills. Or a man may have two farms— one entirely hill grazing and the other wholly arable down on the low ground. Thus the farmers manage to make the best of both worlds, neither of them remarkable for fertility.

Kinross, which is the centre of this region, is the kind of town you might hope to find but very seldom do find in Scotland. It has a pleasant site on the shore of Loch Leven and close to the hills. The Ochils define the limits of the plain a little distance away and the Cleish Hills come in from the west to catch the sunset in the most agreeable way. The setting thus combines the agricultural with the not too sublime, a harmony that the eighteenth century liked. Therefore it is appropriate that some part of the little town should have an Augustan air.

Kinross used to be the county town so it contains the county offices; and, since Kinross is one of the smallest counties, the county offices are small in proportion. They are charming, in the style that the eighteenth century made perfect and the nineteenth century forgot, to our sorrow. There is not a great deal of this good building in Kinross;

the town is not a little Bath; but there is enough to give the town a charming air, a touch of sophistication, sweetness and light. It may survive. The county, being too small a unit, has been joined to Perthshire. The town is not likely to expand, but should remain the shopping centre for the country round about it. There could be no better fate for any little town.

Certainly it is to be hoped that the people of Kinross will never discover an ambition to make their town as big as Kirkcaldy and then as big as Dundee and then as big as Glasgow and then as ugly as Hell. Numbers mean nothing in themselves; the only criterion is the quality of the life that the people live. A town should be of a size, along with the country round it, to have all the amenities of civilization—a playhouse, a good cinema, concerts by the Scottish Orchestra, a full library and an eating-house where the citizens may learn the diviner truths about food and drink. That is not much to ask for in a world where material things are so plenty, nor should a town need to be the size of Aberdeen before it can have them—and Aberdeen has little more. If this were a reasonable world we would arrange our little towns to be centres of amenity for the country-side and we would be careful that they did not grow beyond the size of best utility. As for the people who think that a factory with a thousand underpaid workmen is a sign of progress, we can only hope that God may lighten their darkness. That kind of progress can usually be measured in a sudden rise in ground rents and a gradual rise in poor relief. It means wealth for a few people to-day and a burden for many to-morrow, just as now we are paying for the wealth that was made out of the slums of Glasgow.

Let us hope that Kinross will never be so exploited, that it will remain a pleasant little town setting the standards for the country round about it. There is some little way to go before it will be ideal for its purpose. Some of the amenities are lacking. But it has at least a good inn. The Green Hotel is famous. It is much frequented by anglers off Loch Leven and anglers, however tiresome, do leave good inns behind them. I have done myself well there and been done better by. We have dined there in the summer time off fresh cold salmon and a bottle of wine while the shadows of the trees grew long upon the green and the colours deepened on the Lomond Hills; we have drunk our coffee and our cherry brandy to the murmur of anglers telling immemorial lies; and we have driven home, in and out between the telephones, through the sweet night scented with hay, till we saw the moon rise up, insinuating, above our castle wall. Those are the times when we can wonder at the needless misery in the world; and those are the times when we cease to care.

And when was there ever a misery like Mary Stewart's?

Kinross is older than the eighteenth century. An island stands out in Loch Leven; a castle stands on the island; and Mary Stewart was once imprisoned in the castle. Therefor you can't pass that way without thinking of the fair ghost who so troubled the peace of Scotland and still raises a fine confusion in sentimental minds. In fact, you can't be long in Scotland without meeting that ghost, for her story is part of the national heritage and her worship a soft spot in the national consciousness. I envy the stranger who hears her story with a fresh mind, for he may arrive at something like the truth about her. That is denied to Scotsmen. We were brought up on legends of the glamorous lady born under an unhappy star. The young have either cursed their fortune that they were bred too late to serve her or have joined in a tearful communion over the sorrows of a woman's heart. In later years we may have learned facts instead of legends and begun to doubt our first enthusiasm. But we can never get away from our first impressions. Whatever we may read, our judgement is still enchanted by the ballads; the more we learn the more we distrust our reason.

What was the truth about her?

Now that astrology is becoming fashionable again we may indeed believe that she was born under an unhappy star. The army of her father, King James the Fifth, had just been beaten by the English at Solway Moss. While James lay ill in his palace at Falkland, news came out of Linlithgow that the queen was delivered of a daughter. The double misfortune of a beaten army and a female heir crushed the poor king's feeble spirit. He turned his face to the wall and died, as most of his line had died, in sorrow. Thus events came into evil conjunction at the birth of Mary Stewart.

Yet there was a time when her fortune promised well enough. Her mother was a Frenchwoman out of Guise Lorraine and there was an old alliance between Scotland and France so the queen was raised in France while the queen mother ruled Scotland in her name. It was something to be a queen in those days, even queen of a poor country like Scotland; but fortune held even more for the girl. She married, or was married to, the Dauphin of France, thus drawing the alliance of France and Scotland even closer. If ever the fate of western Europe trembled it might have trembled then when England lay between the consort France and Scotland, like a nut in a tongs, ready to be cracked by a strong man's hand. But there was no strong man. The Dauphin succeeded to the throne as Francis II, but he died a year later; the alliance was weakened; and Mary returned to Scotland after many years.

Now the Stewarts had always had to fight with the nobles for possession of the throne. So when Mary returned to Scotland she had to face the usual intrigues among the ruthless lords. This time the ordinary tale of greed was complicated and made more furious by the Reformation. The peace of the realm was disrupted by rapacious lords and howling fanatics, by the faithful of Rome and the heretics of Geneva; and that fine hell broth was adroitly stirred by English agents, since Scotland's disunion must be England's strength. It was a situation that Elizabeth and Burleigh together might have handled; it was too much for a girl newly come from the Court of France. A born rogue like Elizabeth and one with a remorseless vision of realities might have seen where the good of Scotland lay, might have bargained with the Protestant lords and bought their friendship and then used the authority of the throne to lead the country into ways of toleration and peace. But the old Regent Mary of Guise had been a militant for Rome and her daughter was a faithful Catholic. They could not compromise with what they might have been excused for thinking the devil's work. The result was generations of religious trouble and intolerance in Scotland.

Mary was lovely when she came from France; but something more than loveliness was needed. They say that she was learned, that she could discourse in many languages. We can believe them. For the events of her life show that she had every grace but wisdom. How sad that wisdom should have been the one grace needed then.

Mary was never more unwise than in her marrying. Her second husband was Henry Stewart, her cousin, usually called Lord Darnley. Though he had some accomplishment he was a worthless creature, a fool and probably a drunkard. It was an unhappy marriage and had a mysterious end, for Darnley was killed when his house was destroyed by powder. Mary was then a widow for the second time. There would have been a deal of gossip about that sudden death. The Calvinists saw in it another proof that the queen was the breathing figure, the seductive form, of sin. Even the moderates, if there were ever any such in Scotland, must have wondered and been troubled.

The nation was alarmed by the death of Darnley; it was outraged by the thing that followed after. Mary took

Hepburn, Earl of Bothwell, as her third husband. Bothwell was not loved by either party in the state and could
never have been acceptable to the nation. The marriage
completed Mary's ruin. Matters grew worse. Mary was
imprisoned in Loch Leven Castle; escaped, raised an
army that was beaten at Langside, near Glasgow; fled to
England; was imprisoned again for sixteen years till Elizabeth dared kill her on the falsest pretence of treason.

There has been a lot of bother about Mary ever since.
Chivalrous souls have defended her. Scholars have done
monumental research on trivial incidents in her career.
Novels and poems and plays have been written about her.
And films—oh, such lovely films. They have had a
splendid subject. Against a background of events that
were changing the world she played a tragedy of singular
ineffectiveness. She becomes alive to us only in her relations with a few men—with Darnley and Rizzio, her
Italian secretary, and Bothwell. She appears as it were
only in a few film sequences—arguing with John Knox,
playing games of memory with Rizzio about the fair land
of France, riding over the Border moors to Hermitage where
Bothwell lay ill, escaping from Loch Leven Castle in a
little boat upon the dark water, and laying her beautiful
head upon the block at Fotheringay.

They tell that her father, when he got the news of her
birth, said, ' It cam wi a lass and it will gang wi a lass,'
meaning that a woman would never be able to hold the
throne of Scotland. He may have had a prophetic vision
as he lay so near to death, for it was the tragedy of this queen
that she was a woman and a Stewart. If she had not been
a Stewart she might have had the cool spirit and the
calculating mind to match the Scottish lords and the English
agents with cunning. If she had not been a queen in her
own right she would have been an incomparable consort
for a renaissance prince. But she was born for too great
a place. She fell short of greatness.

You cannot read about the death of her grandfather James the Fourth at the battle of Flodden without feeling that there was tragedy calling for silence in the courts of heaven, for with James there died not only so many knights and serving-men but the best hopes of the renaissance in Scotland. Mary's tragedy was personal to herself alone. You get the idea that she was irrelevant to the greater events of her time, that there was never anything she, being what she was, could have done to change them; that hers was the tragedy of a ruler born with every grace but the power of decisive action. This is a cinematographic age: let us say that Mary facing the Scottish lords and the English agents was like Bergner playing Daniel in the lions' den. Alas for Mary, the lions feared neither God nor man.

It may be that Mary's fate was decided at Flodden long before she was born. James the Fourth was a glorious prince with the dawn coming up behind him. He was a man of the Renaissance—bold, adventurous, decisive, in love with the arts of peace. He had the will and the imagination to have remade Scotland, to have given her the quickening touch of the renaissance. If you care to play at the game of let's suppose, there is nothing he might not have done had he been granted the ultimate wisdom to keep the peace with England. But he could not resist another fling at the old enemy. He marched into England and died at Flodden, and Scotland's hopes died with him. His heir was a child; there were all the intrigues that were inevitable in such a minority; the promises of a glorious future were never fulfilled. The years that might have been spent in learning the new arts that were spreading across Europe —the arts of magnificent getting and magnificent spending —were wasted in faction; and after the faction came the Reformation.

Mary lived in an ill time for kings. The struggle between Rome and Geneva masked a graver conflict—between public duty and private greed. The corruption of the clergy, the infallibility of the Pope, those were fine cries to gather a party, but the real issue was whether a man should be free to exploit the growing wealth of Europe to the utmost for his private satisfaction without any regard for the common good. It was inevitable that the Church and the Crown should lose sooner or later. How could Mary, or any Stewart, or any king, withstand for ever the new commercial classes that were growing out of the old economy of Europe. Mary could neither understand the new forces, nor make peace with them, and so she died.

What is the secret of her after fame ? Was hers another case of all for love and a crown well lost ? Is it a matter of vicarious excitements in lifting the coverlet to see what happens in the royal bed ? Is it that kings and queens, being a deification of the common people, have in their own sorrows a part of each man's suffering and that part so raised above the common state that we feel ennobled because they feel as we. The servant maid that loves the grocer cannot believe for long that her passion will shake the world, but when she sees that the frustrated loves of kings make empires tremble, she, knowing that all love must be the same, discovers in herself community with kings. Perhaps Mary touches with royal state the lives of all who try to maintain the life of the spirit in the hideous deserts of this degraded age. It is likely that there will be some in every age to love her, until the times and the places are forgotten and she is only a legend of sorrow out of some unremembered time.

CHAPTER EIGHT : THE PRICE OF COAL

IT is now time to be stepping down into Fife, that home of stern realities.

There are two ways from Kinross.

One runs by Strathmiglo and Cupar to St. Andrews through fine agricultural land and sturdy little towns. It is a road along which I have made many pleasant journeys and could travel again with great contentment.

We might stop for a little at Auchtermuchty and Strathmiglo, pleasant small Lowland towns that once nourished a breed of grand contentious radicals. We might go down the loan to Falkland under the Lomond Hills where the Palace of James the Fifth stands in the middle of the town like a royal ode in stone, one of the loveliest of our ancient houses. There in the warm garden we could meditate upon the change that has cast down kings and empires and when we had tired of the melancholy sport we could meditate upon the linoleum factory that supports and dominates the town.

We might discover a nice significance in such a factory built in such a place, for it belongs to the Scottish Co-operative Wholesale Society and stands upon what would once have been the pleasure ground of kings. Now the king and the people were a close alliance in the olden time. They stood together—in theory—against the greedy merchants and the lawless barons. Then how just it is, now that kings must stand outwith contention, that the people should still have some part of the ancient heritage —how just, and how surprising. At the same time we may regret that the people have not a royal sense of architecture. Their factory does not add to the beauty of the town. We may regret it; but at least we may also hope that taste is not the prerogative of kings alone; that freedom, being a noble thing, may yet be celebrated in noble works.

From Falkland we could go by shady roads to Cupar, an old country town that still wears some graceful marks of its antiquity. There we would also notice the sugar-beet factory, one of those strange memorials raised to the economic confusions of our time. Then, consoling ourselves with the look of the rich farms along the road, we would go out to St. Andrews on the windy dunes by the sea.

But I have travelled that road too often and know it too well. It is too full of peace, too embroidered with fertility, altogether too domestic and serene. I had rather we took a different road that would lead us through another Scotland. So we will go south between the Cleish and the Lomond Hills till we come to those parts where the coal measures lie beneath the face of the land. There in the heart of West Fife we will find the desolate town of Cowdenbeath.

In the timeless days when I lived in the castle among the Ochil Hills I used to fall into an illusion that the world was very beautiful. Day after day came up in a rosy flame; night followed night of serene and starry dark. We slept in the sun or warmed ourselves by great wood fires or lay soft in our beds watching the moon among her flock of clouds. We had food to eat and books and music and a little strong drink to make us jolly. We lived in an enchanted tower whither the voices of the world came faint and meaningless like a sound half-heard upon the evening.

But there were occasions when we had to go to town. We went down out of the glen in the morning sun into the valley below and there we found as great a peace, with a richness we had forgotten up in the bare green hills. Then we said to ourselves, being Lowland born, ' The world is even bonnier than we had thought.' We got on a train, but even it could not spoil the illusion, for it was a calling train that stopped for a long time at platforms while the officials engaged in conversation. We had to wait a time at Kinross, but that was no hardship when there were roses beyond the line and the mystery of Mary Stewart to beguile us. We left Kinross by the shores of Loch Leven where the anglers' boats lay far out under the silver light like birds upon a quiet sea. The illusion was complete. But like all perfect things it immediately passed away. We arrived at Cowdenbeath and the sternest realities of the modern world.

It was as if we had gone out of Eden into a battlefield; and so indeed we had; for Cowdenbeath and the country round it are part of the battlefield on which the glories of industrialism have been won. I doubt if any modern warfare, with all the resources of nitro-glycerine and poison gas, could have left a more devastated country-side. Men have worked the coal for many years without a plan, always taking the easiest and the cheapest road and leaving their muck behind them. The face of the ground is riven by deserted works and littered with heaps of refuse. The natural drainage has been ruined so that stagnant pools fill the hollows in the distorted face of the land. The result is a series of swamps by which ruined engine-houses stand at the side of mouldering railways. Colliery bings gloom over the waste, black and old and bare, with not a shrub, not a blade of grass to mask their sides worn smooth by the rain. It is a country despoiled by an invading army. The miners have dug out the wealth from the earth and have moved on when the wealth was finished, leaving ruin behind them. The destruction continues. You can see it happen wherever the pits are working. The busy collieries of to-day will be the wastes of to-morrow: and so on and so until the last of the coal has been exhausted.

The wealth that has been taken from under its foundations has not been used to beautify Cowdenbeath. This is a town in which people have to live and get children and make their souls in readiness for heaven. Certainly it is a place that would make people hope for a pleasant life hereafter to compensate for the miseries on earth. It would do well enough for the temporary base of an invading army, but as a place where men and women have to spend their few mortal years it is a sin against humanity. To us, as we used to come down from the hills, the contrast was too awful to believe in; for the town was a horrid nightmare infested with evil. What did I say a town should have? A playhouse. Concerts by the Scottish Orchestra. An eating-house where the citizens could learn the diviner truths about food and drink. You'd hardly dare think of these in the mining towns of Scotland where the people have not got even decent houses to live in. You have only to look at the houses warped by the sinking of their foundations; at the muddy common yards behind them; at the unrelenting gloom of their surroundings to wonder with fear what kind of life can be lived there.

Two families from Cowdenbeath once camped on holiday beside our house. They were four adults and eight children. Their accommodation was one bivouac and a bit of tarpaulin laid over three sticks. The rain fell in torrents, without more than six hours' fair weather, during the week. We could not have imagined anything more pitiable as the children huddled round a poor hissing fire or lay among their wet blankets listening to the rain. But when we commiserated with the parents they said it was at least a change for a single room at home. They were not by any means unique. The miners of Fife can produce enough coal to pay for everything but houses. And Cowdenbeath is not the worst of our mining towns.

The men that must live in such disgusting conditions are not the scum of our population. They are not even the unwanted who may never be employed again. They are men doing the hardest work of the community in the most dangerous places. They and their fathers have brought up millions of tons of coal; that coal has made Scotsmen wealthy; it has paid for magnificent houses and fine pictures, delicious food and generous drink: but it has done nothing for Cowdenbeath except to ravish a whole country-side and build towns that are offences against common decency. Therefore you will not be surprised that West Fife returned a Communist at the last General Election. The contrast between producing wealth and reaping poverty could hardly breed faith in the divine good faith of capitalism; and the inevitability of gradualness must seem both slower and less inevitable than death. You need not be surprised that such men have a revolutionary temper. But it is surprising that they have not rebelled long ago against the inhumanity of their conditions. These conditions are utterly condemned by social justice and common sense. If there is any social justice, then it is immoral that those who produce so much should have so little. If common sense is the judge, then it is madness to make an essential part of the community live in conditions that degrade them and condemn their children to stunted lives. There is nothing that can be pled in extenuation, except the righteousness of greed. That, however, is still enough.

The contrast between Cowdenbeath and our glen in the Ochils horrified us whenever we had to face it. Yet, though they were so very different, the same process had been working in both of them. The decline of life in the hills and the sinful conditions round Cowdenbeath were both caused by people taking the immediate profit without thinking about the ultimate good of the community. In both money has been taken away from the places where it was made and we are left to salvage the ruins. If the traveller sometimes meets with a kind of hopelessness in the lonelier parts of the country and with a violent sense of

6

injustice in districts like West Fife, he may think of the wealth that has gone out of those places to build mansions in Belgravia and fine streets of shops in Glasgow and put stained-glass windows into churches. If he finds that the younger men and women are sometimes a little discontented, he may remember that the great Victorians skimmed the cream of the country and that their grandsons cannot grow fat on a diet of skimmed milk. The west of Fife is not a breeding ground of pious thoughts.

CHAPTER NINE: FIFE AND THE FRINGE
OF GOLD

In the olden time they used to say that Fife was a beggar's mantle fringed with gold, for the wild and hilly interior ran down to a fine strip of farming land and many comfortable little towns along the coast. Generations of good farmers have changed the look of that beggar's mantle. The rough pastures have become arable; the waste has become pasture; and trees have been planted on the hills. The beggar's mantle has been made over into a rich green cloak. And what about the golden fringe? Change has come to the little towns turning their gold into silver, but it is still good metal, sound adornment. The eastern part of Fife is a charming, busy country and the traveller will find it a welcome relief from the desolations of the collier towns.

There never was such a country-side for quiet roads that wander off to make a roundabout to everywhere. They may be a confusion to strangers yet it is no great matter to be lost on them, for all of them lead to some place that may be worth the visiting.

From Cowdenbeath we might go south through Dunfermline to Culross (as they speak it Cu-ros). That ancient town should not be missed if you have an eye for the picturesque, because it is one of the best museum pieces in Scotland. It has the remains of an Abbey. It has a fine palace—the old Scottish kind of palace with many small dark rooms—in which the Office of Works has uncovered some grand craftsmanship of the olden time. It has many cottages with crow-stepped gables, set down at curious angles to the streets. It has a Cross, and wynds, and old men sitting in the sun and an air of genuine antiquity. Go into its crooked streets down under the hill by the waters of the Forth, walk quietly in a humble spirit, and you may guess what a Scottish town was like three—four hundred years ago. Since the life has rather gone out of Culross except at holiday time, you may people the streets with the ghosts of your fancy—with the monks that prepared for heaven by cultivating their gardens on earth and enjoying the fruits in their season; with the gentry from the Palace, proud and arrogant and gaily dressed in the splendid fashions of the time; with the burgess men—merchants and the like—that could enjoy their bottle of claret when another day's profit had been gathered in; and with the common people, the drunken scandalous common people of Scotland. If you stand at the street corners you may hear the news from Flodden come over the firth as heavy as a dirge; may listen to the gossip about Bothwell and the Queen, gossip in which religious horror gives an edge to bawdy pleasure; may catch a note of panic on the wind, that Charles Edward has landed and the Highlanders are on the march for rape and plunder; may let the years go sounding through your head till you have lived again the history of the Scots and you arrive at the latest point of time when a boy offers you an ice-cream block made the day before in London. Then you may be very humble at the thought of the continuing purpose that runs so clearly marked along the centuries.

Go down along the firth from Culross and you may look at the Forth Bridge, surely the bravest work of the Victorian engineers. However you look at the bridge it is an amazing piece of work, an epic wrought in steel. But if you would appreciate its full magnificence you should stand at the water's edge, on the Ferry pier, and look at it between you and heaven. Some bridges are graceful, daring arabesques of stone and lime that go leaping over space.

The Forth Bridge is not like them. It is not a work of the imagination lightly poised on the edge of the impossible. It is as solid, as immutably strong, as if it had been made by the eternal to outlast eternity. It does not span the river; it clasps the riven land together against the encroaching sea. It is a master work and fit to be the memorial to the Victorian Age. That age has other memorials and most of them are dreadful; but it was more than a time of slums and imitation Gothic; it saw man's greatest progress in material things. It had many dubious heroes, but the Engineer best deserves to stand as the symbol of his time; and the Forth Bridge may stand as his memorial, for it is engineering in its most heroic moment.

If you continue along the by-roads—and you must find them for yourself because there is no language to describe their windings—you will find the graveyards of many fine Victorians in the shipbreaking yards of Inverkeithing and Rosyth. I may have said a thing or two about the waste in our present way of doing and I have no doubt that I will say more; but in the shipbreaking yards at least we show signs of a tidy mind. When ships have grown so old that they can no longer earn their keep by the traffic of the seas, they come to their last anchorage at Inverkeithing alongside its melancholy quays. The cabins are stripped. The engines are dismantled. Oxy-acetylene flames reduce the hulls to plates again. In a few weeks or months nothing is left but heaps of metal ready to be passed through the furnaces. A whole fleet from little coasters to battleships has passed through the breakers' yards at Inverkeithing and Rosyth. The biggest ships of the German Navy, after lying at the depths of Scapa Flow, were towed with their bottoms upmost to the Forth and there were broken down to lumps of steel. It was a fitting end to the vanity of arms. But we have not learned the wisdom of it yet. For now the peaceful merchantmen are riven apart so that their metal may be founded into guns. Whether you mourn for the death of good ships or the foolishness of the human race, Inverkeithing will give you something to moralize on.

Fortunately there is enough in the golden fringe of Fife to cure you of sad thoughts. Kirkcaldy will not do it though Nairns and Barry Ostleres make enough linoleum to put a new face on Scotland. Nor will Methil cheer you, for it is one of the outlets for the Fife coalfields and could not be mistaken for anything else. But Leven would maybe lighten your spirits, for that is its trade. It is a seaside resort much frequented by the people of Glasgow who dare the keener winds of the east; and it looks much like every other seaside resort that ever was. It has its streets of substantial boarding-houses where the proprietors lie in wait behind their curtains like spiders behind their webs. There are the usual tents, huts and gaudy little concrete boxes on the front; putting greens and tennis courts and a hard-working pierrot show. You could find a thousand such along the shores of Britain. But there is also the glorious sweep of the bay where the long waves come up the sandy shore and the light spray dances in the wind. I suppose everything else is irrelevant beside that wonder which must touch even the landladies with a kind of dangerous beauty.

I have seen Leven very gay in a dancing wind when the waves were running lines of silver and the red roofs along the front looked warm against the green of the woods. People that have to live in grey cities for fifty weeks a year might have gone drunk on all that colour.

Some did; or at least they were mildly intoxicated. They played in the sea; they ran along the shore; they sun-bathed in suits that were far more nude than nakedness. Most, however, kept themselves well under control. They played decorous games of putting; they ate ice-cream with mild enjoyment; and bared no more than their braces to the uncanny heat of the sun. You often hear complaints about the conduct of holiday crowds, but what does their

deplorable conduct amount to beyond a little thoughtless-
ness and bad manners. There is, alas, nothing dionysiac
about their orgies, for you can't be orgiastic in a Scottish
summer. There is always the danger of rain, always a
sobering sharpness in the wind. So if our seaside towns
are not as seductive to pleasure as we might wish, if they
do not lie open to the sun like passion flowers as is the way
with Mediterranean towns, we may blame the sun that is
not hot enough for passion. It is maybe just as well for
the peace of the realm that it is so.

The Scottish people have a reputation for being very
self-contained; but that does not argue a poverty of passion.
You have only to see them when they let themselves go
with the help of a dram to realize that they have a considerable heat in their blood.

You never know what will blow up out of a dull sky.
When I was still a boy I had no idea of the resources of
the Scottish temper. The older people round about me
seemed to be extremely staid. The fact that the men often
drank too much on market days was considered no blot
on their respectability, and if a girl did have a child un-
timely no one thought very much unless she made a habit
of it. To me who was always getting into trouble, they
seemed a race born to an unnatural canniness. Indeed I
often suspected that they were less than human.

Then I happened to be in their company at a country
sale. There was plenty of drink about, as there always was
on such occasions; the good farmers had their will of it;
and they were merry by the time we left for home.

We were, I remember, seven of us—six farmers and
myself a boy—in a motor lorry driven by the soberest of
the company. But even he was hardly what you would
call stone-cold sober. He drove with spirit and abandon
along the narrow roads, so that the passengers rolled about
on the lorry and swore at him with a great expense of
alcoholic breath. That of course was exhausting work,

so we had to stop at three several public-houses for refreshment. As those visits were prolonged ones, the driver steered an always more erratic course between hedges and ditches and dry stone dykes. It was then, I think, that I first learned the meaning of danger, but the rest of the company were too well fortified to worry about the face of death that seemed to grin at us from behind the wintry moon.

We called at a farm-house. As we had made a certain large provision at the last inn and as our host was himself not unprovided, the gentlemen settled down to enjoy themselves. Being of no age for drinking then, though to be so was my greatest ambition, I went out and talked to the ploughmen in the bothy for an hour or maybe more.

It was, I remember, a perfect winter night when I left the bothy to return to the house. The mud in the yard was frozen into little rills and waves; the sky was a deep unfathomable dark out of which the stars shone in frosty splendour; and to the west the young moon rode in a narrow field of light. Even though I was only a child I stood still and held my breath for wonder at the brittle clearness of the night when even the silence seemed to crack, with a tiny silver noise, under the grip of the frost. But it was not only the frost I listened to. A loud noise was coming from the house, a bumbling rowdy noise that sounded strangely through the still night. It had in it something of an organ and something of the zoo and most of all it was like some force of nature suddenly set free. I stood in the close, a little frightened, wondering what horror had invaded the country-side. Then I realized it was the staid Scots farmers at their pleasure. I ran into the house afraid that I might miss something that sounded like tremendous fun.

Whatever I may have expected, the reality did not disappoint me. The scene in the parlour was like nothing

I had ever imagined. The big low room was poorly lighted by a paraffin lamp that threw monstrous shadows on the roof and left the corners in obscurity. It was better so, for I could see legs and boots emerging from the darkness where their owners had retired from the mêlée or had slipped from the supporting corner to the safety of the floor in unmelodious slumber. At one side of the room a six-foot horse-dealer was playing on the pianoforte and since he did not trust himself on the music stool he was on his knees at the keyboard. He was playing with an excellent sense of time but his fingers were so broad that each one hit a chord at a time. The result was very powerful. And it was wholly in keeping with the rest of the scene. For three farmers were dancing a barbaric dance, an extempore invention, in the middle of the room. So that they could dance the freer they had stripped themselves entirely naked and were leaping fantastically between the shadows in the full glory of their manhood. I stood at the door, completely stricken; for the din of the piano, the shouts of the dancers and the hairy bodies prancing in the gloom made me feel that some ruthless elemental force had been let loose in the room.

My coming in disturbed them. One of them gave a shout and made at me. I just managed to dodge him so that he ran out through the door into the lobby beyond. The other two chased after him. I could hear them shouting and clattering among the pans in the dark kitchen and greatly daring I ran after them. By that time they were out into the close, chasing each other with hideous shouts. Still daring, I followed; and, lurking in the darkest shadow, watched them make half a dozen rounds of the close. Then one of them found an open gate into a field; the others followed him; and, as I stood there in the icy close, I could see their white naked bodies go tearing over the frosty lea and hear their shouts diminish into the echoes of the night while the noise of the piano came grandly from the house in a clumsy but fervent attempt at the Hundredth Psalm.

There is no doubt about it; the Scots have a considerable heat in their blood. Meantime the east wind keeps it well under control. But think what a tropical sun might do. The emotional tangles of Holywood are blamed on the sun that supercharges the young with its vitality. Now it is unthinkable that the bland bodies of film stars could contain any great resources of original sin, yet look what the sun can do with them. How much more would it do to the rich resources within a Glasgow engineer or an Aberdeenshire farmer. How much more exciting the results would be. Who can say what gorgeous dreams it would breed in the mind of a dour Scots elder; what immortal longings it would rouse in a farmer's wife. I'm sure it would release such a fiery tide of repressed emotions as would make Vesuvius look like a penny candle. It would utterly destroy the crooners and film makers that wring a living out of the fringes of love. It would shatter the precarious respectability of Scottish life. It would— but the imagination can go no farther into the wonders possible to the Scottish temper beneath a tropical sun. As long as bungalows must be built and vacuum cleaners paid for, it is as well that we have always the bite in the east wind to make us content with the decorous pleasure of Leven beach.

But the inquiring visitor must certainly visit Leven or some such if he is going to understand the people that live in Scotland. It is an exercise in the new science of Mass Observation. There he will be able to observe our caste system and our tabus. He will observe how some expose almost all their bodies; how some bare only the neck; how some are dressed for ease and some are dressed for Sunday. He will be able to distinguish between those who eat ices openly out of cones and the Pharisees that pay a penny extra for the decent privacy of an ice-cream parlour. He will notice that some take meat teas in their boarding-houses and some take fish and chips to the Follies. He may be a little surprised that the universal brotherhood of man and woman, which is complete in the water, suddenly disappears upon the beach. When he has understood those various distinctions he may be able to follow the holiday-makers to their homes and see that the distinctions are even more firmly held there. Then he will realize that although we are all Jock Tamson's bairns, Scotland being the supreme democracy, we are also like the members of other families in that we don't all speak to each other. He will understand how strong the conventions are that govern our lives, conventions that have as strong a hold in the new paganism as in the old respectability. We are all children of our environment; and our seaside resorts are influenced by the places that support them. Which may be the reason that Leven in spite of its frivolities, remains as douce as a respectable terrace in Glasgow. But like that same terrace it has tremendous possibilities, given a touch of the sun to bring out the Old Adam in all his furious glory.

Leven Beach is as modern as to-day. When you go farther along the golden fringe you will return to an older Scotland. The small towns between Leven and St. Andrews—Anstruther (called Anster) Crail, Pittenweem and Largo have a charming air of antiquity. It is not so much the air of the houses though some of them are old enough, as a feeling that they have known prosperity and a decent living for centuries. They do not belong to any particular time, but have ripened slowly in a good tradition cherished by each succeeding generation. Now it is very seldom that you find such towns in Scotland. There are of course Falkland and Haddington and Culross, the Old Town of Edinburgh and the Aulton of Aberdeen, where you can walk through the streets right back five hundred years. But, considering the age of civilization in

Scotland, those towns are surprisingly few. Most Scottish
towns and villages, even those that have a certain age, look
as if they had been built in very recent times. When the
houses are good they are no older than the eighteenth century and those that have survived from an older time are
quite without distinction.

That may be explained in two ways. Many fine old
houses were destroyed when the towns began to expand a
hundred and fifty years ago. We know that Glasgow
sacrificed its College to a railway yard. The houses of the
wealthy merchants went the same sad road. However,
that sort of thing happened all over western Europe; and,
when you think of the eagerness with which Scotland
welcomed the industrial revolution, you can hardly be
surprised that so little of the older building has survived
in the industrial towns.

But you may indeed be surprised that it is just as scarce
in the parts of Scotland that have been untouched by
industry. You can travel for days and weeks through the
south and west of England and count a thousand villages
that have an air of centuries about them. Broadway and
Chipping Campden, Burford and Corfe Castle, Stratford-
upon-Avon and Ludlow all witness to provincial ease and
culture in the olden time. But there are few such villages
in Scotland.

I have said before that Scotland had a Reformation
instead of a Renaissance. Now the Renaissance is usually
thought of as a time of great cultural flowering. But it
was more than that. It was a time when an increase in
trade brought more wealth than medieval princes had ever
dreamed of. It is not for me to say whether the trade or
the culture came first. It is enough that when the wealth
did come men were willing to use it for the glory of the
arts. Wealth came to the Cotswold Hills; and the wool
merchants used it to build them lovely towns. Thus a
tradition of good building was so strongly founded that it

persists to this day. The wool trade declined and wealth never came again to the Cotswold towns. Their good traditions were never in danger of being swamped by the nineteenth century's ruthless growth. They were allowed to ripen and grow still more beautiful in comparison with the horrors of modern times.

But Scotland did not have that Renaissance. If James the Fourth had stayed at peace with England, the Scottish rose might have had its flowering and the Scottish thistle borne a crop of figs. He would have encouraged trade with Europe and taught his merchants how to spend their money on lordly works. He would have brought wealth into the country places and built fine villages where only hovels stood before. But he died at Flodden, and the years that should have been glorious were wasted in religious and political argument. Then the Reformation came in one of its extremer forms and there was little of Renaissance grace in Scotland to soften the austerities of Geneva. So in the days when Scotsmen had the taste they had little money, and by the time they had the money they had lost the taste. The nobility built some fine houses, such as the castles at Fyvie and Glamis; the merchants of Edinburgh and Glasgow built others; but there was no money for the building of Chipping Campdens and Broadways all over Scotland.

Except on the golden fringe of Fife. The small seaports, thriving on their seaborne trade and the produce of the good farmlands behind them, had wealth enough to build pleasant and enduring houses in the olden time; and they never had enough of the last century's prosperity to spoil their ancient character. They are, to use a very far-fetched image, the Cotswolds of Scotland. Like the Cotswolds they are much frequented by the holiday-maker who looks for something more restrained than Leven Beach. This part of Scotland is a decent Scottish Riviera on a summer day, with a look of innocence that the French Riviera has long since lost and the Cornish Riviera must lose before long. But it is more than that. It witnesses to a chance that was missed; a chance to bring a graciousness into Scottish life that was sadly needed four hundred years ago and is even more sadly needed now.

I like to think of the golden fringe as I saw it one June afternoon a year or two ago. It was a sparkling blue day, one of those that look more like an advertisement than an honest work of nature. We had come from the Ochil Hills between fields of young corn and hedges of vulgar flaunting rhododendrons. There was a tang of growth in the air and light winds ran across the hay like shivers of delight. We felt our spirits renewed as if they too had been quickened by the season. Even the ancient motor car (Ten pounds down and a dubious bargain) seemed to be affected by the easy air. It hummed along the flat, bounded at the little hills and coasted down the braes with a jolly rattle. Then beyond the last rise we found the sea, wave upon wave of blue and silver, sweeping round and far to meet the horizon.

As we looked down across the last fields our mood enjoyed a sea change. Our spirits that had been renewed by the upland airs were now enlarged, set free. Our minds, that had been conscious only of the rising sap in wood and field and all the business of the fruitful earth, were now touched with unknown wonders, as if the salt winds were blowing in from the furthest corners of the world and the blue sky bordered on eternity.

All that afternoon we loitered among the little towns. When the sun was at its warmest around three o'clock we ran our car down on to the beach at Largo and set about enjoying a day at the seaside in the traditional style.

The other two members of the party, a young man and a young woman in all the foolish pride of the comely flesh, went off to bathe; but I remained behind to make the tea. We had, I remember, a kettle that we had filled at a spring; so I went along the shore to look for driftwood. While doing so, I noticed with some interest one of those old conventions that give modern life a delightful flavour. The bathers had of course retired into the undergrowth of the dunes to undress, but the dunes at Largo would hardly conceal a rabbit. Furthermore, a footpath runs along the side of the dunes. So there were my two friends, at a distance of twenty yards from each other, making an elaborate pretence of being concealed while they undressed behind six inches of whins. The general public on the footpath and I myself on the shore played our part in the comedy by looking and yet not seeming to look. If I ever doubted the fable of the king and the imaginary suit of clothes, I ceased to doubt it then. But, for the credit of every one concerned, I must also say there was no small boy ill-conditioned enough to shatter the illusion by calling attention to the obvious. We all, in our various ways, continued to look for driftwood.

That afternoon proved not only the power of an old convention but also the truth of an old insinuation. There is a story, much loved by those who love not Fife, about a man who set out to see Scotland. In order to pay his expenses he used to play a tin whistle and so cozen a few shillings from the village people with the traditional airs of the country. As he had some small skill he did well enough until he came to Fife, but there his fortune changed. He played many a fine spring in Auchtermuchty; he made Strathmiglo ring with his merry piping; he drew melody from the vagrant winds in Cupar. But he did not draw a single penny from the people of Fife, except from one old woman, and she was born in Aberdeen. So, disconsolate and hungry, he approached a citizen of Cupar and asked him pathetically:

'Do the folk o Fife like music so little that they willna pay a penny for a tune o my whistle?'

The citizen of Cupar looked at him as if unable to believe what he heard. Then he asked:

' Man, d'ye tell me ye expect tae be paid for that ? '

The wandering musician said he did.

Then the Cupar man laughed a pitying laugh and replied:

' Huh. In Fife we dae our ain whistlin.'

I have enjoyed that story for twenty years but I never believed it till I went to look for driftwood on Largo Beach. There was none—not a broken spar, not a rotting keg, not a lump of coal, not an abandoned cork. The bones of the foreshore had been picked bare.

It was not till I had walked for half a mile and was among the cottages again that I found some children playing with a soap-box. The spirit of Fife rose strong in me at the sight. I will not reveal the stratagem by which I was able to divert the children's attention. But something makes me confess to the theft of that box. I have no doubt that I disorganized some elaborate game of make-believe, and maybe went off with one of the topless towers of Ilion under my jacket. But I didn't care. In fact I was proud. I had beaten the Fifers at their favourite game.

I went on to the supreme achievement of boiling a kettle on a windy shore. As the grand moment approached the bathers resumed their comedy of manners behind the imaginary whins; and when the grand moment had been achieved we drank our tea on the debatable land between earth and ocean.

I wish I could set down on paper the immediate brilliance of that afternoon but all our words are far too old. I can only think again of that blue firth and the white houses, and the green fields beyond them and remember the shock they gave my senses. For an intolerable amount of literature has passed before our eyes and it is not often that we see things as they really are, for ourselves. It has been the fashion for many years to write as if our skies were always a little grey, as if all our horizons were veiled in mist; as if all our colours were dimmed with an English haze. And indeed there is some justice in the fashion, for it is part of the charm of the English scene that it is softened by a kind of moist air, so that all distance melts into a sweet confusion. But that is far less often true in the harder north. The Scottish scene can glitter with primitive greens and blues, deepening to violet in the shadows of the hills. So it is that, having accepted the English convention of a mellow haze, you are sometimes startled by the brilliant Scottish air. Then you are excited, as if you had discovered a new world on that very instant.

We discovered a new world that afternoon on Largo Beach. We did not say much of what may have been in our minds; nor perhaps did we dare to think very much, for thought is subversive of the established order, and thinking too much, or at all, might upset the decent dullness of our lives. But we could not keep away the thought that a man is more than a bag of tripes to be creeping into a well-sprung bed where his body can prepare itself for the ignoble posture of the grave. England often seems a fine and easy place with nothing to challenge you but fruitfulness and peace. The clear air of Scotland has a harsher challenge—to see the beginning and the end of life and the little space that lies between, and then make sure that that little space is not devoured by fear. For if a man has a mind to comprehend the imperial glory of the sea, he has the power of some nobility in him. But it is dangerous to try a throw with fate. It is better to be safe and humble to them that happen to be in authority over us, and so creep obsequiously into our graves where we will be safe for ever.

It is a bad thing to be susceptible to scenery. As we climbed out of Largo we saw, as it were, the whole of Fife lying clear before us in our minds. We saw the coal-mines of Cowdenbeath, the mills of Kirkcaldy, the docks

7

at Methil, the good farms and the fishing towns all under the brilliant afternoon. Then we said to ourselves, ' what couldn't we make of this if only we had the courage. There was a good life here when money was coming in by land and sea. Life has good moments still, when all our wealth has grown a thousand times. But if only we were men of courage and goodwill there is wealth enough in Fife to make a golden age upon the earth.' We drove on through the little towns half-drunk with the dreams of what might be; half-maddened at the thought of what was not; afraid to think of the courage that we lacked. If only we had had a leader to give us courage we might have started then to build a new Scotland on its old foundations. But there was no leader; and as we came to St. Andrews under the spacious evening light we were glad to be received again into the arms of picturesque antiquity.

Lowland Scots : The Shepherd

CHAPTER TEN: ST. ANDREWS

St. Andrews is the jewel that hangs at the end of the golden fringe of Fife. It is an old town with a ruined abbey, a ruined castle, a University, the offices of the Royal and Ancient Golf Club and many fine old houses in the Scottish style. In term time it has the peculiar charm of University towns when the tides of young and foolish creatures surge about the ancient walls. In summer it has the easy spirit of a holiday place without the more excessive vulgarities. And it is always romantic. You may go into a very modern shop to buy a modern specific for indigestion but when you come out you will see a crow-stepped gable between you and the moon, or the ruined walls of the abbey among the stars. The University, founded in 1411, is the oldest in Scotland and the Royal and Ancient is the most famous golf club in the world. Therefore you would expect St. Andrews to be the guardian of the best traditions in learning and in sport in Scotland; and indeed tradition could not find a fairer home.

If you go in search of history the ruins will speak to you of the Scottish kings and the princely Scottish churchmen. They will speak also of the Reformers, of Knox and Wishart, of those that were persecuted for Christ's covenant, and of those who persecuted whenever they had power. You will see the town houses of the local gentry, built in the native domestic style; you will see the houses of the common people that are, perhaps, the most eloquent of all. There was a time when kings and prelates were my constant companions, and I would rather have spent an hour with James the Fourth than inherited a thousand pounds.

But somehow the kings and bishops, their parasites and mistresses, have lost their power over me, and I would rather have a night in an alehouse with some old St. Andrews worthy than hear from Knox himself his views on Mary Stewart. Kings and bishops are creations of their own time, living in a remote world of their own, but the worthies in the alehouse are eternal, the enduring stock from which the rest must be renewed. So, if you walk abroad in St. Andrews looking for the picturesque, I hope you may see, beyond the cavalcade of kings and scholars, some ghosts of the common people—the hostlers and fish-wives, the respectable tradesmen and disreputable servants, that were the commons of Scotland.

If only you could recapture a little of the life there must have been in the little alehouses down by the port or up in the wide and windy streets of the town, you might have a new idea of Scotland. One gets tired of kings and their wars, of Mary Stewart and her lovers, of Charles Edward and his invasion; of Knox and all the rest of the clericals. They made such a deal of noise in their time and have so monopolized our history that you might think the people of Scotland were always furiously involved in the affairs of state and religion. But I suspect that those troubles affected the common people very little, except that they kept them poor. Whether the king was a Stewart or a Hanoverian, the thirsty citizens wasted their substance in the alehouse; and there were as many bastards under the rule of Geneva as there had been beneath the rule of Rome. So the commons lived, sometimes a little more respectable than at others, but always adapting their religion to human limitations, and always, I think, managing to enjoy their pleasures without undue regard for consequences.

St. Andrews was a fine town and a man might have been proud to have been its citizen. It is still a fine town; a place whither a man might retire to cultivate a quiet mind, without going out of the living world. There are the old houses to remind him of the strange mischances of the past : the students to make him hope a little for the time to come ; and the worthies, those ripe and native characters, to be his constant refreshment. There is also the golf; but what can I say about a game that calls for so much seriousness in hitting a ball over waste ground. Golf is a good enough way of passing an hour when you cannot be bothered with anything else, like contract bridge or going to the pictures. In St. Andrews, however, it has become an art for some, a religion for others, and a livelihood for many. As a livelihood it is no worse than many and much better than some—it at least does nobody any harm. But as an art, a religion or a social duty it invites laughter, tolerant laughter perhaps, but laughter without respect. So much seriousness about something essentially trivial is, I suppose, a form of escape. If so, it is an extremely unfortunate one, because the woes of a man who has lost both honour and fortune are hardly greater than the anxiety of a golfer off his game. It is one of the most fascinating of human aberrations, and St. Andrews is the place to study it in.

I take leave of St. Andrews conscious that I have done the old town less than justice. She has in her something beyond criticism, something that makes our fashions and our systems and our philosophies seem trivial, almost irrelevant, something of rare beauty that has endured out of all the years of Scotland. It is the good custom of the students to hold a pageant every spring in honour of Kate Kennedy, the niece of good Bishop Kennedy who lived in the olden time. A beardless bejant, a student in his first year, takes the part of Mistress Kennedy, and other men students walk in the guise of the great men that have honoured the town. So they walk through the streets in a procession of varying solemnity.

It is, I suppose, just another show. But once, when I had gone into St. Andrews unaware that it was Kate

Kennedy's day, I heard music on the wind as I was walk-ing along the street. I thought it might be Scouts or the O.T.C. or something of the like and dismissed it as no great matter. Then I saw what made me stop and wonder if I had not been drinking unduly. For a figure came round the corner of the street some distance away, a tall figure in a monk's gown, holding a blue St. Andrew's cross before him. As he stepped, slowly, over the worn stones, he was followed by other grave figures, soldiers and priests and scholars, a beautiful girl in her carriage, a scowl-ing prelate in his coach, and some of the common people in the dresses of a former time. They came a little distance towards me then turned down into some other street, and slowly, like a pageant of all dead ages, they passed out of sight. Seen thus at a distance, whence I could not distin-guish the grease paint and the powder, the figures had an extraordinary effect on me, for the heart of St. Andrews did indeed become alive in them. I realized then, as I had sometimes guessed in King's College in Aberdeen, that a University and a University town have something in them that is both noble and enduring. The fashions and the heresies of one time and another may distort and abuse that noble quality, turning it to the service of a furious religion or some dreary respectable way of living; but the quality will outlive them all. And that quality is a faith, held by different men at different ages, that there are two things valuable above everything else on earth—knowledge, that calm clear light, and reason, crowned, imperial. St. Andrews is founded upon that faith.

CHAPTER ELEVEN: THE LAD O' PAIRTS; OR, WHAT IS SCOTTISH EDUCATION?

THE love of knowledge upon which our universities is founded is a very noble thing that will endure long past our day. But unfortunately that love is not constant in all ages and conceptions of knowledge are apt to change. Universities though they serve the eternal must also be affected by the spirit of the times. Therefore I should say a word about Scottish schools and Scottish colleges and that Scottish phenomenon—the lad o' pairts.

You will soon hear about the lad o' pairts when you come into Scotland. He is a poor boy of undoubted talent who makes his way to the University by his own hard work, the sacrifice of his parents and the generosity of the educational system. He does well at the University; wins a prize or two by heroic industry; takes a good degree; and proceeds to Oxford or Cambridge. He is never heard of again except when he produces some textbook or monograph of appalling accuracy and dullness. Or he passes into the Civil Service where he spends himself in the vehement defence of precedents like his forefathers defended their independence three hundred years before him. He is one of Scotland's chief exports and we are proud of him, perhaps because we have so little else to be proud of. He is the fine ripe fruit of our educational system.

Now the English are often inclined to treat the Scots as a comic race, and they have reason, for the Scots often lose their sense of humour when they cross the Tweed. But the English always make amends by saying how well educated we are, that Scottish education is the best in the world. If that is true it may account for a lot of the confusion in the world to-day.

Of course it all depends on your idea of education. If you think the best education is that which turns out a standard wage earner in the shortest space of time, then I agree that Scottish education is very hard to beat. The Scots are good engineers; we are masters at building intricate machines that have everything but souls; and we have engineered an admirable machine for education.

As soon as a child is five it is taken in at one end of the machine and remorselessly worked on until it is fourteen. Then, if it is not very malleable, or if its parents are too utterly poor, it is ejected from the school and becomes a juvenile labourer.

The children who are better adapted to the machine, or who have parents not in urgent need of their earnings, are carried into the second part of the machine, the high school, until they pass the leaving examination at seventeen or thereabout.

There is a second winnowing: many (and those the more enterprising) go into the labour market. The rest pass, by the easiest of conveyors, to a University.

It is, or at least might be, one of the glories of the Scottish education system that there is no wide gap between the high school and the University, such as there is in England, or such as there was to the lower classes until the foundation of the provincial Universities. The Scots Universities have never been the preserve of the well-to-do. The fees have always been low, and there is a great deal of assistance for poor students in bursaries from private benefactors and in the statutory provision by local authorities. Therefore any boy or girl, except the very poorest, can attend a University if he or she is able to satisfy the entrance board. This often means a good deal of sacrifice at home, but a sacrifice that is very proudly made.

After four or five years there is yet another winnowing.

Most of the students, dignified with the title of bachelor, or master, go out to look for positions of some authority and respect, in teaching or medicine or business. A few, and those the finest products of the system, are gently conveyed to Oxford or Cambridge for a final polish.

As a system, this education could hardly be improved on. It reminds me of a machine that my brother-in-law, a farmer, uses for sorting his potatoes. The potatoes, ware, seed, dirt and dross, are shovelled on to a conveyor belt that carries them up to the top of the machine. There they fall on a series of riddles, of decreasing mesh, so that the fine big ware-size potatoes are retained on one riddle, the seed on another, the brock on a third, and the dross falls down to the bottom. Each grade falls out at its proper spout and is collected in sacks and sent to the appropriate market. The only essential difference between the educational machine and the potato sorter is that the potato sorter seldom makes mistakes, and the mistakes are not important, whereas the educational system is always making mistakes and the mistakes are fatal.

The weakness of the system is obvious. It is a weakness of mass production. I know that mass production is a wonderful thing that could, if it were properly used, set us free from an intolerable amount of drudgery. But mass production demands that the material used maintain an even standard of quality and texture. It works very well with an inanimate substance like iron that can be forged all of a piece, but not quite so efficiently with wood that, having once been alive, has unexpected knots and varying grain. Thus the mass-produced razor blade is usually a better thing to look at than the mass-produced Jacobean table.

Now, if it is not quite satisfactory to apply mass-production to things that though once alive are now dead, it is less satisfactory when applied to things that are not only alive but are still in the best years of their growth. But that is just what the Scots education does to our children. It

takes all those young minds, full of strange needs and
original curiosities, and subjects them to a standard in the
hope of turning out a standard article. It succeeds in its
aim, for it does turn out a child with its originality killed,
its curiosity dead, a child that will be obedient and uncritical
and stupid, the ideal patron of the cinema, the unquestion-
ing supporter of political parties, the good and wholly
unintelligent citizen of the modern state.

But you may believe in the older idea of education which
is a drawing out of the various capabilities that are in every
child, so that the result may be an intelligent man with
harmony among his various parts, a man that may be of
the greatest service to the commonwealth. If you have that
antiquated notion then you will see that the educational
system is a godless machine that kills the loveliest things in
the victims. True education entails the understanding of
every child, so that he may be given the opportunity to
develop those powers in the best possible way.

The Scottish system, being a machine, cannot do that.
A teacher is given a class of thirty or more, and so many
hours a week, and must return the children at the end of
the year in a certain higher standard of proficiency. But
you cannot measure true growth by examinations. Every
child has a problem, or a number of problems acting on
each other—problems of home life, of communal life, of
learning—a network of fears and hopes and needs. If
education means anything at all it should help the child to
solve those problems and the conflict between them and
so be able to live on equal terms with its world.

An educational system that is a machine cannot deal with
such intricate personal affairs. It can only discipline the
children, problems and all, into some sort of a pattern. But
if people, at the end of their schooling, are a mass of
unresolved conflicts, how are they going to master their
world, or live on good terms with it ? The answer is that
in most cases they don't. The hopeless, the neurotic, the

useless, the feckless, the ill-adjusted and unhappy, the unreasonable and incurably silly people that make up so great a part of the Scottish nation are the typical products of the Scottish educational system. So too is the fable that the system is the best in the world. It is not a good thing to be ashamed of your own countrymen; but when I have heard, as I have heard too often, one of them telling an intelligent English company that of course he is far better educated than they, and doing so in the loud assertive voice of one who is conscious of a slight inadequacy within him, then I have wished for the night to hide me.

This lovely system of education, then, is concerned mostly with inessentials, with the three R's instead of the eternal verities. It produces wage earners instead of intelligent and happy men and women. It puts a kind of polish on the surface, instead of fostering a harmonious growth of body and mind. And, of course, it is blighted with snobbery.

The chief end of education at the primary stage is to fit a child for making a few shillings a week at fourteen. The chief end of higher education is to qualify the child for a position in the middle class or higher up. It is the ambition of all good parents that their children should be a little better off than they themselves have been, and education is one way of securing that advancement as it is so concerned with the external things. It teaches children to be more refined than their parents and the people they grew up amongst. Now true wisdom lies in knowing yourself, and that self is very largely the product of your earliest years. The onwards and upwards kind of education, by teaching refinements of speech and action as vitally important things, cuts children off from the people to which they belong. It interposes something alien between them and their sources. It leads them in time to deny that those sources have any value. But how can they even know themselves, if they deny their most vital part? As a result, they lose the refreshing contact with the soil they sprang from, they are never quite at ease in the refined society into which they graduated; and so they live on a kind of margin, without security, always striving to consolidate themselves, always afraid that they may slip back to their beginnings. It is a poor end to twenty years' continuous education, a fine reward for being a lad o' pairts.

I was a lad o' pairts myself, and I offer my own experience as a tribute to the system. This made it very difficult for me to write about St. Andrews because when I was a student in Aberdeen, I had only to think about St. Andrews in the rain and superlatives came winging to the point of my pen like a flight of doves. I thought no life could compare with a comfortable post in a University town and a good golf-links to play on; and, since St. Andrews had the air of divine appointment to learning and certainly a divine appointment to golf, it became my dearest and most secret ambition to live there all the days of my life. It was a beautiful ambition for the son of a servant girl and a ploughman.

St. Andrews had a monastic air, for it had once been the seat of the Catholic primate of Scotland. So, being in love with the antiquity, I imagined myself leading a quiet monastic life in one of the old houses of the town. I would hold, I decided, a lectureship of some kind in the University, that would give me five hundred pounds a year in return for a little instruction of the young. I would be elegantly witty and detached about Chaucer and Donne for an hour or two each morning; I would play golf in the nicely tempered sun each afternoon; and in the evening, with a glass of brandy at my side, I would make charming researches into the private lives of the Renaissance churchmen. There would be long nights of conversation in winter-time when the sea-gales tore at the walls of the town and the moon rode furiously across a riven sky. There would be summer nights of music in the gardens, with the tall flowers moving in the arms of the night wind like

dancers in a waltz. And there would be little excursions
abroad to Italy and the Isles of Greece where women were
not restrained by a Protestant morality and love was a bird
singing for ever in the woods.

You see, after fifteen years of education, I was in a very
troubled state. I was full of unresolved conflicts and adolescent fears. I was very conscious of the common world's
brutality; and I feared that I would never make for myself,
nor long maintain a place within it, so I made a virtue of
my own fears and would have withdrawn from it with a
contemptuous gesture.

But two things were against me. There came a time
when I had no more money for studying the Anglo-Saxon
authors and others who have increased but not enriched our
literature; and about that time my superiors made plain to
me that, even though I continued, I would never be called
to a University appointment. These alone might not have
wholly discouraged me, and I might have gone on in spite
of them, if I had not made two further discoveries—that
my golf was never likely to be more than a tribulation to
myself and others, and that a single glass of brandy after
dinner would put a final to my researches. The rest of my
dear illusions followed. There are, I discovered, only a
limited number of things one can say even about God, and
these become tedious at the hundredth repetition. I had
also to admit that I had no understanding of music.

When I had made a sacrifice of conversation and music,
there remained only love. I could not tell you how long
I guarded that last illusion after I had left the University
of Aberdeen without distinction; or how many nights I
lay in my bed just off the Great Western Road in Glasgow
defending the nightingales against the noises of the town;
but the leagues between me and the Isles of Greece grew
longer, till the day came when I realized that I had not
the voice for singing in a garden, nor the figure to be
climbing a lady's window. I resigned the academic life

with a sigh, and turned to the reality of life in Glasgow on three pounds ten a week.

The reality was not, as I had expected, stern. But it was often intolerably dull. My work consisted of arranging copy for a morning paper, of dressing up speeches according to the rules of grammar, of gutting and filleting murders and divorces; and disinfecting stories of too lively passion. I had often heard of the rush and bustle of a great newspaper office, but I can hardly remember a time when our monastic calm was disturbed by any excitement, except once or twice when somebody (usually myself) made those little mistakes which readers love, and editors, curiously, fear. It was a little less than the adventure I once thought the free life of a young man would be. But I knew that I was fortunate. My employers were just: my superiors were amazingly kind; and my associates were amusing, friendly people. But I was completely lost and gone astray. I didn't know why I was there nor what I wanted to do. I did not seem to belong to anywhere, I had no roots. I was just one of a great class of slightly educated young men that put up with the little they had because they were always hoping for better. I had, of course, relations, farming people, but after my so much education I felt I would not understand them, nor they me. My education had cut me off from them, and had given me three pounds ten a week in return. I was, as I have said, a little lost, a little disappointed.

There were, however, some compensations. We were, I think, six or seven of us, young men of a like age, in a boarding house off the Great Western Road. We worked at the things young men work at, agreed no better than most, and saw each other as little as possible. But, perhaps because we did not associate during the week, we made a common occasion of Saturday night. On Saturday afternoons I used to attend the Rugby football matches, being paid to do so after having learned the art of the game out of the *Encyclopædia Britannica*. As soon as I had written my report, and adorned it with bits of Shakespeare and the Bible (for I had just become a disciple of Neville Cardus), I was ready for the evening's excitement. It began with a pie and several pints of beer in a public-house in St. George's Road. During the first half-hour there was, I seem to remember, a certain constraint, as if we were still possessed by the inhibited dullness of our working lives. But at the third pint we attained our freedom. We suddenly discovered a lot of things that we must talk about, and we developed fine arguments in which complete strangers unexpectedly joined and from which they, as unexpectedly, disappeared. We were quite ordinary young men in ugly clothes, sitting at the corner table of a Glasgow public-house. During most of our days and nights we were unhappy at the vast indifference of the world, at our total insignificance under the wheeling sun. But on Saturday night we became superior to the world; and equal to the sun. If we could not master our world, we could at least escape it.

We usually separated when we had reached that happy state. Some went after drink, and some went after women and some to endless arguments about the ' dogs '. Tom and I went after music. I cannot draw you Tom in this little space. A man of such various nature and so abounding humanity could not be miniatured upon a postage stamp. Let it be enough to say that his face seemed to look out of an earlier and ampler time, even when it was crowned with a bowler; and that he could talk about Bach while washing his drawers on a Sunday afternoon in a way that made music and washing both arts and equal. He was a man of such forthright tastes and total enjoyment as did not belong to this decrepit age. Nor, when I remember, did he belong to the polite audience that gathered together in the St. Andrews Hall to hear the Scottish Orchestra. There must have been something disparate between the listeners, all a little discouraged by the enormity of life, and the monumental harmonies of Bach that, drawn from gut or blown upon human wind, rode upon the night, remote and immutable as the bow of heaven. It seems to me now that most of us listened to music as an escape, but music was an art in its own right for Tom, not a substitute but a part of life. In music I acknowledged him my master, and in most things else, for I had not been long in his company before I realized that while I knew only the names of things he understood the substance.

My University had hardly prepared me for the curious chances of this life. I had planned to deliver aphorisms about Chaucer to the intellectual young; but there I was reducing murder and rape to grammatical politeness on a Glasgow paper. I had imagined myself drinking my wine, elegantly, as befits a scholar and a gentleman, in some old house in a University town: but the reality was beer in a Glasgow public. I had wished for sighing soulful music in a twilit garden; and there I was half-drunk in the St. Andrews Hall thundered against by Wagner's trumpets; while Tom, beside me, cursed the fat conductor that impeded the beat with his mass of stupid beef.

It was my first contact with the living art. During four years I had studied the best authors, had seen them dissected and heard them explained; and even learned why one poet was good and another bad, why one critic was almost right and another wholly wrong. As my dreams have shown you, I had learned how to plan, if not to achieve, a tidy life spent upon the edges of eternal things. I thought I knew a lot about art. But if that was art, what was the furious thing unloosed in the St. Andrews Hall? At the first hearing it was a confusion of noise haled out of gut, blown out of lungs of brass, a furious riot without form or meaning that gave me no pleasure yet disturbed me profoundly. It shook me, as you might shake a bottle of beer, and sensations ran up my spine, to make my head dizzy like a hive of bees. So it was for a few Saturdays. I was disturbed, but I did not understand the reason. Then I heard a bit of 'Le Coq d'Or' and a tremendous thing happened. I suddenly understood what it was all about. I think my hair stood on end, but I'm not sure about that. But I know that my excitement rose on the brazen clamour of the music until the last chord delivered me into a new world. Then, as if it had been a flash of lightning in a pitch-dark night, I saw how little and foolish all my dreams had been. The aphorisms, the golf, the brandy, the music at midnight and the Isles of Greece were all an escape. I could have had them all and lived no more than a refined old maid in an almshouse. Nor were the disinfecting of adulteries and the drinking of too much beer a tolerable end for any man's existence. I knew, suddenly and beyond all question, that I had been living in a kind of twilight, that the music had broken down the walls, and that I had seen the real world in an awful instant. The shapes of that world were exultations, agonies and love and man's unconquerable soul. I saw then for the first time the struggle that lies at the heart of life, for on the one side there is greed, stupidity, ignorance and fear; and on the other side there are knowledge and reason and the will to glory. On one side compromise from day to day and the harlot comfort: on the other glorious worlds without end to be fashioned out of chaos.

I discovered all the joys of one who had been saved from an heretical and false religion. Tom introduced me to a life that was, at first, incredibly rich, inveterately bawdy, and endlessly amusing. Never was anyone more surely born again. Or it was like the Renaissance that followed the Middle Ages. (Forgive these so personal matters, but if you understand what happened to one young lad o' pairts you may understand something about life in Scotland.) You see, as I have told you in another place, I was born of a race of farmers that had never been troubled very much by anything but desire and drink. I should by rights have

8

been a ploughman, and fathered many children a little too soon and all too frequently. But I got the chance of learning and I took it. I went to a good school (though not as good a school as the improvers would like to make it) and then to a University for the final touch of culture.

I was a little confused by the school, for Latin and all that had no relation to the life of an adolescent boy. I was wholly confused by the University. Of course there was one thing I did know, that the end of all the schooling and all the culture was a job that would enable me to live in a respectable way. But that was the source of all the confusion, for it made the learning a means to a living, not something that had a value of its own; and besides the eventual living was of far more importance than the education. More than that, it was a means to a certain kind of living. Once you studied culture, you rose into a cultured class, equal perhaps to the less substantial tradesmen. It was the accolade of middle class with all that middle class implies—the compromises, the restraints, the respectabilities, the desperate holding on to what you have in case you may slip back to the class you sprang from. That was the fate that the University had delivered me to—either an incredibly refined academic life, the distillation of pure selfishness, or the ineffable respectabilities of the middle class. As I had not the ability to gain admission to the first, only the second was open to me. These then were my Dark Ages when I tried to work hard and be a good citizen and rise in the world, and achieve the consummation of a Scottish education. It was a time when my body and spirit grew away from each other. For my natural inclination was to follow the ways of my fathers, to be that for which my first years had fashioned me, a peasant; but the training of my later years made me aspire to be the shadow of a gentleman. So the two influences pulled in opposite directions. The bad part would have won fairly soon and I am sure that I would have made an excellent head of some department, besides earning a modest competence; and the natural part of me would not have exerted itself except in the occasional orgies that are excused when a man is away on deputations.

But I was saved, and I doubt if any one ever enjoyed salvation more. I can't quite say how it all happened. There was of course the revelation of the music. The glories I saw there had nothing to do with morning coats and assured positions and knowing the names of thirteen kinds of wine. It reduced them to agreeable but not essential amenities of a civilized life. Though that was a great deal, it was not enough. I still thought that a taste for music and books set men apart from ordinary beings, that it must entail a refinement in everything—a genteeler way of eating and drinking and speaking—the marks of culture as we had learned them at the University, the stamp of middle class.

Then I had a second revelation.

It was our custom at the interval in the concerts to cross the road to a public-house for a draught of beer—I, because I thought that beer and music had a mystic affinity, Tom because he had a thirst. While we stood drinking, some members of the orchestra used to drop in for a glass to renew their wind, after the expense of a Wagnerian idyll. I was thrilled to be so near men that blew their breath so divinely into the sounding air, and I edged near them, so that I could listen to their conversation. I was sure that divine mysteries would be revealed to me. They were. The musicians, the elect who lived with Mozart and Beethoven, devoted the interval to discussing that day's races. I looked at them again, and saw that I might easily have mistaken them for honest tradesmen, joiners or the like; and their dinner-jackets might have been evidences not of culture but of their annual ball. Then indeed I realized that I did not need to be a gentleman in a dinner-jacket because I had a taste for Mozart. And from that it was easy progress to the day when I realized that a dinner-jacket was indeed ridiculous.

Then I could enjoy the incredibly rich and endlessly amusing life that flowered about Tom wherever he went. I had, as it were, come home; because that was the life that my fathers had lived for generations, and the life to which I had been born. It was a renaissance, a real new birth, for I went right back to the day when I first went to a good school, and, without thinking about it, became myself again. The unhappy years at school and university, those years in which I had worshipped so many idols stuffed with straw, became tiresome memories of futility, compared to the new ease I had discovered.

The change was not very much when you add it up; it only meant that I did not pretend to be anything more than I was, that I began to enjoy music and food and drink for the pleasure they could give me, not as the marks of class and culture. That I did things because I liked them; no longer to please convention or to spite it. And also that I could explore the great richness of my heritage, without any foolish inhibitions and any explaining away of the coarseness and vitality of my fathers. Things then became real to me; and I lay back on my heritage, like a tired man lies down on a grassy bank, in thankfulness for the solid earth and the green shade.

Like that same man, I rose, refreshed. The work remained the same: it was something to be done as well as possible and then forgotten. Our pleasures were the thing. Those Saturday nights have made Glasgow dear to me above all other towns. When the concerts were over and the tympanist had exchanged his thunders for a glass of beer, we used to go down to an eating-house in the lower part of the town. There we ate sausage and mashed and tried to recapture some melodic line until we were forced out into the streets again. We did not go alone, for it was our custom to load ourselves with bottles of beer in paper bags, and so like two good asses in panniers, we rolled back to our lodging through the crowded streets.

We all gathered in the common room about eleven o'clock. It had a long sideboard on which each set out the provision he had made, and there were times (if Saturday fell at the end of the month) when I have seen it covered with bottles from end to end. At this time the landlady and her daughter, two of the most understanding people that ever lived, came in to wish us good night and, I think, God-speed. There was a little silence when they had gone out. Then Tom would look round the company and say, ' Gentlemen, we will have a little beer and a little music.' So saying he took a tuning fork from his pocket and the corkscrew from behind the clock.

We always began with a service of praise, raising the line of the Scottish psalms and casting it like a challenge to the godless winds of Glasgow. Thereafter the evening became wholly secular. The Admiral, a man of unexpected humour and curious animosities against the Vatican, used to sing ' Sur le Pont d'Avignon ' to a little dance of his own invention. Then Tom brought out his clarionet and mixed strathspeys with Mozartian *divertimenti*. We sang, we drank beer, we conducted arguments in corners, and so the night grew vague and luminous, till suddenly we found ourselves out on Great Western Road at four o'clock of a Sunday morning, fulfilled of glory, while the Admiral danced on the bridge of Avignon before us. Those, and not the years I have spent in learning, were the days and nights of my true education, for they taught me what my fathers had always known, that a man has certain fruitful powers that must be enjoyed early, for death comes soon, and that a society that destroys such powers is mortal foolishness.

And so I came to say good-bye to the dinner-jackets, the assured position, the aphorisms, the golf, the brandy, the music at midnight and the Isles of Greece. I did not lose them all at once, and some of them remained with me after

my conversion. But I got release at last, and that, very
curiously, in St. Andrews. I had gone there on some business or other and found myself in the middle of a student
celebration. After I had finished my business I joined the
revellers and found myself paired with a comely young
woman. We agreed very well, and, to make a short end
of the sad story, finally wandered down to the edge of the
sea. It was a night such as I had imagined on the Isles of
Greece. The crescent moon shone delicately on the quiet
sea, there were distant lights, and music, and the gentle
surge of the tide upon the rocks. It was a night compounded of subtle harmonies, of delicious thoughts and
exquisite sensations. We, heirs to all the culture of the
western world, sat upon a little grassy place in a quiet out
of which an absolute beauty might have flowered. I was
a man enchanted, waiting a sign from heaven. She drew
in the sweet night upon her breath. The world hung in
the balance of her lightest action. Then she opened her
mind to me, and talked about the wonders of the British
Empire, solidly, for thirty minutes. As I went back to
town alone, I heard, or thought I heard, a mournful echo
on the waters, where the Isles of Greece lay for ever drowned
beneath a tide of heavy words. That, I think, was the
final end of my University education. And that was the
end of a lad o' pairts.

That is all I have to say about Scottish education—that
it isn't education at all. The system does allow a great
many people to go to the universities and graduate into a
respectable way of life. But even then it is vitiated by what
is sometimes considered its greatest glory.

You will hear about the students of the olden time so
poor that they came to college with a sack of meal and a box
of herrings as their only food; you will hear of modern
students so poor that sixpence spent on a bath would be an
unthinkable extravagance; and you will be asked to admire
them and the system that produces them. They are sanctified

and blessed by the Lady Poverty: but they can't always enjoy her blessing. The best part of a university education is in the society of living minds. The poor student hasn't the coppers to buy a place in that society. The sort of development that is true culture demands a certain amount of ease; the poor student has not that amount of ease because he is too worried about paying his way and too uncertain about his future. There are too many students at the Scottish Universities who must spend three or four years (that should be the most exciting years of their lives) in poverty and soulless labour to get the degree that will make their parents' sacrifices worth while. What happens to them ? Many of them are worn out by the end of their course; finished. Most of them take what jobs they can get and never dare say or do anything to endanger them. Four years at a University should be one of the greatest privileges of a civilized state, the road to a splendid intellectual freedom. But, as things are, a boy or girl who gets a decent job in an office or workshop has often a better chance of real education than one who goes to a University without either money or outstanding brains. We might look to the Universities for the leaders of an enlightened democracy. We do not get them from the Scottish Universities. Nor will we get them until we send only the best to the Universities and assure them of humane conditions there. Then the Universities will be something better than front-doors to respectability. There may be real education when a young man from the joiner's bench returns to his bench after three years' study at a University. And when the community is wise enough to leave him there.

CHAPTER TWELVE: DUNDEE: THE
PRICE OF IMPERIALISM

AFTER the discussion of so many serious matters, it is a great temptation to go straight from St. Andrews to the softer delights of Perthshire, but my sense of duty forces me to a roundabout by the city of Dundee. You see I am an Aberdonian and Aberdonians like not Dundee, any more than the people of Dundee admire that deplorable city of Aberdeen. That is a fact to be remembered—if you wish to please the natives of either city tell them that the natives of the other are a set of unmitigated thugs and they will give you anything you ask them. There is great rivalry between the towns, being near neighbours and almost of a size, and the rivalry has been fostered by sport that binds together peoples, in enmity.

We are, as I have said before, the folk that our childhood made us; and those that were children in Aberdeen at the end of the war will always hate Dundee. We were all the devoted followers of the Aberdeen football team (it was my bravest day when a misguided lady presented me with a pair of stockings in the team's colours—black and gold). We lived for the time when Aberdeen would stand at the top of the League table, or, O height of glory, win the Cup. The team did not encourage us, for they were indifferent performers, but now and then they would show signs of climbing to real distinction. It was then that the horrid shadow of Dundee would fall across our bright hopes, for we knew that the team must fall and we knew that the Dundee team would be the cause of it.

We were too often right. I can remember New Year's

Day matches and cup-ties when we stood on the shilling side of the Pittodrie ground at Aberdeen and prayed for the total humiliation of Dundee. But we prayed in vain. Our forwards would move sweetly down the field, passing the ball from wing to wing with lovely ease, and we cried to ourselves ' Now ! Now ! ' Alas, we cried too soon. There was in the Dundee team a full-back called Napper Thomson, a man of amazing foresight, a dreadful man fated to destroy the sweet precision of our forwards. They would go down on the Dundee goal, accurate, and seeming irresistible, and you would have thought nothing could have prevented a score. But, just as we were drawing in our breath to cheer, a bald head would rise across the line of the ball, there would be the sore impact of leather upon taut skin, and Napper Thomson would be running after the headed ball to complete destruction with a long kick up to midfield. The hiss of breath released on the shilling side was a bitter compound of frustration and hate.

The Scotsman shares the passion of the English for football and it is a pity that, coming in summer, you will not see that passion in full flower. Football has reversed the seasons for the true fanatic; winter has become the summer of his contentment and summer is a time of hibernation, a tedious long weary time that must be passed with bowls and cricket. June and July are a time of mortification, but there is a re-birth of life in August and joy and sorrow are renewed when the matches begin at the end of the month. It is curious to see the almost universal interest in the game, or at least in the results of the matches. That may be a kind of local pride, though a team may be local only in name, the majority of its players having been born round about Glasgow. But no matter how many Irishmen are included in a Scots team, people will buy a newspaper to see the result of a match who would never pay a shilling to see the play. I myself have not seen a professional football match for seven years, yet I can never be at peace on a Saturday night until I know if Aberdeen have won and my evening is slightly flawed if they have lost.

But then no one can suffer, as I suffered when a child, without a permanent mark upon his spirit. I could not always go to Pittodrie on Saturday afternoons. Sometimes I had to stay and work in the garden. That was hard, for every male person over the age of fourteen in our village at the edge of the town used to go off to the match, leaving only my neighbour, an aged man, and myself at home with the women. We, the aged man and I, pretended to work in our gardens, but it was very little work we did from the minute the teams ran on to the field. You see we were only a mile from the football ground and we could hear the sounds the crowd made as they followed the play. We knew those sounds as if they had been words spoken clearly in our ears. There were the deep murmur at some bit of clever play, the surge of excitement at a threatened goal; a sullen troubled noise that showed a goal scored by the opposing team; and the mighty triumphant roar, a minute long, when Aberdeen had gained a point. We stood among the potatoes, the aged man and I, making our ears and our imaginations do the work denied our sight. At the sullen roar we returned to our digging; at the great roar we threw down our forks and shouted too. And sometimes we quarrelled. The old man was rather disillusioned and occasionally a roar I counted as a goal he discounted as a penalty saved. Then we grew angry and threatened each other across the wire fence and the space of seventy years. Only another and triumphant roar saved us from unforgiveable insult. Now you cannot live through such hours and then completely forget them. Football was once my passion; Dundee teams frustrated that passion too often; so it will always be impossible for me to speak without prejudice of Dundee.

If you go north from St. Andrews you will come to Newport on the Firth of Tay where you can get the ferry across to Dundee, on the Angus shore. As you cross the blue water (though it is often an inhospitable grey) you will see the railway bridge, an extreme contrast to the mighty work that spans the Forth. It is a plain and unpretentious bridge, just a railway track laid upon strong pillars at some small height above the water. You might indeed wonder that anything so frail could bear the weight of the London train, and if you cross it you may have good cause to wonder, for the stumps of an earlier bridge still show above the water line. You will not stay long on the East Coast without hearing about the Tay Bridge disaster. There are old men who can make your blood run cold when they tell how people on the Fife shore watched a train crossing on a wild night and how the lights ran slowly above the darkness of the water till a fearful moment when they fell like a shooting star, down into the firth. Many people were drowned that night and a large part of the bridge was destroyed, but the new bridge stands firm to thrill the imaginations of those who cannot forget that stormy crossing.

And as you cross the blue water you are sure to be impressed by the lovely situation of Dundee, for the town lies on the south slopes of a hill with the water at its feet. Nature could have done nothing more. I have known people, of the town-planning sort, struck dumb at the opportunities given. They saw a broad street fronting the river with terraced gardens down to the water. They saw an harmonious row of offices a mile long, the whole design locked together by a Customs House in some classical style. They saw more broad streets running up to a square in the middle of the town. They saw the residential parts rising terrace upon terrace up the sunny slopes of the hill. And they saw the factories collected together beside the docks away down the river at the east end of the town. They saw and were struck dumb—at the opportunities lost, for Dundee has grown up all anyhow, like most other towns. There is no fine waterfront—only a railway yard and factories and stores. The town has turned its back to the firth. The result is as nice an example of *laissez-faire* as you will find in these islands.

The town has suffered in other ways from that economic heresy. Its fortunes were built on jute and there was a time when it prospered exceedingly. However, the profits were not quite evenly divided so that the shareholders got more than they needed, though the workers had perhaps a little less. The fortunate ones had to find some way of investing their surplus. So they invented the investment trust that is such an important part of modern finance. But, more important for Dundee, they invested some of their money in jute mills in India. As the standard of wages was even lower in India than in Dundee, the profits were even greater. So the moneyed people of Dundee grew even richer. Unfortunately, as often happens, the colonial enterprise began to harm its parent. The jute mills of India, many of them financed from Dundee, have taken away the home manufacturers' markets. Thus, although some investors have grown richer, both the home manufacturers and the workers have suffered many years of depression. It is the logical end of *laissez-faire*. Unemployment in Dundee is the price we have to pay for imperialism.

If you are travelling in search of the picturesque you would be as well to avoid Dundee; but if you really wish to know about modern Scotland then I think you will find a great deal to fascinate you there. You will see how individualism without a plan can waste a beautiful situation and you can study in its simplest form the conflict between home enterprise and foreign investment that seems to be inherent in the present order.

You will also be able to see how a still wealthy town is dealing with those problems. For a long time the mills have taken people from the country; now the mills can no longer employ their children; so there is something of a return to the land. At Dryburgh and Claverhouse two big farms have been turned into small-holdings where unemployed men are being trained for the farming life. It is at least an important experiment, and a proof that progress can go so far that it completes a circle and ends up where it began.

A great deal is also being done to reorganize the centre of the town. What used to be a confusion is being changed into a fine square with a magnificent public hall, and there are signs that Dundee is beginning to realize the beauties of its situation between the firth and the hill.

The people of Dundee have suffered and their troubles are by no means at an end; but you should go there to see the spirit that is left in the people. Spend a day there and I will be surprised if you do realize the tremendous possibilities that lie in such a town. What could 180,000 people not do if they set their minds to it ? Perhaps there may yet come a time when even the Aberdonians will be forced to admire Dundee.

CHAPTER THIRTEEN: THE GENTLE PERTHSHIRE

THE road from Dundee to Perth runs west through the Carse of Gowrie on the north side of the Tay. I hope you will take that road and enjoy it; for the Carse, although typical of a certain kind of Scottish country, has nothing of the brown heath and shaggy wood about it. Like the land around Stirling it was originally swamps, but the swamps have been drained and the heavy soil carries a great burden of fertility. You will see good cattle on the deep pastures and fine crops of corn, and fields of garden fruit. There is a warm air, sheltered by the Sidlaw Hills. There are many old trees that shadow the little villages. And at an odd time you may see a coasting boat weigh up between the meadows to the quays at Perth. It is so rich an agricultural scene, so warm and contented, that you might say to yourself, ' This isn't Scotland at all, but Worcestershire or Warwick.' I have said as much myself in the days before I realized the variety of Scotland. Even now, when I think of my childhood in Aberdeenshire, I can hardly believe that a part of Eden lies on the north side of the Tay. I have gone along the Carse on a hot summer afternoon when the small fruits were ripe and the air was so sweet that you might have thought God was making jam all over Gowrie. But do not think, because you have been to Worcester, you have no need to come this way. The Carse can give you an experience that is peculiarly Scottish. If you go out from Dundee to Monifieth you can walk on the sharp sea thyme and smell the tang of the waves. Then only a few miles away you can run deep into the mild sweetness of the Carse. That contrast can give a sharper edge to the pleasures of a summer day; and it is a contrast that belongs to the eastern part of Scotland.

If you have spent a night in St. Andrews (which I hope you will have done if only for the sake of the twilight) then you might spend another night in Perth. This city, at one time the capital, has had a long experience in entertaining travellers, and it has still a few hotels where you may lie in comfort. It can also give you some amusement. Its situation on the banks of the Tay is very pleasant and it has two fine parks called the Inches along the river-side. It is of course a great place for history of the bloodier sort —but you will be able to read all about that in the little books, price sixpence, that make up so big a part of our current literature. If you incline that way, you can walk through the Inches where the famous fight between the Clan Chattan and the Clan Kay was held before an enthusiastic crowd; you may inspect the house where the Gowrie conspiracy against King James was planned, and you may spend an hour in the beautiful Church of St. John. If your interests are more modern you can see Pullar's dyeworks and the whisky warehouses of Dewar and Bell. Also for my sake I would have you look at the terraces of eighteenth-century houses along the North Inch and in particular at the front of the old Academy. Though they have a little declined they retain something of the flavour of a time when taste was more regarded than it is to-day. Altogether you should find Perth an agreeable though not quite a beautiful town; and I wish you a sound night's sleep, for there is a great deal to see on the morrow.

Perthshire is the most delectable county in Scotland— but then I may be prejudiced because I have spent so many pleasant days there. From whatever point you start there is always a circuit of a hundred miles with a good hotel for tea about the half-way mark and many other houses of call where you can get a drop of something to put a final bloom on the scenery. If there must be highlands let them be like the highlands of Perthshire. As you approach them from the east or the south, you pass through the peculiarly Scottish kind of scene—varying farmland well cultivated and sheltered with breaks of trees—good lowlands with a line of mountains to the north and west. You do not leave civilization when you enter the glens. The mountains heave up their barren rocks; the lower slopes are heather and tough grass; but there are many villages by the rivers and the long blue lochs. These highlands are picturesque but not desolate. You may be excited by their occasional grandeur but you will not be overpowered by their loneliness. They have a glory, but the glory has a domestic air. A man might be at home in those glens and cultivate ease of mind under the shadow of those hills.

If you have slept a night in Perth and then are in the mood for a day of varying pleasures, I would advise you to make the kind of excursion that I have often made through the centre of Scotland. You need only the fortitude to endure a bus or the patience to drive your motorcar in a leisurely way. Then, if the weather is fine, you may gather some rare impressions of a charming country.

Since you are at my mercy inside the covers of this book, we may go by a route that always pleases me though I have gone that way a hundred times. Go down the Methven road from Perth till you come to Crieff. Thence you may go along Strathearn to Comrie and St. Fillans, but I would rather you took the Stirling road through Braco. All this way you will be running through mixed country between the Highlands and the Lowlands, unexciting but attractive like the people that live there. In case you may think it sounds a little dull I'd say that the country-side is diversified with fine gentlemen's houses that have been supported and beautified with the increase of the fields. And just before you come to Braco you may see the remains of our earlier masters, the Romans, in a pasture on the left-hand side of the road. When you reach Dunblane you should hold on down the Stirling road, till a little distance short of Bridge of Allan where you will find a road on the right going over to Doune and Callendar. Follow it to Doune for the view of the ruined castle that you get from the bridge beyond the town, on the way to Thornhill. You are back into the valley of the Forth at Thornhill, a wide place bounded by the Gargunnock Hills along the south. Like the Carse of Gowrie it was once a swamp but generations of good farmers have turned it into land bearing fine crops of grain and hay. If you have the time you might run over to the far side and spend an hour in Kippen and Gargunnock, two pleasant villages with an old Scots character and interesting churches for them that like a touch of the ecclesiastical on weekdays. You should also look at Thornhill—but not for long because it is the perfect type of another and commoner Scottish village. Having appreciated its quintessence of grimness, you should take the Aberfoyle road by the Lake of Menteith.

This is, if I remember right, an indifferent road; certainly a narrow and winding one; but the Lake of Menteith will repay your trouble. In the first place it is the only piece of water in Scotland that may be called a lake, all other pieces of water being lochs on this side of the Border —a bit of information that marks off the educated tourist from the other kind. In the second place it can be extra-ordinarily beautiful. It is a lonely water and so still that the fir trees along its banks live a second and remote life, mirrored upon its quiet face. I have never known in any other place so great a peace as lies about its shores, the peace that might lie about a mystery. Perhaps there is a secret; for an old ecclesiastical house stands on Inchmahome in the middle of the lake. Cunninghame Graham lies buried there and those who attended him to the shore have told

9

me that as the boat was rowed across the water they felt it was carrying away for ever something noble that had endured a long time in their country's spirit.   I don't know: but if there is a place where the soul of an older Scotland could lie in peace it is on Inchmahome in the Lake of Menteith.   You may visit the island to see the ruins of the Priory; and, if you must, I pray you go in quietness; but it would be a kinder thing to turn away and leave the dead in peace.

It is only a few miles from Menteith to Aberfoyle and by the road-house you meet on the way you will know you are coming into tourist country.   It is all that and more—it is Scott country too; and all beyond it lie the Trossachs and the teas and the souvenirs and Bonnie Scotland.   God bless Sir Walter and them that have come after him.

You may gain some respect as a knowing one if you refer to the clachan of Aberfoyle, clachan being, I am told, the Gaelic for a village.   That sort of thing goes well round Aberfoyle, for this is right at the heart of the pseudo-romantical kind of glamour so widely spread over Scotland by Sir Walter.   Some of the action in *Rob Roy* and *The Lady of the Lake* is set in this part of the country, and you will no doubt find references to Bailie Nicol Jarvie and the Lady in quite unexpected places.   In short, you cannot go to Aberfoyle without thinking about Sir Walter.

That being so you may wish to know something about such a remarkable reputation.

Scott was an Edinburgh advocate who combined the practice of the Law with the aspiration for county gentility that is still a mark of the Edinburgh man.   His love for everything old led him to collect the ballads of the Scottish Border.   Then he spun some adventure stories in verse that pleased the taste of his age.   Finally, he took to prose and wrote the long succession of the Waverley Novels, that made him famous all over Europe.   He was a safe man,

Lochearnhead in the Highlands of Perthshire with Glen Ogle beyond

a sound Tory, with a fine estate at Abbotsford, and books and medals and broadswords and that love of the antique that has been a notable Scottish infirmity since his day.

The worship of his books has become a cult that has little to do with the books themselves. The stories, being classics, are set in schools for the teaching of grammar, history and appreciation. Therefore most Scots people can say quite honestly that they have 'read Scott'; but very few have done so after they left school and fewer still have enjoyed the tales. So you need not be familiar with anything more than the names of a few of them in order to pass as an educated traveller. The important thing to remember is that Scott, having incurred a debt of £100,000 in business, literally wrote it off with his pen and thus became a great national figure. If you know the story of the debt you do not need to trouble with more. Very few Scots people do.

However, it would be a mistake to dismiss Scott too lightly. He had a very considerable talent. He could tell a story. He could draw a courtly scene. He could sketch a good Scots peasant. He had a sense of humour and an eye for idiosyncrasies. But he missed true greatness; he had not a grown-up mind. He wrote novels, as other people wrote histories, with a grand eye for the picturesque and the trivial, but he had not a sense of wonder that man, so small and weak a creature, should walk so valiantly with the eternal all about him. He had a poor sense of the heroic; he saw it in the clash of swords, not in the passionate marches and counter-marches of the human spirit. He was a country gentleman with the limited vision of his order. He could see as high as the king, but he could not see as high as heaven. He was the greatest entertainer Scotland has ever produced, greater than even Sir Harry Lauder; but he never knew the ecstasies of heaven or the spiritual terrors of hell. He was ignorant about the more passionate parts of life; or did not choose to write about them. That was his strength as a popular novelist in his own day but his weakness to posterity. Yet when all that has been said there remains his very considerable talent. Though the chief characters in his books are wooden contrivances, some of the incidental characters are lively types of the old Scots peasantry, excellently observed, from above. He was also a master of the common speech. These alone would be enough to give him reputation in a country where genius of the literary sort has always been rather scarce.

I envy you the chance of going to Aberfoyle without the Scott business in your mind, for you will be able to see that romantic country as it really is—picturesque and sometimes amazingly beautiful when the sun throws curious shadows on the hills. You may eat well at Aberfoyle and then climb the high but excellent road to the Trossachs. If you go up to Loch Katrine you may sail on the still water under great crags, and invent all sorts of romantic fancies about the clans and the stirring affairs of the olden time. Afterwards in the evening you can run into Callendar and there bide the night with the certainty of comfort.

If it should be a golden evening you may walk by the river to the Falls of Leny or climb up the shoulder of a hill to watch the sunset making a splendour of blue and gold upon the mountains. Then you will indeed be civilized if you are not possessed by romantic notions. Plain honest men, stockbrokers and the like, have been so ravished by a night in Callendar that they have taken to kilts and learned to play the bagpipes. But the midges will likely save you. The insects in the Highlands are the most ferocious I have ever met and people they like have been bitten almost beyond recognition. I'm afraid nothing can be done about them. The strongest of tobacco in the foulest of pipes and all the lotions that the chemists have sold me have never discouraged those furious creatures. They are a bit of the price you must give for a Highland holiday. But a summer evening in Callendar is worth a little discomfort. If you have come to Scotland in search of glamour there is the place and then is the time. A glass of whisky neat will make the experience perfect.

The road goes up from Callendar by the side of the Leny to Loch Lubnaig and Strathyre. It is Highland country all the way—hills and water and a narrow road between them. When you come to the Kingshouse Inn you may turn into Balquhidder and go a long way into a secluded glen where the sun and the clouds make strange contrasts of light and shadow on Loch Voil. As there is no way out at the top of the glen, unless you go on foot, you must come back to the Kingshouse again and follow the road to Lochearnhead. There is, I believe, some dispute as to which is the prettiest village in Scotland, a very foolish way of wasting time. Lochearnhead would have to be reckoned in such a contest and indeed it is a charming village. Not that the houses have any distinction; but they are so beautifully situated at the head of the loch, such a graceful viaduct crosses the mouth of Glen Ogle behind them; and there are so many trees to soften the brilliance of the sun on the water, that Lochearnhead is an harmonious and delectable place. It has also one house of rare beauty. Go up the side-road on the left, a little short of the village, till you see Edinample among the trees below you. It is a white-walled castle on a level ground beside the loch and that is really all I can tell you about it, for I do not know any words delicate enough to hold its spirit. It is the most beautiful house I have ever seen and I would give everything I have to possess it.

Up Glen Ogle on the road to Killin you will find the more desolate Highlands. The glen is bare, a wind-swept place where the gales play hell in winter. Then you will come to Loch Tay and the glamour again. I would weary myself and you as well if I tried to describe this part of the journey in detail, because this kind of scenery is all alike, however much the colours and the shadows may change. So you may follow the road along the north side of the loch to Kenmore knowing that it will be all you could ever have imagined and hoping that you may see those occasional flashes of turbulent colour, or utter peace, that happen in those parts. At Kenmore you may visit the big hotel to get an idea of what a great Scots nobleman's house looked like in the days of Victorian glory. Then you may go on to Aberfeldy and look for the road to Perth through the town of Dunkeld. By that time you will have gotten into a daze. Hills and rivers and towns will have lost their distinctive forms and will pass before you like a rich cloth of many colours blended into something lovely and soothing. It is a kind of drunkenness; and to be drunk with Highlands is a curious experience you may care to try before you resume your travels north across the Lowland country.

When I look back I see I must have given you an impression of Perth as a holiday county; if so, I hope you will forgive me, because it has always been that to me and I have spent so many delightful hours along its roads. The impression is not wholly a wrong one. This is an agricultural county, a land of farms and small towns that depend on farming and the tourists for their living. There are no manufactures and nothing to remind you of the more deplorable part of urban life. If you can believe that agriculture is an idyllic trade than you will find Perthshire an idyllic county. Even if you know farming for what it is, you may still think you would rather farm in Perthshire than in many other places. The life is easier there than in the north-east. The hills of course are under sheep and the herd's life is not a soft one. But down on the big Lowland farms round Crieff and Coupar Angus there is a kind of richness that we do not associate with the hard-won north. Of course that richness is enjoyed a little more by the farmer than by his servants yet everybody can share in a more generous atmosphere. It is difficult to express the generous quality; I'd say only that there are trees and flowers around the cottages and that the fruits of the earth come willingly to ripeness. The soil has a warm heart, and that comes out a little in the character of the people.

Perhaps that is why, when we think of Scottish cricket, we think of Perthshire.

Of course there are people so misbegotten that they say we are incapable of cricket this side the Tweed. They will admit that we can produce a Peebles, a Baxter or a Kennedy once or twice in a generation, but those, they maintain, are only sports of nature. For they think it is not in the temper of a Scotsman to appreciate the true inwardness of a game that is the fine flower of English earth. When they assert their belief with the quiet arrogance that other nations can seldom understand and seldomer forgive, it is difficult for us to deny them. What are our few bright stars against their constellations? What are our hitters of ten against their hitters of thousands? What can we say when their bowlers are almost as fast as our trains? It is not only in accomplishment that they are superior, for even their Saturday afternoon cricketers wear their flannels with a more elegant air. You could say that, while some Scotsmen achieve flannels after much effort, every Englishman wears them as his birthright. So what with one thing and another, it might seem as though there were really no cricket in Scotland. I would almost believe it myself, but for Perthshire and Uncle Thomas and the Local Team.

We had never suspected that there was any cricket in Uncle Thomas, for he is a Scottish farmer and we had always thought that he kept his devotion solely to his farm and the profits thereof. When we went to see him one night we were sure that we would find him on some vantage point, keeping an eye on his corn and pasture. But we were wrong. There was no sign of him about the

steading and the fields. That was alarming. Any one
or all of a thousand disasters might have been happening
in his absence.   The fowls might have been taking paralysis,
the swine taking fever, the cows taking the corn, and
weevils, warbles, blight, and mildew coming down in
every direction.

'For sure,' we said to ourselves, 'it must be something
extraordinary that is taking Uncle Thomas away at this
season of the year.'

We were right. He was up at the cricket, watching the
Local Team.

Now, if it is true that we cannot play cricket in Scotland,
we can at least do it honour in the matter of pitches, and
I have never seen it more honoured than by the Local
Team. We found them playing in a wooded place where
the beauty of summer had taken on an everlasting air. It
was, I believe, the grounds of a mansion house but the
house had fallen into ruins. We did not miss it, for the
old trees stood round the field ampler and more tall than
houses, casting their black shadows beneath the evening
sun. Through their branches we could see down along
Strathearn, a pattern of green meadows and red clay fields
with the river, in the middle distance, a stream of gold.
There was life down in the haugh-land—cows walked
through the long grass with followers at their heels ; horses
stood tossing their heads in the corners of the fields ; and
little trains ran home to Glasgow with a flash of fire from
their windows. That was not all nor was it the most
wonderful. Whenever we looked between the tops of the
trees we could see the hills—a comfortable shoulder to the
south and a tumbled mass of deep blue peaks swinging
from the west far into the east and evening. Nature could
hardly have done more to pleasure us.

For once man did nothing to spoil the scene. The
Visiting Team were in. Two powerful young men were
knocking the ball in every direction while the Local Team

either hurled themselves (one at a time) in the general line
of the wicket or chased the ball into the deep grass or stood
in poses of rustic immobility in the outfield under the trees.
Their white uniforms were in perfect harmony with the
green of the field and the gold of the sunset; and the static
poses they assumed at every chance were only a little less
immobile than the eternal hills. Surely if a man had set
out to find the perfect field for cricket he need have looked
no farther. And if he had been looking for the perfect
spectator—there was Uncle Thomas.

They say cricket is best at Lord's where you may realize
it is the Englishman's religion. Well, I have been to
Lord's and I have seen the old gentlemen in the stands
facing excitement with supernatural calm. But their
restraint, the mark of the true cricket spectator, was nothing
to Uncle Thomas's. He stood under a copper beech with
his hat well down over his eyes and his hands well forward
in his trouser pockets, and a complete lack of any expression on his face. Only the short sharp puffs of smoke
from his briar pipe—puffs that were costing him one-and-
seven an ounce—showed the intensity with which he was
following the game and the sense of disaster that was over-
taking him. The Local Team were having a dreadful
time. You see, the Visitors included a few men that
played for the county, and a county reputation is worth
a handful of runs on any local ground. So although the
gardeners and ploughmen bowled till their shirts were
sticking to their backs, the gentlemen of the county hit fours
with lordly deliberation and got themselves out more by
acts of courtesy than as any admission of defeat. Mind
you, all runs were fairly scored. The batsmen had to
contend not only with the eagerness of the fielders but also
with the grass that grew ten inches high within a few yards
of the wicket. Sometimes of course the striker got an extra
run when the ball was lost in a bunch of perennial ryegrass
but that did not compensate for the drives and cuts, all

potential fours, that were stopped by impassable thickets of timothy. Still, in spite of every obstacle, the score went up to the hundred and beyond it. Uncle Thomas said nothing but pulled his hat farther down over his eyes. It was an exhibition of calm in the face of misfortune that the old gentlemen at Lord's must surely have envied and, silently, applauded.

It is said to be another attribute of the true cricketer that he never knows when he is beaten. The Local Team were true cricketers to the last man. Though the visiting bowlers had the prestige of county—and of a county that had Wilfred Rhodes behind it—the Local Team batted with vigour and abandon that must have alternately thrilled and desolated Uncle Thomas. Wickets fell quickly and the score was slow to rise. Night too was falling. The light grew enchanting, for curious shadows came down between the trees. Things that had been distant now seemed near and things that were near went glimmering away into the distance. At such a time the true English cricketer would have appealed against the light and the match would have ended ingloriously as a draw. The Local Team did not bother about the light; they were determined to have their innings. Besides, there was always the hope that the ball would be lost among the fescues in the outfield. So the game went on till the players moved about the dark field like white moths in the twilight. Uncle Thomas still said nothing, but drew his hat farther down upon his brows and brooded over the scene like the figure of Night.

They say there is no more heartening sight than the defence of a forlorn hope. What could have been more forlorn and therefore more heartening than the last wicket stand by the Local Team. At one end a ploughman and at the other end a little man in his working trousers interposed themselves between the bowlers and their wickets. Having small skill they offered what they had, their bodies ;

and let the mortal flesh take what they had no art to withstand. It was heroic; but, like so much that is heroic, it was useless. Five minutes from time the last wicket fell. The Visitors had won. But the Local Team had the glory. As we watched the players go into the shadows and the twilight take possession of the field, we wondered what besides skill had been lacking in the game that an English team would have given us on an English field. And honestly, with our hands on our hearts, we answered ' Nothing '.

' Well,' said Uncle Thomas, ' that's that. Now come down tae the steading and see the pigs.'

I can't think of any other county in Scotland where we could have enjoyed such an evening. They play cricket in other parts; but cricket is more than a question of runs and wickets; it demands a harmony of atmosphere, and that is why cricket in Perthshire is different from cricket anywhere else in Scotland. There is something in the mellow air that suits the game. And that is why Perthshire itself is different. Down in the Lowlands it is rich and mellow; up in the Highlands it wears a softness in its grandeur. I wish you all joy of it wherever you go.

CHAPTER FOURTEEN: ANGUS: PETER PAN AND POTATOES

THE next part of the journey I would propose for you runs from Perth to Aberdeen through Angus and the Mearns.

These are names that may not be familiar to you, and it is unlikely that you will find the Mearns on your map; but I like them and I use them partly because they have an exact meaning and partly for the native character in the sound of them. There are many such in Scotland. Some of them are alternative (and perhaps older) names for the counties; others are natural divisions of the country ruled over by nobles and chiefs in medieval times. All of them have a meaning for the people that live there; they are a part of the Scottish heritage. Their existence is not peculiar to Scotland; you find districts like the Isle of Ely and Purbeck and Wessex in England; but the lovely-sounding names are peculiar to themselves and are worthy of observance. It may please your humour to know them and to know how to speak them on this side of the Tweed.

First there are the alternative names for the counties. Berwickshire is sometimes known as the Merse, though not often, and you may not be understood if you refer to it as such. Then there is the district of Lothian. It is divided up into West Lothian or Linlithgow; Midlothian or Edinburgh and East Lothian or Haddington. It is probably best to refer to the whole district as the Lothians and to the individual counties as West Lothian, Midlothian and East Lothian. But I admit the business is all very confusing, because you will hear people speak of Linlith-

North through Angus to the Buchan Coast

gowshire and Haddingtonshire, but never I think of Edinburghshire. Fife, as you know, is sometimes called the Kingdom of Fife which pleases the natives very much; and to use it is a sign of the knowing traveller. Angus is unique. That old form was lost, officially, under the alias Forfarshire for a long time until the county council, recognizing its superior beauty, and the strength of tradition, restored it a few years ago. Thus you will find many people that still refer to Forfarshire but more that speak of Angus. Kincardine (Kin-càr-din), immediately to the north, has not followed Angus's good example, but if you call it the Mearns you will be using the idiom of the people. To be a Kincardineshire man is nothing much; but to be a man of the Mearns is to feel the heartening warmth of local pride. The counties of Elgin and Nairn together are Moray (Murray); but curiously enough, the term Morayshire often seems to refer to the county of Elgin alone. It would appear that the name of Moray, an ancient territorial form, has been narrowed to one of its parts; so that I have heard the two counties spoken of as Moray and Nairn; yet we still refer to them collectively as Moray. The last of this group is the Stewartry of Kirkcudbright (Kir-còo-bree). The origin of the first part of the name is obvious; and the survival of the old form is a blessing; for Kirkcudbright is a very outlandish name and it is usual to use only the easier half. So it is known by most people as the Stewartry.

The second group are the natural divisions of the country. Now they are many and I could never name them in detail, but I may be able to give you some help in finding them. For instance, the part of Stirlingshire to the south of the Campsie Hills is called Lennox. The land around the upper waters of the Forth is Menteith. One part of Inverness-shire is Lochaber. Another part is Badenoch. The north-eastern corner of Aberdeenshire is Buchan; the part immediately inland is Formartyn (For-màr-tyn); the centre is the Garioch (Geery); the fine tongue of land between the Dornoch Firth and the Beauly Firth in Ross-shire is the Black Isle. Ayrshire is divided into three parts: Kyle in the north, Cunningham in the middle and Carrick in the south. Then the valleys take their names from the rivers. It is impossible to give a sound rule about these because there are at least three forms. In the Borders you will find that the country is named by adding -dale to the name of the river, so that the country along the Teviot is Teviotdale. In the middle part of the country you can use the word valley and speak about the Valley of the Forth and the Clyde Valley. But you can also speak about Clydesdale when you mean the land around the upper waters. North of the Forth there is a fair division between strath and glen, as in Glenfeshie and Strathdon. It is always advisable to find out the local style; because, though people might understand you if you spoke about Glendon, they will understand you much sooner and like you better if you use the proper name. Besides these there is the suffix -side, used, I think, in all parts, except the true Highlands. You can say Tweedside, and Tayside, and Donside. You can say Nairnside or Strathnairn and you will be understood perfectly, if you sound the *r*'s. In some cases, as in Deeside and Ythanside, this is the only form used; for although Strathdee is a common surname, I have never heard it used for that fashionable district. However, just for the sake of confusion, I should mention that the desolate waste around the head-waters is called Glendee. It is impossible to make any rule about this matter except that you had better not use the -dale form north of Stirling or the glen and strath form south of it. But even that rule is broken when you go down into the south-west where an old Celtic kingdom has left Glenluce and Glendee and Glentrool and Glenkens as a legacy.

Since we are on this matter we may try to find some rule for the counties, for there may be a difficulty when

the county and the county town have the same name. I
have heard people make a rule that in such a case you
should always use the shire form when you mean the county
—as, Ayr the town and Ayrshire the county. In the case
of Elgin county you would say Morayshire though there
isn't a town of Moray. The composite Ross and Cromarty is often called Ross but usually Ross-shire, though
there is no town of Ross. It is never called Cromarty or
Cromartyshire, which is curious since there is a town of
Cromarty. On the whole I would say always use the shire
form in every case, remembering that the natives often use
either—as Aberdeen or Aberdeenshire, meaning the county
in both cases. There is, however, one form they never use
—the English contraction as in Beds. and Bucks. It
annoys the people of Clackmannanshire very much when
their glorious mouthful is contracted into Clacks.

As to pronunciation I have no help to offer you. If you
see a strange name like Kilconquhar, be very wary of it.
The natives probably call it something very different.
Finally, I would pray you to be a little modest about our
guttural ochs and achs. The Scots are rather proud of
them and really the laugh is not always to the visitor. It
is perhaps as funny for the native to hear the visitor call
Brechin ' Breekin ' as it is for the visitor to hear the native
pronounce it correctly. The weakness, if there is any, is
not in the people that have the guttural but in them that
haven't it. A certain modesty becomes the traveller in
strange parts and that modesty is the only fixed rule I can
give him in this matter of names. Try to discover the
local form wherever you go because that is a compliment
the natives will appreciate. People have a strange but not
uncomely pride in their own regions. A man that is not
very sure if he belongs to Peeblesshire or Selkirkshire will
be fanatically proud that he was born in Teviotdale. Thus
you can imagine how annoyed he will be if you call it
Glenteviot. Never be afraid to show your ignorance by

asking the native. He will appreciate the compliment and he will be delighted to instruct you at great length. In fact it is sometimes a good thing if you pretend to be more ignorant than you are. I once asked a man how he pronounced Friockheim (approximately Freekam) and before he had done he told me some of the most enchanting scandal about the Angus country-side. There is a kind of tact that repays the traveller an unlimited per centum.

You need not be afraid of any vernacular traps as you go up the Forfar road from Perth. The great valley that runs north and east has a name as broad and stately as itself —Strathmore. That may recall Ouida's novel; and when you look across the broad fields and the mansions that stand among old trees to the line of the Grampians against the north-west you may think it a country fit for Ouida's guardsmen. There are, however, few of the guardsmen in Strathmore and fewer still in its northern extension, the Howe o' the Mearns. The Strath is wholly agricultural. Of course there are mills in Forfar and Kirriemuir but a five-minutes' drive from their market-places will take you right into the heart of the tillage again. You can run for thirty or forty miles along wooded by-roads between heavy crops of oats and potatoes, through small villages where the only excitement is a flock of hens playing touch last across the road, past whitewashed farm-houses in tidy gardens and mansions hidden in well-tended woods. There are rivers to pass on bridges high over ravines; burns on bow-backs that throw you high into the air if you go too fast; and lochs to delight you with their silver ripples and the cooling winds. When you want to stop there are at least five good inns where the food is edible and the drink will do you no harm. There is surely nothing more you could ask for, unless it is a fair at evening; and if you go to Trinity outside Brechin at the beginning of June you may find that too.

You will see plenty of good earth, sometimes brown,

10

sometimes red, and always in a high state of cultivation. But if you are the kind of person who goes into ecstasies about nature, I would advise you not to throw yourself on the bosom of the good brown if it is bearing a crop of wheat or potatoes. The men of Angus do not understand a nature-lover's ecstasies. They have been growing potatoes so long that the Golden Wonder has entered into their souls. Do not invite them to admire the primrose at the river's brim, for the innocent flower may turn out to be an agricultural pest. Nor would I seek to dazzle the natives with the latest wit from town. A good new story about going to bed is always a passport to society, but the cheap wisecrack will get the reception it deserves—the long cruel stare and then the hearty spit which indicates wonder that the God who made seed potatoes could have made anything as silly as you.

Angus is the place for real country pleasures. It is enchanted with little streams that contain excellent trout for which you can fish at small expense, except of time and patience. They are generous with their fishing in Angus. If you wish a day's or even a week's fishing, find out the owner of a stretch of water, speak him nicely, insinuate that you are a fisherman, and I will be surprised if he does not ask you to make yourself at home in his burn. You do not need to catch any fish. When you are tired of casting your flies upon the water and seeing them rejected by the cunning trout you can strip under a beech tree and spend the rest of the afternoon in the water. Nobody will mind, for there will be nobody about to see you. Nor I think would any one object very much if they came upon you in a state of nature. The people of Angus have a fine indifference to strangers.

They play cricket in this part of the world. I remember a July day at Kirriemuir when I saw a tremendous battle between two local teams. The cricket ground was at the top of a hill from which I could see the country for miles

around. I lay on the scented grass beside a whin bush
half asleep. Sometimes I looked at the cricket and sometimes at the hills and sometimes I fell asleep altogether.
When I woke the hills were still standing against the north
and the fielders were still bounding after short singles or
hunting drives among the whins. Both the hills and the
game were in the nature of things eternal.

The slope grew almost precipitous on the far side of the
pitch and a fielder would sometimes trip and go rolling
down the hill to reappear some time later picking whins
out of the seat of his trousers. Meanwhile the beauty of
the village paraded the boundary, displayed their silk stockings and ate as much ice-cream as the youth would buy
them. Between the cricket and the girls I saw as much
country comedy as a quiet man could ask for on a quiet
Saturday afternoon; and when I tired of laughing, there
were the hills before me where the sun and the clouds
played shadowy games as the evening came on.

The hills are a great glory in Angus and the Mearns.
Villages like Edzell, Fettercairn and Auchenblae are
pleasant in themselves but they would lose half their character if you took away the hills. Even Laurencekirk, ' the
Mile o' Misery ', becomes less grim when you look over
the houses and see the Grampians stretching in an endless
blue rampart against the north. Seen from Strathmore
and the Howe o' the Mearns, the Grampians seem to define
the limits of the civilized world. On this side there are
peace and plenty, gardens and fields and pleasant homes.
But on the other side—who knows what horrors there may
be ? You should see for yourself; and the way lies on
foot through the glens where the streams come down. You
can go up Glenclova, Glenlee, Glendoll, Glenmark or
Tarfside, first of all by motor-roads and then by tracks and
old droving roads over the watershed and down into the
valley of the Dee. They are romantic roads, once the paths
from the Highlands to the south over which the drovers

brought the cattle to the fairs and the Highland girls came down to gather the harvest in the Lowlands. They are disused now, except by small bands of walkers whose songs come sweetly down the evening air or whose curses salute the esurient midge. But the Grampians are wide enough for all to sing and curse in without creating a breach of the peace, and by the Water of the Mark you will find all the peace you have ever desired.

You will have gathered that there are three sorts of country in Angus and the Mearns—the rich strath where Glamis and Kinnaird stand in witness to the ancient state of the Scottish nobility; the foothills with their little towns and ruined castles like Edzell and Kincardine that fell with the passing of an earlier glory; and then the glens that run up through increasing poverty to the magnificent desolation of the hills. If you are the kind of traveller that does not fear to leave the mainroads you will be able to see a little of them at no great expense of labour.

First the strath. Take the Forfar road from Perth by Coupar Angus and Meigle and look about you as you run through that easy country. You can't learn much in an afternoon because the ways of a country-side take years of knowing but you can make a comparison with the land around Lochearnhead and Aberfeldy and you will realize how rich and settled it is. Just before you run through Glamis (Glaaaams, not Glarms) you will see the gates of the Castle, where the Lyons have ruled in Strathmore for many generations and in which Queen Elizabeth lived as a girl. A few miles farther on you will come into Forfar, the county town. I would like to say nice things about Forfar, for I have always liked the town, mildly; but I can't think of anything notable in it, except that its bakers make, or used to make, a delicious kind of meat pie called a Forfar bridie. And it has a public convenience adorned with flowers.

You have a choice of at least three roads out of Forfar.

You may go east to Arbroath and bathe in the very modern pool, down to Carnoustie for a round of golf on the championship course, then up to Montrose, a quiet little town with an eighteenth-century air now a little troubled by the dubious amenity of an Air Force school. If you are in a hurry you can go straight on from Forfar to Brechin, where if it is market-day, you will see the farmers of Strathmore making their bargains with a complete disregard for the value of time. But I think you will find it most amusing if you take the third road and turn west to Kirriemuir. The other name of the town is Thrums, the earthly capital of the Barrie Country.

I have often wondered why people go to foreign parts for their holidays. It can't be to get away from their neighbours because, nowadays, the neighbours go too. It can't be for novelty because most travellers take their own domestic atmosphere with them, and the more they travel the more determinedly they are at home. Maybe it is just because they have got to do something with the leisure they so greatly value and so little understand. But there are some who travel with a purpose, to visit the country made dear to them by their favourite writers. Well, there must be about five million of those who wish to spend a day at Kirriemuir, hoping to get right to the soul of J. M. Barrie in the place that nourished his immortal whimsies. However I may deplore (and my prejudice against the works of the Little Master is as great as my prejudice against Dundee), my duty is to act as the honest broker and guide you into the Never-Never Country.

Kirriemuir is an interesting little town. I do not doubt that people who have admired *A Window in Thrums* will take one look at it and say 'How quaint. Just what we expected from the book.' It has an old Scots air and you might be sure of finding worthies of the kind so nicely drawn in the stories. The young man in the grocer's might be John Shand; the young woman, so plain and respectable, might be Maggie unexpectedly learned in the things that every woman knows. You might be sure you are in the place where Barrie found his deep understanding of men and women; and when you look over at the glens running back into the enchanted secrets of the blue hills you know where Barrie found the magic of his other-world.

But are the people of Kirriemuir like the people in a story by Sir James? If so, they are unlike the people of any other place in Scotland. The difference is so marked that we say the characters are quite unreal and we say they are bad art since Barrie would have us believe they are living men and women set down on paper. There is no necessity for characters being like real-life. It takes nothing away from Sexton Truggin and the Reverend Silas Dottery that you would never meet them in Dorset, for Mr. Powys never pretends you would. But Sir James invited us to believe we were seeing mortal men and women through his window in Thrums. We say they are not mortal men and women but conventional figures displayed with great skill, in a Scots kailyaird.

Kailyaird is an expression used about a great mass of Scots writing. The kailyaird is the kitchen garden and, according to an old song, a rose or two can grow in it. The connotation is domestic, homely, full of homely joy and homely sorrow. Writing of the kailyaird type became very popular about sixty years ago when a vast official respectability came over Scots life. Then there grew up a market for stories that showed simple people as amusing, humorous and idiosyncratic, people that might have rough exteriors but certainly hearts of gold. The silver-haired old grandfather; the erring child that fell because a tall dark man looked over the kailyaird wall; the candle in the window to light the dear one home—all the stock situations of melodrama were softened with a Scots mist of humour and watered with bountiful tears. Thus we inherited a body of writing, like the stories that might be told by a dear old lady in her garden of a summer evening. Sir James touched that kind of writing with something near genius. Whatever else he lacked he had technique; he mastered the technique of the story before, and just as, he mastered the technique of the stage. Anybody can write about real people—he has only to set down what he honestly thinks about his relations; it takes talent to write about people as they would like themselves to be, and then make them believe in the picture. Sir James, like Sir Walter, gave the public what they wanted and prospered exceedingly thereby. It was certainly magnificent, but was it art ?

In the matter of taste it is well to speak with some humility because there can hardly be an objective standard of good and bad. Therefore I had better just say that Barrie's work is not my taste, and leave it at that. But facts are different; and it is an amusing fact that the town which produced *Auld Licht Idylls* also produced, or inspired, the bawdiest of all the bawdy songs of Scotland. I wish I could quote you the politer stanzas of the ' Ball o' Kirriemuir ', but even they could hardly pass in a Latin footnote, let alone in the shameless Doric. That may give you some idea of the Rabelaisian masterpiece. Place that beside Sir James's blameless works and you will understand why some of us regard the auld licht as a rather smoky candle. ' The Ball o' Kirriemuir ' set in the idylls would be like a muck midden among the roses in the kailyaird. But curiously enough, muck has its place in a kailyaird: without it there will eventually be no roses. Perhaps that is why Sir James's roses are beginning to wilt too soon—they were grown with an artificial fertilizer.

There is a nice parallel between Sir James and Sir Walter. Both had talent, great talent: both were enormously successful; and both refused to grow up. They were Peter Pans—in Sir Walter's case because he couldn't help it; in Sir James's case perhaps because he deliberately chose that way. They were both essentially frivolous writers, being without great passion. They were incomparable public entertainers that satisfied, in a magical way, the needs of the average readers of their time.

There has been, as you may have gathered, a kind of reaction against the kailyaird school. There are still a few Scots writers that are content to master the technique and do very well out of it, for the public likes technique though it does not understand the reason why. The 'serious' writers (very foolishly) despise technique but concentrate on what they think to be the truth—a little nearer the 'Ball o' Kirriemuir' than *A Window in Thrums*. But when the truth and the technique are combined then we have writing, imperial, beyond question. *A Scottish Quair*, by Lewis Grassic Gibbon, shows a passion and a magic that have been scarce in Scotland since Burns wrote *The Jolly Beggars*. *Sunset Song*, *Cloud Howe* and *Grey Granite* are immeasureably the best work in the new spirit as *Auld Licht Idylls* is the best in the old; and curiously enough, all deal with this part of Scotland. If the idylls are like the stories told by an old lady in her garden, *A Scottish Quair* is like the conversation of a peasant in the byre at night when the cows have been bedded down. But it is inspired conversation. The story is nothing much, but the incidentals make the ordinary part of country life stand up, muck and all, with devastating reality. The adulteries, cruelties, treacheries, and hatreds—everything that Barrie passed over —have been set down with a furious delight. Can you wonder that we look on the books as something rich and strange. Of course it is only the complement to the kailyaird. Grassic Gibbon dared to say what had been too long left unsaid but he was inclined to omit some things of some importance—that although men are guilty of sudden beastliness they occasionally show surprising kindness. He missed out something—the heat of passion that lies behind so many cruel and treacherous actions and the lust for enjoyment that ends in so much suffering. But when all his faults have been numbered he stands on a different earth from Barrie's. He was at least trying to see the truth although he died before he saw it all. Barrie was perhaps clever enough to see all the truth and cleverer still to suppress it. If you want to understand the people that live in Strathmore and the Howe o' the Mearns, read Gibbon's books as well as Barrie's; and then temper both views with what you know about living people.

As I sit here and write in my book I would be glad to be going with you along the side-roads of Angus and the Mearns about three o'clock on a late summer afternoon when the corn is ripening. I would not put any bounds upon your journey, for any side-road is as good as another. You may go as you please, out and in across the plain, or up into Glenclova and Glenesk. But I think you might visit Edzell where there is a fine golf course, a few good hotels and a magnificent ruined castle. You could lie the night very agreeably there and go out a short distance to the mouth of the glen where the Esk comes down over the Rocks of Solitude. Then, while the dew is still on the grass in the morning, you might play a round on the course that stretches away to the river and the hills. You will be sure of a good game and you may see, as I have seen, the Mearns farmer in his glory.

I played there a few times with a farmer of those parts, a choice spirit, free from all self-consciousness. As it was the holiday season fashionable people were out on the course, some that occasionally got their names in the papers and more that hoped for such happiness. Their clothes were more accomplished than their golf. But my opponent was, as always, dressed in large boots and trousers very tight in the leg. He had taken off his jacket and waistcoat for freedom's sake, showing a pair of virile scarlet gallowses on a gentleman's pin-striped shirting. He had also undone the button at his neck and the first button at his waist.

The result was something noble and free. While the correct but tiresome young men and women stood around looking disgusted, he teed his ball in front of the club house, rolled up his sleeves, settled himself comfortably into his trousers, and then hit the ball a nice 250 yards up to the green. The County and near-County raised their noses, but my opponent just said, ' They canna sniff away a drive like that.' The game continued in that spirit. My opponent was a man who knew the glory of language. When things went well he cried on the ball with agricultural idioms; when things went ill he addressed his clubs and the world at large in glorious commination. Then it was indeed amusing to notice how the polite young men would try to shelter their women from the gross assault of such dreadful words in best tradition of the (late) Anglo-Saxon male. I had a suspicion, however, that the young women showed a juster appreciation of my opponent's genius besides of the scarlet gallowses that flashed a challenge to propriety in the morning sun.

When you leave Edzell you might hold on between the hills and the plain to Fettercairn, a charming village with a good inn and an arch in honour of Queen Victoria. That is all I can say about Fettercairn; it has nothing notable, nothing to justify a sixpenny guide-book; and yet it has something—personality, atmosphere, an elusive quality that may delight you if you have any taste for things that can be plain and subtle, both at once. And if you happen there at the right time you may attend one of the most characteristic occasions in the rural year—a cattle show. You must see one somewhere if you are to get the real flavour of country life in Scotland.

There is often controversy as to the value of cattle shows. They are intended to raise the standard of breeding in horses and cattle, but there are critics who say they do positive harm. That may be true in the case of big shows like the Royal and the Highland that encourage the breeding of fancy animals irrespective of whether they may be the best types. Just as old families can be bred too fine so with cattle and horses; and it may be that the big shows, having once done valuable work, are now doing harm. But that is a matter I am not qualified to speak about. The local shows, however, are not likely to endanger the community. They do some good by encouraging farmers to think about quality at a time when in agriculture as in everything else there is a danger that quantity may become the only test. They give a fine chance for rivalries to be settled in public without the use of violence. And they are a grand excuse for a day out. Perhaps the last is their best justification.

Go to a small country show like the Fettercairn one if you want to see the country-side on parade. There will be the best horses and cattle of the district stalled and penned under the trees around the field. If you go in the morning you will see the farmers and the attendants giving the beasts their last brush up, the final tittivation that may catch the judge's eye, for judges being human are susceptible to a touch of artifice. Then you may watch the animals paraded in their classes round the judging ring and drawn up before the judges for cross-examination. You may have difficulty in deciding between animals that seem all equal and magnificent, but if you listen to your neighbours at the ringside you will hear defects analysed at length in the choicest language, as 'widegaen ahint' and 'boggit in the hochs'.

The forenoon is devoted to serious competition; the afternoon is given up to pleasure. There are sports. These range from the ridiculous to the homeric. That athletic curiosity, the slow bicycle race is a favourite, a rare test of equilibrium on a bumpy field, and I have seen surprising exhibitions by surprising people on the greasy pole. There are better things. You should see enormous young farmers trying to pitch a sheaf of broom over a fifteen-foot bar; or two of them taking the opportunity given by a pillow fight to settle a difference over a woman. Or you may be fascinated by the spectators. Many will look quite ordinary because farmers are no longer the distinctive race they ought to be. But you are sure to see some grand faces twisted and gnarled by passion and circumstance, the perfect expression of the natures behind them. And you will see others that might belong to an earlier time. The cattle show attracts men from remote farms that would not turn out for any other occasion. So you may see, as I have seen in Tarland, wild black whiskers and antique coats that would not have been out of place at Flodden.

The shows are convivial affairs. There is always one refreshment tent and sometimes several, but never in my experience too many. As the beer flows the tongues wag looser. The seemingly dour countrymen become almost animated. They make assertions, accusations, innuendos. Their language grows rich, very rich, till they seem to speak with the voice of their native earth. You too might have a drop of beer in the tent and listen to them. Even if you can't understand very much, you may like the rhythm of their speech, its depth and character. It is not musical, even when oiled with bitter; it has always a touch of northern hardness, of the east wind; but it is man's speech without any degenerate refinements. So with the thought behind it. Country people have still the power of making a phrase that catches all their meaning in a flash of words. Thus their conversation is conducted with many pauses for thought and there is none of the incessant flutter of words with which fashionable people try to express nothing in particular. There may of course be an impetuous eloquence later in the night; but that is a sign that much liquor has set free thoughts engendered through a whole year's sobriety. And later still there may be song around midnight when the road curtsies to the moon and the stars are in solution, going home.

If you are fortunate there may also be dancing on a board

in the open air. If the show is a fairly important one there will be a band to discourse music, for brasses, all afternoon and then to play for the dancing. If not, then you may have the highest felicity of hearing a local and amateur combination.

There was one I remember—and I pray they are still alive though I fear they have been assumed into a superior music—that used to play for the dancing after a very local show. It was composed—and how could I ever forget it —of a fiddle, a string bass and a cornet played by a farmer, a roadman and a blacksmith, not for money but for the love of music. Of these three the fiddler alone had much accomplishment; it was even said that he could play at sight. The string bass player was a case of heredity; he had inherited the string bass from his wife's uncle. He had never learned to play tunes on the thing because what was a tune on a string bass anyway; but he could bring out notes like the strokes of doom at strict intervals which was a good thing in a dance. The cornet player was, they said, self-taught. He was also an artist; in fact he played swing of his own invention long before swing was heard of in the south. They were an irresistible combination that gave, and still give me in memory, immense pleasure. The fiddle gave out the tune, the string bass added its boom boom in strict time; and the cornet improvised wonderful variations that became incomparably sweet as they died away through the wood. The three honest players sat on a wooden platform and all the youth of the country-side danced on the board at their feet. They were as I remember them three jolly gods of the fields that wove music for the country boys and girls between the haytime and the harvest. Like gods they had immortal vigour; and, whoever might tire in the dance, the three old gentlemen kept their places. Reels or strathspeys, one-steps or waltzes, their elbows were always as supple, their fingers as lively. Refreshed by an occasional glass of whisky, they played on till the sun went down and the owls, entranced, added their woodwind notes. Then the field became mysterious, for lamps were lit around the board and the old gentlemen seemed to play tenfold among the shadows. Round one o'clock people began to go home or at least to leave in pairs for the dark paths through the woods. At two o'clock the band played the last strathspey, the lamps were blown out and the show was over. Then there was only silence broken by the hooting of the owls or the snore of a ploughman abandoned under a tree. That's how they used to do it; if you are fortunate you may find a place where they do it that way still. Then you will be fortunate beyond the lot of ordinary men.

There are several ways you can go from Fettercairn. One runs along the foothills to the Clatterin Brig whence you can go up over the cairn o' Mounth and down by Glendye to Deeside. It is a picturesque road through Highland country with some magnificent views. But if you wish to understand Aberdeen you should approach it from the main road. So you may go from Fettercairn to join the main-road at Laurencekirk; or turn east from the Clatterin Brig through Drumtochty by Auchinblae to Drumlithie, a quaint and curious place. Beyond that a little you will find the Aberdeen road. After you have passed Stonehaven you will find that the land becomes poor and cold and you will have the rough sea by you all the way. The rich fields of Strathmore and the Mearns have given place to a windy scarp between the hills and the brilliant blue of the sea. Plenty and easy living are left behind; the bite of the east wind is in the air; and the stony fields betoken a sparse amenity. The quality of the scene has hardened, as if the land, narrowing between the sea and the hills, had taken on the colder qualities of both. This inhospitable inhuman air increases as the hills run down to the sea, until at Girdleness you stand on eternal rock beaten for ever by the green waves. You may think then that you have reached a point where the ancient enmity of sea and land leaves no place for mortal men. And looking northwards over the bay you may think you have found a new dead world of insentient things. For there, glittering silver and cold as death, are the granite towers of Aberdeen.

CHAPTER FIFTEEN: ABERDEEN

ABERDEEN is a town that you will likely respect at sight, but you will not stay there long enough to love it. I have known it so long that I have lost the respect and only love remains, because my first twenty years were spent around it, and I am in some ways its child. So the fact that prejudiced me against Dundee prejudices me in favour of Aberdeen. It may be well to keep that in mind when I tell you about the north-east.

You will likely respect Aberdeen at sight, because it has an air of imperishable newness. As you get to the top of the last hill, either by the railway or by the road, you see half the town rising up on the other side of the Dee—glittering white houses among trees, with the cold blue waves to the east of them. It looks a clean and prosperous town from the distance: and the streets that lead into the centre will confirm that impression. If you are accustomed to yellow brick, or to sandstone well grimed with smoke, this granite town may strike you as cold, hard and even repelling. One visitor, who had never seen granite except in the form of tombstones, said that three hours of the town was enough for him, because it reminded him of a colossal burying ground without the flowers.

Granite is always uncompromisingly granite, a hard bright stone. You can try to disguise it in any way you like. You can carve it into twirlie-wirlies and pretend it is butter, but it will always defeat you; will always remain an unconquerable stone to be used in great square blocks or not at all. So you may find the town inhospitable, too obviously something built of stone, too obviously unsoftened by the

150

dirt of industry and unsophisticated by romantical twirly-wirlies. If the weather is fine it will have too much glitter; if the weather is cold it will be too grim. But that is right. You are out of the rich carses. You have crossed the Grampians where they meet the sea. You have come into a poorer country where life has a sterner discipline. And Aberdeen, the chief town of the country-side, is that sterner discipline in stone. So it is a fascinating town: but it is more than stone and lime—it is the expression of unconquerable human will; the perfect expression of everything I mean by Lowland Scots. It is a temper more than a town.

What is there on the town side? There is Union Street, the true centre of the north-east: a good enough street in an unimaginative way, but you should overpraise it to please the Aberdonians. There is Marischal College, a miracle in granite and also, some think, a miracle in bad taste—but an undoubted miracle either way. Just off Union Street there are one or two most dignified squares, and straight up beyond the top of Union Street there is one fine terrace, where the granite has been treated with understanding. There is the Fish Market, where even the dullest people must be amazed at the strange fish that come out of the sea. And there are all the usual things that make up a big town—the slum clearances, the west-end villas, the many miles of bungalows and tenements, the churches, the picture houses, the public assistance department and the rest. Then, out towards the river, you will find the Aulton, a beautiful antique among all that modernity. It is very little, just a long street with King's College at one end and St. Machar's Cathedral at the other, and a delicious little comical town house in between. Down by the sea there is a fishery research station: out in the country towards the west there are the Rowett Institute, made famous by Sir John Orr; and the Macaulay Institute for Soil Research. Near by them you will find the College of Agriculture and the Craibstone School of Rural Domestic Economy, the first, and perhaps still the only school of its kind in Great Britain. In short you will see a modern town admirably equipped to serve its hinterland—the efficient capital of a distinctive province.

That would be a lot to see; but even if you examined it all you might not discover the temper, the unique flavour of Aberdeen. The secret of the town lies in the country round about; for Aberdeen is so closely linked to its hinterland that one cannot be understood without the other. That, I think, makes it unique among big towns. You cannot imagine that Leeds or Hull would be vitally affected if agriculture stopped in Yorkshire. Glasgow would still flourish if all the cows in Ayrshire died and Dundee would hardly notice if no more Golden Wonders were grown in Angus. But the prosperity of Aberdeen depends on the fruit of its surroundings—on the harvests of the land and the harvest of the sea. Aberdeen stands on the disputed margin of those elements: its prosperity depends on them; so inevitably something of their nature can be seen in the nature of its people. To understand the town and the people you must look at the land and sea.

If you are interested, go out the coast road through Ellon and Cruden to Peterhead. Go from there to Maud, and look at Mormond Hill rising drearily out of a dreary plain. Then run down to Methlick and up through the Howe o' Fyvie to Rothienorman. There you may turn towards Aberdeen again, by Wartle and Pitcaple, and into town by Inverurie and Tyrebagger Hill. It is not a long way, not a hundred miles, even allowing for detours when you lose your way, but if you watch the country through which you will pass, and the cold sea that washes it, you may come at the real secret of Aberdeen.

I once called the north-east the cold shoulder of Scotland, and I have not felt anything since to make me change my mind. It is a county made up of indifferent soil, some of it woefully thin, some of it sullen clay. There are wonderfully good stretches—in the Bonnie Howe o' Fyvie for instance—but these are lonely islands of fertility, into which, you might think, nature had once gathered all the poor resources of the country-side. There are lands that have a generous heart; that seem to invite men to seed them and gather harvests from them, and live on them in peace for ever. There is little of that in Aberdeenshire. At one time—and that is no great distance away—the country must have had great miles of waste so cold and forbidding that you'd have thought no farmer would have dared lay hands on them. Yet the wastes were put under the plough, and they have been kept in such good heart that Aberdeenshire is reckoned one of the best farmed counties in Britain.

If you go the round of it you will see hundreds of crofts and small farms on land so poor that you may wonder how the people make a living. They make their living in the same way their ancestors made those farms—by the hardest labour and the strictest economy. The kind of life lived by the crofters and small farmers is a discipline that most people would find intolerable. There is no genial conspiracy between the farmer and the earth; the land is by nature wild, and fertility is, you might almost think, something imposed on it against its nature. So farming in those parts is a struggle to keep back the waste. If the crofter takes his ease, then the rushes and the dirt will eat away his pasture and choke his corn. That lovely but how thin veneer of sweet grass and yellow corn is indeed maintained by the sweat of the husbandman—and it is the most precarious beauty in the world. After all, even in much better farming land, fertility depends not on the inexhaustible riches of a deep-delved earth, but on a thin layer, a few inches deep, enriched by manure, and sweetened by the sun through generations of tillage. You can imagine then how few resources there can be in the stony soil of the poorer land, and how much harder work it must be to make them the foundation for the mysteries of growth in corn and cattle. And you can also imagine how small a surplus such fields can leave the husbandman at the end of the year. So that is the discipline of a great part of the north-east—unremitting labour in return for bare subsistence.

There are still families that work hard fourteen hours a day, six days of the week, in all kinds of weather, and never have any money among their hands. They have the necessities—food, clothing and shelter—but the other things that people, wisely or foolishly, want they do not have; and cannot have until the children go away to work in the towns. Of course they have other things—independence, a place of their own, the job they like (though the children seldom like it as much as the parents) and everybody puts a different personal value on these things. Perhaps you think they are worth the hard work : I think not; but that does not matter, as far as this book is concerned. What does matter is that Aberdeenshire is a county where men started with many disadvantages—a cold climate, a poor soil— yet they have brought its farms to a state of rare efficiency in good times and bad times, by care and labour. And all of it has been done on the slenderest margin of profit.

I can't tell you much about the other kind of life that has gone to the making of Aberdeen. I have always feared the sea, ever since I was a small child and lay awake at night, listening to its noise, that was said to be the howl of the Black Dog, a grim rock along the shore. But I suppose I don't need to tell you about a fisherman's life, because the English are a seafaring nation, and the waves are for ever beating on the shores of their hearts. The men that sail out from Peterhead and Fraserburgh would be the same kind of men that go out from Bideford and sunny Appledore, and get no more for doing so. There is a convention that fishermen love the tossing waves; that they sail their craft like the Vikings did, exulting in the battle with the incontinent seas. That may be true. But I have stood at my cottage door, outside Aberdeen, and watched the drifters pitching across the harbour bar into the grey wastes; and I have seen the waves go lashing over the tops of the harbour lights on the north pier for days on end: and then I have doubted if the little men in bowler hats could still be exulting. They do it because it is their job. Like the small farmers they make an endless struggle against a part of nature that can be managed but will never be tamed. And they do it for rewards small out of all proportion to the labour.

Now Aberdeen has been built up out of the farming and the fishing, and they have decided her nature. When you see the town on a grey forenoon you realize there is dourness and defiance in the set of the houses. Just as the farmers keep back the waste, and the fishermen drive their boats into the force of the storms, so you might think the town has been built as a challenge to wind and weather. The houses do not flower out of the earth as Georgian houses do on the kindly English earth. They have been put there forcibly by determined man, to stand for ever. I would not say that Aberdeen was particularly well planned in the olden time: but, of all the commercial towns I have seen, it most gives the impression of having grown up with a clear design. Looking at it, you can understand that it was built by the sons of the men who imposed their will upon the moors and ruled out their little square fields from the waste. It is an order imposed upon wild nature, like the fields themselves.

You can see the influence of their background in the people. They are, of course, notorious for meanness. There are, I believe, stories, diverting stories, built upon that reputation. But the stories are a little less than the truth.

Aberdonians are careful with money in business matters, for a reason that must be obvious by this time. There are no great natural resources to play with: there is no great staple (except fish) to speculate in and make a thousand pounds before lunch. The whole business of the north-east is done on small margins (except in the fish trade which swings from fabulous losses to fantastic gains). So, inevitably, the people realize that they must pay their way by careful management, and will bargain desperately over the last half-crown, just as their ancestors haggled with the butcher over the price of their chickens, and their cousins still do in the wilds of Buchan.

But as soon as the deal is made, the Aberdonian changes. After he has spent half an hour to gain another half-crown he will spend a whole hour and five shillings standing you whisky and telling you stories to celebrate. Just as the country people can show tremendous passions below all their hard-working respectability, so the careful business man can show convivial powers that terrify the stranger. Two men from the south—men that have never been known to flinch at the sight of drink—have told me that the Aberdonians' taste for whisky scared them. Decent, respectable, God-fearing men, they said, would take half a dozen doubles before lunch, and then go back to business quite sober, ready to start all over again before dinner, after a hard afternoon in their offices. Of course drinking may be just a habit and mean nothing at all; but it is true that the careful Aberdonian can be most reckless and generous in his pleasures. It may be a sign that he is not long civilized; it is indeed a sign of his ancestry. People that work hard for very little, fishermen and small farmers and ploughmen, have few chances of a celebration, but when they get a chance they celebrate in a kind of primitive glory.

You cannot appreciate the north-east, or any part of the Lowlands, unless you realize the power of wild delight that lies far under the outward respectability. There are a lot of churches in the north-east, and most villages seem quite dead on Sundays. But in Aikey Braes, in Deer, on a Sunday afternoon in July, you will find a most vigorous and entertaining carnival. This festival is held on the eve of one of the old horse-fairs and once was only a prelude to the serious business of the Monday. Now, of course, the Mon-

King's College in Aberdeen

day's business is nothing, and the eve has become a riot. To Aikey Braes go all the showmen of the north-east. The mechanical organs blare out their secular music on the Sabbath air; games of chance are everywhere on a day that should be devoted to making certain of Heaven. Even worse, there is strong drink; and worst of all the strong drink has been known to go to people's heads. Thousands of revellers come from all Aberdeenshire to the devil's work on Sunday, and, in spite of the Evangelists who call them to repentance in the quieter corners, they do that work with pleasure. Aikey Braes is admitted a scandal by all right-thinking people; but it will survive much effort to put it down, for it satisfies a need in ordinary people. There is a limit to the amount of patient well-doing and quiet respectability that people can endure without any reward of money or praise. An occasion is necessary, as an acknowledgement that life is rich and various.

A cottar wedding can be a wonderful pagan festival of drink and music and dancing though there isn't a penny in the house. Those who live such hard lives have a sort of lust for pleasure when it comes. I think there is still something of that furious delight in the ordinary Aberdonians. They are careful and restrained in their business, and at ordinary times, but a stranger should beware when they let themselves go: they have farther to go than most.

That is the idea that I would like you to have of Aberdeen—a town where a great deal has been made of very poor resources, lived in by people that must make their own way in the world. They make that way particularly well, again because it is a tradition forced upon them by the croft and the farm. The men who broke in the waste were strong brave men: they were also mighty begetters of children. The poor land was not enough to feed their sons and daughters, so the younger ones had to seek their fortunes elsewhere. To begin with, many of them went to Aberdeen and started businesses there. But the opportunities were limited, so they held south to Edinburgh and Glasgow, and finally to London.   The young men and women have been holding south ever since.   They do very well for themselves in England which is a way that Scotsmen have.   Our system of education, which places importance on facts and discourages imagination, turns out young men and women that take easily to an office life.   They are careful, trustworthy, and clear in the head—the very people to become heads of departments.

There is a much-loved joke about that, and I'll tell you it now so that you will be able to deal with it whenever you meet it.

A Scotsman who had visited London was asked on his return what he thought of the English.   He replied: ' I don't know.   I didn't meet any.   You see I interviewed only the heads of departments and they were all Scots.'

There is only one retort—that the English would have been the directors; and, perhaps, that the directors would likely have been controlled by Jews.

I don't apologize for telling you such an old story, for I think it is a very true one.   The Lowland Scot has a clear head that makes him a grand executive.   He has tenacity and endurance and the power of waiting.   He has everything that you might expect in the products of such a background.   The one thing he wants is imagination—the one thing that you would never expect from his country-side. These are marks of the Lowland Scot, and, in the highest degree, the Aberdonian.   So, if you find yourself admiring Aberdeen but unable to love it, the reason may be just that the people have always lacked a touch of the high imagination because they have always had to work too hard.

Have I given you the impression that life in Aberdeen and the north-east is hard and lacking in grace.   If so, I have done very wrong.   You will not find anything more graceful and civilized than King's College on a fine summer day. I have said hard things about Scottish education; but I must also say how grateful I am that I was allowed to spend some time in that College. The learning was not particularly useful, for I suppose I was too immature to know what I wanted, though mature enough to know that I was not getting it. Yet I got something—four years of comparative ease spent in a very beautiful place. I passed a lot of time looking for 'curious' books in the library, in playing tennis, and in lying under the trees in the summer vacations. It was perhaps just the very life to counteract the persevering philosophy I was brought up to at school. There is a dignity about the College; and a great age. Just now and then they suggested that the struggle towards the head of the department might not be worth while. I interpreted the admonition obediently then, as I have told you in the piece about Scottish Education. I saw it as an invitation to an academic life, withdrawn to the fringes of existence. But my wrong interpretation does not take away from the beauty of the College, or its power to move others with a better purpose. If you have any humility or any hope, go there on a summer afternoon. Remember that it was planned by the good Bishop Elphinstone to the glory of God and the service of posterity, four hundred years ago. If you stay there long enough, in peace, you may see his faith built in the walls and, neglecting what is, be a little moved at the thought of what might be.

It might be an entertaining experience for you to see Aberdeen on Friday. That is the market-day, when the country people go in to sell and buy, the day when Aberdeen is most the capital of its province. If you wished to get the full experience, you might get up very early and go to the Fish Market to see—and hear—the fish being sold. Then, after breakfast, you might go out to the auction marts at Kittybrewster, where you will see the farmers conducting their business with superhuman self-control. Back in town again, you might go down to the Green, where the country butter and egg merchants haggle with the careful housewives. About two in the afternoon you might go along to Hadden Street where the Corn Market is held. You may have some difficulty in getting into the little street, because of the absolute immobility peculiar to a farming crowd, but it is worth the effort. Stand among them quietly, and you will hear real conversation. The long pauses, the profound silences, the utter incredulity, or the sharp attack and reply of individual wit, all in the hard broad speech of the country-side. Of course you must not expect very much. Like so many other small pleasures I've thought up for you, this depends entirely on the occasion suiting your mood. If the mood is wrong, pass on with an easy mind. After all, more was lost at Mohacs field.

Then I think you might continue your investigations in Union Street, which, at three o'clock on a Friday afternoon, is most the main street of the north-east, the true setting for the crowds that take their pleasure there. You will soon discover the main types of this province. As I have written in ' Scottish Country ', edited by Mr. George Scott-Moncrieff :—

Business men dressed immaculately after a pattern step out smartly as if to build their fortunes on the last half-crown of discount. Beautiful ladies from the West End, dressed as immaculately as their husbands and cut as much to a pattern, take the air so graciously that it is unthinkable their elegance could be founded on so low a thing as trade. University wives go past, less well-dressed than the others but trying to show thereby that beauty bought by trade is vulgar. There are other wives who have little to do with elegance—I mean the bustling ladies from the tenements who walk a mile to save a penny and have a genius in the art of beating down the merchant. They are always in a hurry in case a good thing just eludes them. An occasional country gentleman stalks along, very tall, very thin, very tweedy and very wrinkled about the hose. He has a far-away look in his eyes, as of one who seeks the far horizons or is touched with incipient paranoia. Bands of three or four students may try to imitate his careless stride but the brightness of their eyes betrays their interest in the world around them.

And then the farming people. You might study their variousness for hours. Thin hairy men, with enormous hands and feet and trapped expressions on their faces, carry unwieldy parcels in the wake of round little weather-beaten women whose heads are full of bargains. Others stand on the kerb in twos and threes, talking and spitting and looking about them with no more sign of excitement than if the street were their twenty-acre fields at home. Bigger men in every way, men who can take an overdraft as if they were doing the bank a favour, carry their bellies high and engage each other in a grave discourse. They are representatives of a new order just as the others represent the old. And occasionally you may see one who represents something older still—a man or woman with a ruddy face and white hair, who sees the town in quiet wonder and in whose look there is the innocence of a simpler age.

There is the north-east on market day—a crowd of types though superficially different yet essentially the same. At heart they are all products of one environment and, if you discount their strange sophistications, a common character remains. Its elements are a good conceit, a keen, off-taking wit, a measured though not a mean economy, a due regard for all the public virtues and a private taste for all the pleasant vices. Simple people with a simple faith—that they have inherited the earth and in due time will succeed to the Kingdom of Heaven.

Last of all you could go out to the Aulton in the twilight, about ten o'clock. You might go up the Chanonry to St. Machars, where the twin spires are raised to heaven in a pious benediction over the graves of our drunken fathers. It will be very quiet then, for there will be no sound but the rooks going to bed in the high trees, and the Don falling

over the weir in the shadowy field. Peace comes down
upon you there, like the dew on the silent woods, and you
feel as if all the generations of mortal men were offering you
their wisdom. You walk down the High Street to the
gates of the College, and find your mood quickened by old
and lovely things. Now that you have seen so much of
the hard north-east, you may let your imagination free upon
King's.

It is beautiful in design: its chapel is indeed a holy
place enriched with pious craftsmanship. Its library is
full of noble works. Yet these are not the whole of King's.
Greater and more lovely is its air of wisdom, as if knowledge flowered upon its walls, and the love of the Lord
were its true foundation. Set in a land where life is a
bitter personal thing, the College keeps its witness to calm
eternal truth and with its great age corrects the little age
of men.

CHAPTER SIXTEEN: THE NORTH-EAST: PIONEERS IN SCOTLAND

THERE are several interesting roads from Aberdeen to Elgin, and I will describe them briefly in this paragraph. First the coast road by Peterhead, Fraserburgh and Macduff, Banff, Portsoy, Cullen, Buckie and Lossiemouth. The country it passes through is always bare and often grim, but if you go that way you will see something of fisher-life and the traffic of the little harbours.

The second is a variant of the first. It runs out to Inverurie and then up to Banff, thus giving you a various agricultural scene before you come to the fishing towns.

The third is the main Elgin road by Inverurie, Huntly and Keith through a mixture of highland and lowland country.

The fourth is the railway, where again you have three choices. You may go straight through by the main L.N.E.R. which will reveal to you some of the majestic aspects of the River Spey. You may choose the L.N.E.R. coast-line that leaves the main line between Huntly and Keith and swings round by Cullen. Or you may change at Keith to the L.M.S. Of the three the main line passes through the most picturesque country, where the hills, the Spey and the distilleries, singly and together, will delight and tantalize you.

There is another road for the slightly adventuring motorist. It goes by Deeside to Balmoral Castle, then turns north across the hills to Donside, by a steep and narrow way. After crossing the Don it climbs again over a lofty hill and then runs down a steep narrow glen and carries you to

Tomintoul, one of the highest villages in Britain. This is a military road, built as a result of the Jacobite troubles in the eighteenth century. It has, however, been very well repaired since then. You have a choice of two ways from Tomintoul. If you have had enough of the switchback you can run down to Elgin along the Avon: if not, you can go over the hills again to the Bridge of Brown and so down into the valley of the Spey at Nethybridge. I have never been the first way, so I cannot tell you anything about it. I have been the second way, and I can assure you it will give you magnificent prospects of mountain and river, besides some interesting hills to try your car on. These, then, are some of the roads to Elgin.

Whichever way you go, I hope you will do it at the time of the harvest. There are places that are divinely wedded to their own particular season, as Purbeck to March, when the first primroses are coming out under the windy downs; the Vale of Evesham to blossom time when the orchards are white round Elmley Castle; Ludlow to summer when the hills are blue along the Marches. So the harvest gives a kindliness and a warmth to the north-east; and the conjunction not only softens the country-side but gives a new meaning to harvest. When you look up to the hills and then across the corn ripening in the little fields along the road to Elgin you may indeed realize that a miracle has been achieved; and you may understand why the harvest home must have been a real festival of gratitude, that so much should have been made out of so little. Then, I think, is the time to draw up your car at the top of a hill and, looking down upon the tidy farms, to remember the men and women who worked such wonder upon the face of Scotland.

Aberdeenshire can look fair enough on a harvest day when the sun is shining, the pastures are a lively green, and the corn stands up proudly in the little fields. Then the landscape takes on a humaner aspect, a fugitive grace as tenuous and as desperately maintained as the sweet pastures that lie so close to the rocks.   But the grace passes with the sun; it is an illusion from heaven, not the quality of earth. In spite of a hundred years of honest farming Aberdeenshire is still a poor land.   How much poorer it must have been a hundred years ago; how much poorer, how wild and grim, the home of all the cold north winds.   How defiantly the rocks must have affronted the lowering sky; how inhospitable the sodden moss and the spouting clay.   Surely no man who looked over the monotonous rise and fall of that desolate land would have imagined that it could fill his barn and bring joy to the mice in his girnal.   But there were brave men a hundred years ago, men so hungry for land that they would have tilled the Mither Tap o' Bennachie. They cast their eyes over the waste and swore to make it bloom fair to their glory; and, as we look across their fields a hundred years later, ' Let us now praise great men.'

Though those farmers left such brave memorials in the little fields won with such patient labour, their names have been forgotten.   Their latest descendants learn the names of the kings and battles of far away and long ago, yet they are ignorant of the men who made the very fields that feed them.   Perhaps we are not to be blamed too much that we have forgotten, because the farmers were not conscious of any particular glory in their work, and few left any written record behind them.   But it is my good fortune to have read an account by one whom I might almost call an ancestor, of how he trenched and took in his land from the moss.   He was a great man and did his work so well that men are still gathering harvests from his fields down to this very day.   His words deserve to be written in gold for later men to read and marvel at.

The record of his work, which was prepared for the Highland and Agricultural Society, is a manuscript of twelve foolscap pages written in a fine hand without a single error. Did the old gentleman write it?   Who knows?   It is unlikely that a hand so skilful with the spade could have been so expert with the quill; nor do the sentences, so dignified and balanced, have the ring of the Buchan speech and thought. One may see the dominie's hand in the final polishing of the phrases and in the admirable penmanship. But one should not be too hasty about a conclusion. A man who could impose his will upon a peat moss in Buchan may well have been able to deal as successfully with the no less intractable wastes of the written word.

That is immaterial; the story is everything. In the year 1820 this man took over his farm on a nineteen-year lease. The farm consisted of 101 acres, of which fifty-one were peat moss and the other fifty acres arable land 'completely exhausted and unfit to bear any crop of grain. The dwelling-house and steading were most dilapidated' and 'could not be inhabited in safety either by my family or bestial'. It was not an easy sit down, but industry was in the farmer's bones, and by the end of 1822 he had repaired the houses, cleared the arable land of all the old fences, and laid out the fields so that they might be cropped in some rotation. Then he was ready to start on the moss.

It must have been an uncompromising sight. 'A great deal had been cut up for fuel, leaving peat banks, holes, and pits filled with water. (The rest) was boggy and muirish ground, covered generally in water and producing rushes, bent, and heather, intermixed with a coarse and scanty herbage upon which a few stunted cattle subsisted in summer.' In the year 1823 he experimented with four acres of this wilderness. At the beginning of his tenancy he had dug shallow ditches through the moss, and thus drained off the standing water. Now he began the real business of reclamation. First, he dug 170 yards of drains which he filled with stones to a depth of three feet. On to the surface he carted 600 loads of clay as a mixture for the moss. And three-quarters of an acre of old roads, rocks, and quarry holes had to be trenched and covered with mould. The whole expense of this field was only £19 in money, but how much more in human labour? However, there was an immediate reward. The first crop of oats ran out at three quarters to the acre; next year the turnips were worth £4 an acre; and in 1825 the oats ran out at fully four quarters, a mighty crop for Buchan in those days.

The first success heartened the farmer for a much bigger job. In 1824 he began the improvement of seventeen and a half acres of 'moss and marshy ground interspersed with springs'. Here he cut over a mile of drains and filled them with stones, which cost him in all £60. Then, as the surface was very uneven, ten acres had to be levelled with the spade. After taking a crop of oats off this new field, he top-dressed nine acres at the rate of 600 loads of clay an acre —5400 loads, all to be filled and driven across the soft moss land. There must have been many sore backs before that job was finished. But in 1828 that field yielded nearly five quarters of fine oats, with the appearance of a close and excellent bottom of young grass. Eighty quarters of corn off what had so recently been a wilderness must have gladdened the old man's heart. Perhaps they are not wholly wrong who look back to that time as a golden age of husbandry.

Finding that his methods were successful—and, I hope, remunerative—the farmer drove on the work of reclaiming the rest of the moss, 'the greater part of which was in the most rugged and most uncompromising state possible, being full of deep pits, bogs and springs.' He dug nearly three miles of drains and over a mile of open ditches. In some parts the ground was so spongy that no cart could pass over it and the stones for the drains had to be carried in wheelbarrows. But no difficulty could beat the farmer. By 1828 the last of the moss was under the plough.

That experience multiplied a thousand times makes up the story of how Aberdeenshire was won to the plough. So if you find pleasure in the country on a summer day think with gratitude of the pioneers who made it beautiful with corn and pasture, and in your prayers remember that good man, Mr. Yull of Mains of Fedderate, in the Parish of New Deer, District of Buchan and County of Aberdeen.

Except for the magnificent reaches of the Spey, and some prospects from the hills if you go by the Lecht and Tomintoul, I do not think there is any surpassing wonder between Aberdeen and Elgin that I should make a song about. There are some fine historical places to see, like the castle of Tolquhon (To-hòn), a beautiful sixteenth-century ruin, just off the Tarves (Tàr-ves) road; and there are the great sea cliffs, like the Bullers of Buchan, at Cruden Bay; but these are things that anybody will direct you to, and there are always printed guides that have the great advantage of being accurate. Besides, I have come to distrust sightseeing. It is so very rarely that the mood, the place and the moment come so divinely together as to make a perfect experience. The things I remember about the places I have been to; and especially the things that come to my mind again and again, with a growing loveliness in tranquillity, are chance encounters, quite unexpected conversations, a sudden harmony of light and shade, a sound of water falling, or music played in the distance, peace beyond understanding and understanding beyond words. These experiences cannot be planned, nor may they be compelled: they just happen along the road to such travellers as are willing to enjoy them.

You may find them along the Elgin road. In trying to give you an idea of the great labour that went to the taming of this country-side, I may have given you also the idea that you will find little grace beyond the Dee. That, of course, is not so. There are many delightful corners of Aberdeenshire and Banff where trees have been planted and you will find a deep shade at noon. As you go along the roads, you may hear children's voices in the woods, and see the cottar girls picking wild rasps, themselves burned ripe as any fruit by the hot sun. I have come through the Den of Logie, at Pitcaple in the beginning of August and seen a crowd of boys, about nine or ten years old, running in and out among the trees and the sunlight by the Ury's side, naked, their bodies stained with the juice of the berries they had been picking. When I came upon them unexpectedly, they stopped in their play to stare at me, surprised and taken aback. Then one slapped the other on the bare hip in a way that echoed through the stillness. Just as a shot would have raised a flock of pigeons, so the children jumped round and ran down, shouting, and dived into the river. There they kicked up little fountains of shining water and cried out in their shrill voices, and never heeded me again as I passed on my way.

At another time I have sat on the bridge and watched the Ury flowing down between the wood and the pasture at the end of an August day. The mood, the place and the moment were in perfect conjunction so that I wanted nothing more than I could see with my two eyes. There was a black-and-white cow (she would have had a touch of the Friesian about her) that came down the pasture, taking an evening walk in the milkiest humour, with her head, her udder and her tail, all swinging gently and her ears twitching, without malice, at the attendant flies. She had come to look at me, for cows are inquisitive beasts, friendly and gregarious creatures, and a cow will sooner have a man for company than no company at all. There were wood pigeons, cushie doos, in the trees on the other side of the Ury. They had no friendliness. Troubled, perhaps, by a conscience guilty from the theft of a farmer's corn, they flew out of the wood with a loud slapping beat of their wings, and disappeared, like sinners before the thought of judgement day. The river flowed very gently in the least perceptible motion, as if it had been a floor of green glass for the midges to dance on. They danced endless ballets, now high, now low, in a delicate interweaving of airy motion, so dramatically broken by the small trout that leaped through the air, like the intrusion of fate into the climax of the dance. A heron stood on one leg by the far bank, watching the trout as the greater fate might watch the less. There was a peace on every side of us, even in the sky, where the wildness of the sunset had mellowed into a rosy afterglow. I sat on the bridge and smoked my pipe, content that the midges should dance, that the trout should eat, that the heron should watch, and that the cow should inspect with such great eyes of wonder and such blowing out of gusty breath. That was enough; but it is at such moments that nature can add a touch of the high fantastic. So it was on this occasion, for an old crow came up from the east, cawing raucously as he flapped his way home to his nest in Logie. He sounded a very angry crow and there was something in the way the light touched him that made him more than a bird. He somehow suggested a very angry rural Dean pedalling home on a rusty bicycle from a meeting of the Chapter at which the junior clergy has been profoundly disrespectful. Or again, there was a touch of the furious Calvinist in his sombre angry progress as if the rusty old bird were rebuking the twilight for a meretricious and sinful beauty. He was the discord that raised the quiet of the evening to the heights of the fantastic. When he had disappeared still swearing, into the west, I too went home. The evening could give me nothing more, nor I receive it. You may, if you travel with an easy mind, see no less along the road to Elgin.

CHAPTER SEVENTEEN : OVER THE HILLS
TO MORAY

THERE is yet another road to the north—the road across the hills. To go this way you should take a train to Ballater and then a bus to Braemar. Thereafter you must walk on your own two feet to Aviemore, whence you can finish the journey to Elgin by train, either across the open moor by Forres, or up Speyside, to join the L.N.E.R. main line at Craigellachie. This walk will take you through some of the loveliest country and grandest mountains in Britain by crossing the Larig Ghru, a wild pass 2,000 feet up in the heart of the Cairngorms.

Like most of the people that live in this country, I have always been fascinated by hills. We cannot go far, even in England, without seeing a line of ample slopes that define the horizon; and I am certain we would feel very insecure without them, as if there were no rim to the world and we might be blown off by the winter gales. I certainly have always thought them an inevitable part of any scene. When I was a child they were the first things I saw from my bed-room window in the morning—the near hills of Dyce, reputed by old men to be a haunt of fairies, and Bennachie (Ben-na-chìe) a fine upstanding peak that terminated the west. The Ben was almost a personality in those days. It was my old grandfather's weatherglass, very anxiously inspected every morning. If the clouds were high on the Ben, the weather would be fine. If they hung so low that the Mither Tap was obscured, the outcome was very dubious. And, if the Ben was invisible, then we prepared for the worst.   There was a rhyme, the earliest piece I learned, that said—

> When Bennachie gets on a tap,
> The Garioch lads will get a drap.

meaning that a cloud-top on the hill augured rain.   What with the power of the verse and the old man's example, I took the notion that Bennachie controlled the weather.   My prayers for good days were all directed to it, and when they were answered, the hill received my boundless gratitude. So it was that hills not only seemed an inevitable part of the country-side but they also had a magic in them, when I was a child.   We do not forget such things when we grow old.

Yet it was a very long time before I went to the hills. Though I have been seeing Bennachie off and on for more than thirty years now, I have never climbed the top of it, and indeed I would have an uneasy feeling of sacrilege if I did so.   It was not till I was twenty-seven that I first committed myself to the awful silences and the experience was so delightful that I hope you may be able to go, as I went, and enjoy as much.

It was, I remember, a spacious evening in July, when I walked over the Bridge of Dee at Ballater, on the road to Glen-muick.   The day had been intolerably hot, but now a cool wind was flowing in beneath the sunset, and all the burdens of the heat were changed to pleasure in an air so cool and yet so warm.   I stepped out very lively in spite of the load I was carrying.   It was my first venture in camping, and I had very little idea of things required for it, but I had made the smallest possible selection.   That soon began to feel quite a lot.   There was a tent, neatly rolled up as it had come from the shop, and far neater than it was ever rolled again.   There was a rucksack, stuffed with a ground sheet, a blanket, pyjamas, socks, tea, a loaf and a dozen white puddings.   And there was a nasty little billycan that banged on my hips with every step I took. Not for the first time I began to feel myself a man weighed upon with many possessions.

That feeling soon passed off as the light turned always more golden down in the valley, and the evening air more cool. I must have been walking at an unaccustomed pace, because I could hear the sound of a pony and cart behind me as I climbed up alongside the Muick. I expected to be overtaken, but after a couple of miles I was still in front. Sometimes the pony trotted, and came very near me, though I could not see it because of the trees; then it changed to a walk and slowly dropped well behind me. I became very curious about the beast I could so outdistance, so I slowed my pace, until it did overtake me.

That was the sort of chance any traveller might hope for. One glance showed why I had been able to keep in front so easily. The pony was old and comfortable, and it was harnessed to a high dogcart, in which a stout old lady sat among innumerable parcels. She was a charming sight, a farmer's wife with a brown face and jolly blue eyes under a really remarkable bonnet. She was stout, but there was something beautiful in the stoutness—a generosity rather than an excess of nature. She was so like everything a farmer's wife should be that I could hardly believe she was real. But she was; and she invited me to ride in the dog-cart beside her, which I did; and so we drove on, behind the fat old pony, very well content with the chance that had brought us together. By the time I got down at her road-end, I felt as if I had known her for a very long time, and there was real sorrow in the thought that I would probably never see her again.

That mood, grown very mellow in the twilight, lasted until I came to a waterfall, where I pitched my new tent on a grassy ledge. Then a night came on as lovely as the day. Since it was midsummer, there was never any dark, only a grey ghost of light near the earth, and a high green colour that swung round, slowly, from the west through the north and into the east, attending sunrise. I sat outside my tent by a fire of twigs and peat and watched the smoke rise straight up like a flower that opened to the sky. I seemed to be the only living thing in all that world of moors and hills. There was no motion, no cry, no light down towards the lowlands—nothing but the fire and the silent smoke and the river tumbling into the pool below the falls.

It was tranquillity so complete that I feared it : I had been so accustomed to an excess of noise and people, that peace was something new, a little strange, a little terrifying. I pretended to be calm, but I was really tense, listening, with all my powers, for the things that might come out of the silence. I went to bed, to listen; and I must have lain there a long time in a doze, still listening, but comforted by the occasional brightness of the dying fire when a light wind stirred it, towards sunrise.

Then the sky lightened in the east; a single bird went crying over the moor; and, at last, a ray of the sun swept up across the arc of heaven. I rose then, walked over the wet grass, and bathed in the river. The water was still warm from lying all day in Loch Muick, and I remember the gratitude with which I slid into it, away from the chill wind that was blowing down off Lochnagar (Loch-na-gàr). I stayed there like a curious fish in a pool, till the sun had gathered sufficient strength to warm the morning, then I returned to my camp for breakfast.

I was very tired by the time I had finished my meal; and the sun was gathering strength for another torrid day. I could not think of marching on through the heat, so I lay in the shade of my tent in my pyjamas and slept till three or four in the afternoon. The sun was then fulfilled of its glory and my thin pyjamas were so hot that I could hardly bear the touch of them. I went again to bathe in the river. This time the order had changed, for the water was now cold and the air was hot. The touch of that brown river drove

away my sleep, and as I lay on the bank to let the sun dry
me, a delicious peace succeeded to the apprehension of the
night before. I looked at the moor and the river and the
grave hills as if they had been my friends. I cried good
afternoon to a lizard that watched me from a stone. I
thought about the farmer's wife and the old fat pony.
Then, as I lit my fire again to boil my tea, I sighed in
contentment. The promise of that spacious evening had
been utterly fulfilled. And, having gone down to bathe
again in the river at midnight, I looked up at the hills from
the face of the brown water and knew that they still possessed
the wonder they held for me when I was a child.

I spent seven or eight days beside the waterfall, and in
that week I did not walk more than five miles. I intended
to explore the moor, but there was never time. I lusted
after pleasant food (a thing you will understand if you have
ever tried to live on white puddings for a week) but I could
not make myself walk down to a farm-house for milk or
eggs. I just lay in the sun, or bathed, or slept. Once, and
once only I talked to a shepherd, and one day a man who
had walked over the hills from Angus cried to me as he
passed. He wanted to know who had won a test match
somewhere, and he wasted no time on me when I told him
I did not know. Maybe he guessed that I didn't care.

Nor I think will you care if you go up among the hills.
You might tramp from Ballater up Glenmuick to Lochnagar then down the other side to the Cairnwell Road.
It is all good walking in fine lonely country without any
difficult climbing unless you try the rock faces on Lochnagar. Then you might go up the side of the river to the
Linn o' Dee, cross there to the north side and commit yourself to the Cairngorms. Even if you have little time and no
experience of the hills, you should still go through the
Lairig Ghru. It is neither dangerous nor difficult in
summer-time and it will be an experience you can always
be proud to remember.

When I was looking after the Youth Hostel in Ballater, two ladies, no longer young, asked my advice about walks around the hostel. I advised them to try the Lairig.

But, they said, they would never dare.

I laughed and said there was nothing to it.

They protested; but I noticed they were not quite certain.

Then I found out they really wanted me to send them to the pass, to persuade them into what they wished, but feared, to do.

I persuaded them and they went.

The next two days were among the stormiest in a stormy summer; and I regretted having sent the two poor ladies into the wilds. But the regrets were wasted. Some days later they sent me postcards saying the journey had been terrible, the boulders unimaginable, the wind and rain pitiless, and the experience one they would not have missed for worlds of comfort.

You may find the same. Go up to Derry Lodge from the Linn o' Dee, then follow the path into Glendee and up into the dark Lairig. The summit of the pass, over 2,000 feet up, is hard to cross, for there is nothing but stones, but it is not really difficult and there is no danger. You will have an incomparable view from the top down into Rothiemurchus and a few hours' walk will take you into the valley of the Spey.

There are several ways to do the journey. If you are in good order you can walk the thirty miles from Aviemore in a day without undue stress. Or you can take a tent with you and lie the night on the Derry side of the pass. Thus you may have an easy walk on the first day and get over the hardest part of the road in the fresh hours of the morning. If you are motoring in a party you can drive as far as Derry Lodge in the morning, then one can take the car round to meet the rest of the party in Rothiemurchus. The driver will have plenty of amusement; for, if he goes by Corgarff, the Lecht, Tomintoul, the Bridge of Brown and Grantown on Spey to Rothiemurchus, he will enjoy a continuous switchback crossing the foothills of the Grampians. But I hope you will have time to spare and that you will go, as I have gone, with a little tent. I hope you will make your camp at the side of running water on nights of dark and quiet with only the stars for light. Then for a day or a week you may stop caring about test matches and all such trifles.

The Province of Moray

The Province of Moray, or the counties of Elgin and Nairn, is one of the blessedest corners of Scotland. It consists of two, or perhaps three parts—the glorious rocks and sands along the Moray Firth; a strip of rich land called the Laigh o' Moray, some of the best farming country in Scotland; and the Glens of the Lossie, the Findhorn and the Nairn, running up into the Grampians. Although it faces the open sea, it has a surprisingly generous climate, which has made it a very popular holiday resort for the more respectable kind of person. Lossiemouth, with its fine golf-course, attracts many gentry in the late summer: Forres and Nairn do the same; and Elgin is much favoured by those who retire to bridge after building the Empire. There is nothing of the Blackpool kind about Moray; no grand wheels, fish suppers and sixpenny hops. It is upper-class, and slightly aristocratical. Whatever vulgarities the season may bring they are not of the common sort. That is, perhaps, as it should be, for Moray wears the purple in autumn. It has a spacious air about the time when the leaves begin to turn. There is brilliant sunshine on the dunes, warm enough to bring out the sharp sweet smell of the herbs and yet tempered by a light wind off the firth. Those rays have a quickening power in them. When you address your ball on a tee at Nairn you feel that you could drive it right across the firth and hole out in three on the top of Morven. If you go inland towards the hills you will find the trees that grow along the rivers have been turned to so warm and so subtly mingled colours, that they hang like rich tapestries half-way up to heaven. I have said that each country-side has its own season. Well, autumn is the time for Moray, because there autumn has most of the summer's beauty and least of the chill foreboding of winter. There are grace and spaciousness and warmth there in autumn; in the sky as well as on the earth, for the sunsets over the firth and the Sutherland hills are glorious beyond the power of words to describe, as if all the colours of the earth were caught up and turned to fire along the sky. So, when the year is falling to ruin in other places, it comes to its complete and final richness in Moray, surely one of the blessedest corners of Scotland.

Elgin is worthy to be the capital of such a province. It is an old town, set very nicely on the Lossie's banks. It has the ruins of a great cathedral, and just enough of the older style of domestic building to give it an air of pleasant antiquity. If you walk down the main street and along by the cathedral in the evening, I think you will find it easy to imagine the kind of life there must have been in the town. You will be able to see priests and bishops going in their solemn parade to the Cathedral, or walking privily among the shadows to some unhallowed assignation. You will be able to bring the gentlemen's coaches on to the cobbled streets again, and hear, upon the reminiscent air, the polite music from the halls and the assemblies. It is a town where you may be very curious about the years that have passed. Behind the hot jazz from radio machines you are conscious of the priests chanting their Latin: behind the machine-made frocks and costumes you can see the clumsier home-spun. If you have faith you will see a continuing purpose in the age of the town; if you have not you will at least acknowledge the long continuing; and in either case you may notice that the lovelier things fall into ruins while the uglier persist in ugliness. But Elgin retains its air; and

that air makes it an experience you cannot get very often in
Scotland. We have no longer any Cathedral towns with
all the traditions of a religious order—I mean the sort of small
country town that is dominated, physically, by the bulk of
a cathedral, and socially by the well-ordered pyramid of
clerics with the Bishop at its apex. That may or may not
be a good thing: I myself do not regret the lack of it; I
can only say that it is something distinctive you will not find
in Scotland. But I think you will feel that Elgin is still
something of a cathedral town. It is dominated by the
great ruin and I have often felt that the ruin still has an effect
on the life of the town. It can be only the slightest influence: I may be trying to create something out of a
shadow; and so I leave you to prove it for yourself. But
I am sure you will find a distinction in the town that makes
it worthy to be the capital of a rich and lovely province.
The very names of Moray and Elgin have a ring of beauty.

I warned you that I have no great taste for ruins; but I
would like you to go out to Pluscarden, a ruined priory
among the hills behind Elgin. It is a long time since I went
there, and I have never gone again; yet Pluscarden stays in
my memory as something rare and very beautiful. It is,
as I remember, a plain ruined house, set in a glen, with
cornfields round it and a line of hills for shelter. It was a
Valliscaulian house, and the Valliscaulians, like all the
religious orders, built their houses in pleasant country.
They could not have chosen better than that quiet valley.
The house is surrounded by peace, a divine peace for the
contemplation of holiness. The corn-fields would have
belonged to the monks, and the box hedges are still growing
in their garden. You have to stay there only a little time in
quietness to feel their personality round about you. The
monastic life is a little difficult to understand—rather an
anticipation of death. Yet the quiet discipline of prayer in
the chapel and work in the garden, year after year, with no
worry about material things, must have been very pleasant

in Pluscarden, if you found chastity not hard to bear, or if an occasional sweet sin was a mighty aid to repentance. I hope you will go to Pluscarden in harvest time, and see it as I remember it. I can't tell you if the architecture is notable. But I do know that Pluscarden, like Elgin, has an atmosphere that can help you to a knowledge of how people lived in the olden time. And I do know that it is beautiful in itself. Besides, it is part of the Scottish heritage; and we cannot understand the present unless we know something of the past. Finally, it is a most romantic name, a name for a ballad or a love song. Let these be enough to recommend it.

While you are in Moray you may see another and less holy part of our heritage. The Bishop was not the only lord that influenced the life of the country-side. There was also the Earl of Moray at Darnaway Castle near Forres and the Earl of Huntly at Gordon Castle in the Bog o' Gight near Fochabers. The Earl of Moray was a changing quality: at one time he was Randolph who fought for Robert Bruce; at another time he was a member of the house of Douglas; and yet again he was James, the bastard half-brother of Mary Stewart and leader of the Protestant lords. The Earl of Huntly was always the same—head of the house of Gordon. An old rhyme says that the Gordons were the greatest scourge ever seen in Moray. They were more: they were typical of the greatest scourge in Scotland—the power of the great territorial lords. A Stewart may have been King in Edinburgh, but the Gordons were as good as king in the north-east. One of them, nicknamed 'Cock o' the North', had a court famous for its royal splendour; and all of them, at some time or other, stood outwith the law. Once at least they fought against the royal army—and that was a curious affair. It was in Mary's time: Mary was a Catholic: Huntly was one of the few great lords that remained faithful to the old religion; thus the Catholic Queen and the Catholic lord might have been on the same side. But it so happened that Mary wished to give the Earldom of Moray and all its lands to her bastard brother James Stewart. Huntly hated James and did not wish to see him established on his flank in Moray, and besides he had possessed himself of part of the Moray lands while they were in the hands of the Crown. So Huntly let it be known that he was opposed, violently opposed, to the Queen's wishes. Mary, perhaps because she was fond of her half-brother, perhaps because she had no choice, led a small army into Aberdeenshire to impose her will. Huntly raised all the Gordon men and led them against her. The armies met at Corrichie in the Hill o' Fare in Aberdeenshire and the good generalship of James Stewart defeated the Gordons. Huntly died as a result of the fight, and a few days later Mary attended the execution of his son in Aberdeen. Thus she was fated to make war on one of the few great nobles that might have been her friend.

But it took more than a battle to reduce the power of the Gordons. They persisted through all their troubles and the nineteenth century found them better established than ever. Lord Byron was the son of a minor branch, and, in the next generation, a Gordon of Haddo was Prime Minister as Earl of Aberdeen. Even when I was a child the house of Gordon seemed to divide all the power and the glory among them, for the Marquis of Huntly (Cock o' the North) held one part of the lands; the Duke of Richmond and Gordon held a second; and the Earl of Aberdeen held a third. Besides them there were many others that owned estates throughout the north-east. But the power and the glory are sadly diminished in my short life-time. All the Huntly and Richmond and Gordon estates and part of the Aberdeen estates have been sold. The Crown (in the form of the Inland Revenue) has at last been able to reduce the proud Gordons. There would be one or two Bishops of Moray that turned over cosily in their graves to think that they had been revenged at last.

There is a great deal of antiquity in this chapter, but that is Elgin's fault, for the old city pitches the note of all her province. Go there in the evening and walk by the Lossie under the ruined walls of the cathedral. Go out to Pluscarden and smell the box hedges in the afternoon sun. Go to Darnaway and think about the feuds of the Scottish nobles. These are our past. We have spent a lot of time in prayers and killings.

And that brings us to the Highlands by Culloden Moor.

CHAPTER EIGHTEEN: THE HIGHLANDS

I<small>T</small> is, as you will have guessed already, rather difficult to say where Lowland ends and Highland begins; but I would risk saying that the next part of the journey lies in the essential Highlands. It will take you from Moray through Inverness, west to Beauly, north to Dingwall, north again to Bonar Bridge, west to Oykell Bridge that lies in the heart of the moors, west again to Ullapool, round the sea-lochs by Gruinard to Gairloch, down by Auchnasheen to Strome Ferry, across the sea-lochs there and at Dornie, over the hills to Glenshiel, thence into Glenmoriston, down along the Caledonian Canal to Fort William, through Kinlochleven to Glencoe, then through the Pass to Crianlarich, whence you can go on to Glasgow by the side of Loch Lomond. It is a long journey over adventurous roads in a most romantic land. If there is a Caledonia stern and wild it is between Inverness and Loch Maree. Go in search of it and my blessing goes with you.

It is utterly impossible for me to write about the journey in detail. First because it would need too many words, and second because it has been done so often already. There is a third reason, better than the others. As I promised you at the beginning I have written only of the things I know a little about and the things that have made me a Scotsman. That is why I have written a lot on some parts of the country and little upon others. It is not enough to have lived a week or a month in a place. You must have known it or lived in it for years. Now I have been to the Highlands. I have walked in them and motored in them and passed through them in trains. But all I know about them is that I know

very little about them; if, after all, there is much to be
known.   Of course I could vamp up some fine chords
about the glory of nature but that would not be of any
service to you.   And I could make a réchauffé of Celtic
raptures, but that would only mislead you.   So I had better
become a visitor along with you and look on the islands
with stranger eyes.   But there are two Highlands.   One,
about which I know little, where a dying race maintain a
precarious existence between the inhuman wastes of moor
and ocean.   The other a body of legend and history about
which, alas, we have heard too much.   I will pass quickly
through the first.   But the second—how will I deal with
the Highland Problem ?   The culture of the Gael, the
'15, the '45, the Clearances, the empty glens—these have
had their influence on the Lowlands and some still oppress
us with the sense of a problem that cannot be solved but
refuses to die.   That is something I must try to make clear
to you.

First of all the Highlands that you will see.

Going out of Moray towards Inverness you will come to
the battlefield of Culloden a few miles from the town.
There you should step aside and be a Jacobite for Charles
Edward's sake.   Then you may run into Inverness.   The
town is called the capital of the Highlands and it is worthy
of the name, but I cannot tell you much about it, for I have
never made any contact with its spirit.   All I can say is that
it has some good expensive hotels, that it can be an agreeable
place on a fine day, and that it has a very beautiful cemetery.
It is also one of the few towns I know that have made even
tolerable use of the rivers running through them.   Towns
either use their streams as industrial sewers or hide them in
concrete gorges.   Very few have made them centrepieces
of design.   Not that anything wonderful has been done
with the Ness; but the water is clear and the citizens have
not built their worst houses along its banks.   There is just
enough amenity to excite you with the thought of what

might be done not only in Inverness but also in much wealthier places. It may be the memory of the broad river sweeping down through the August sunlight; or the fact that I have always had a good lunch in the town; or the effect of the one on the other that has given me an impression of Inverness as a town I would like to know.

There is one curious thing you begin to notice hereabouts —the people speak rather nicely. It is not what you would expect. As soon as you venture from home, you meet the tedious business of accents and dialects. The Scottish dialects and accents are notoriously comic and obscure and you might expect they would get worse as you went north. So perhaps they will until you reach Inverness. There quite unexpectedly you will find the common people speaking recognizable English with an inflexion that gives it a charming sound. It may not be as pure English as they use in Kensington yet it can be understood at the first hearing. That remarkable fact has quite a simple explanation. The people of the Highlands have their own language, the Gaelic, and it is only in recent times that they have learned the English. Some Highland people have been English-speaking for only one generation; some have learned English as a second language. Thus they speak English with the precision of those to whom it is something new. If there can be such a thing as pure English it is most likely to be spoken by those who have had to make an effort to learn it, whose English has not settled down through generations of local use and wont into a dialect like Cockney or Lancashire or C. of E. The English of the Highlanders has not had time to settle down, to become idiosyncratic and vernacular. It is one of the more delightful surprises in Scotland.

But that is not all I mean when I say that the Highlanders speak very nicely. They use words with the aim of pleasing you; and a traveller will be very unfortunate if he does not find himself the subject of that pleasant art. The Highlander delights to please the stranger—not because he likes the stranger but just for the art of pleasing. A Highlander will speak you fair, praise you tactfully, flatter you, disagree with you for the sake of admitting you right and send you away feeling yourself no end of a personage. But you needn't think he is of the same opinion; in fact the more he can flatter you the more he despises you. He is an artist; and an artist does not bother to admire the bit of canvas on which he lays his colours. This has got the Highlander a reputation for smooth speaking and treachery that he does not deserve at all. The cruder natives of Yorkshire and the East Coast of Scotland, having no subtlety, make a virtue of their simple reactions because they have nothing else to speak from. The Highlander can keep his reactions to himself and makes play with the crude reactions of other people, which is a very fine accomplishment. So, if the Highlanders speak you fair, do not make the mistake of thinking them a dear and much-wronged people. Be even more careful not to expose the naïve emotions that their delightful manners have raised in you. And, most of all, do not be hurt if they try to overcharge you two hundred per cent at the end of the day. It is all part of the social game and the simple Gaels are accomplished players. They have what is left to so few of us, some skill in the art of living.

Half an hour's chance conversation with an old Highlander can be a perfect entertainment and a lesson in the art of talking. Once upon a time I had the good fortune to travel round some part of the Highlands with a gentleman who seemed to know everybody that ever lived there. While stopped at a public-house, we fell in with the local blacksmith and began discussing the country-side. The blacksmith was a huge old man with a massive head and everything about him was in proportion, including his knowledge of country scandal.

'Do you ever see X?' my friend asked.

A Short View of the Highlands

'Mr. X?' the blacksmith repeated. A look of intense disgust came over his face as he told us the worst about X.

That subject exhausted, my friend asked, 'And what has Sir D. been doing?'

The blacksmith's disgust gave place to delight as he outlined the latest adventures of that gentleman.

So they took the country-side through-hand, my friend with innocent but very real pleasure and the blacksmith acting all emotions from spite through immoral appreciation to righteous anger. I had not thought it possible that a pair of blue eyes could be so eloquent, but at last I decided that nothing the blacksmith would do could surprise me.

Then my friend asked 'How is old Y doing?'

The smith put on his best act of all.

'Old Y?' he asked in a sacred kind of way. 'Old Y?'

'Aye,' my friend said.

The smith drew a deep breath, cast up his blue eyes to Heaven and replied, 'They've taaken him hoome.'

My friend was puzzled by that and repeated, 'Taken him home?'

'Aye,' the smith said; 'Taaken him hoome to Jaisus.'

In his eyes there was profoundest pity that men must die, and in his voice wonder that man so frail can yet become immortal. He stood there, motionless, a man in tune with the infinite. My friend and I could say nothing; we were dumb, as before a seer. Then the smith broke the silence.

'But that old bitch his wife——'

His expression changed, as swift as the thought, to that of a strong man denouncing a shrew. He would have been willing to continue the act for as long as we cared to listen, but we had to say good-bye. We left him on the road, and as we drove away I saw him at the door of the miserable public house giving a magnificent impersonation of an old Highland gentleman entering an expensive hotel.

Matter-of-fact people find it difficult to appreciate a genius like that.

Let us be stepping on.

It is an agreeable road from Inverness, across the river, along by the canal at Clachnaharry, then out along the side of the firth to Beauly. Then it goes north to the Muir of Ord, once a great place for cattle markets, where you have a choice of ways. You may turn east into the Black Isle a tongue of very rich agricultural country with comfortable farms and some charming villages like Rosemarkie. Or you may hold straight on by Conon Bridge to Dingwall.

The county town of Ross and Cromarty is a small place quite remote from Leicester Square, and I think you could live very pleasantly there on two—three hundred pounds a year. There is nothing much to the town, except that it has a meaning and a purpose. It exists by and for the country-side it serves and the work of the people that live in it is closely related to that country-side. That is the ideal for a small town—to be a part of the country-side, not something that eats into the good fields and kills fertility with a burden of stone. I hope you will see Dingwall as I like it best—at the evening of a summer day. After passing through moors and fields, hour after hour, under the brilliant sun, I have come to Dingwall about nine o'clock when the sun had gone down and the shadows were investing the town. Lights came out among the trees; smoke rose up from a hundred chimneys; men stepped easily down from the public-houses. The town was very comfortable and domestic, and I felt I had come home to it, as the farmer goes home to his steading. I felt then as if the whole of Ross were my farm and Dingwall my farm town, with lights and fires and soft beds for the night. Since then I have always thought of Dingwall in that way.

Now you have a choice of roads from Dingwall, for you may go west by Achnasheen to Gairloch or out along the Cromarty Firth and north to Invershin. I would rather you took the second road for the sake of the wildness of Wester Ross.

But first you must look at Strathpeffer Spa.

That delightful purgatory is only a few miles from Dingwall along the road to the west and though you are tired of watering-places you may find some entertainment there of the quieter sort. The waters have a medicinal quality and do something to correct the evils of over-indulgence, but the purging and the penances are only minor parts of the ritual. If you play the game of mass-observation, you could spend a profitable hour or two in Strathpeffer. You would see the procession to the well in the morning and the valiant drinking of much unpleasant water. You would see the little promenades in the forenoon under the trees; the motor rides in the afternoon to visit the Falls or the beautiful moors; and the games of bridge in the evening, when recrimination is not at all softened by chalybeate water. You may observe the nice distinction between hotels and private hotels; between private hotels and boarding-houses, between boarding-houses and common lodgings. You will hear all the philosophy of the comfortable about life and death, babies and morals and bridge, stated with a certainty that admits no argument. You will find a society of like-minded people, confirmed in everything including their diseases; a society in which everything has become convention, and from which all delicious inconstancies, humours, speculations and desires have been excluded, till life has been reduced to the simplest form of observing a quiet routine. You may in short observe a home-spun comedy of manners in the idyllic highland glen. You would discover more about Scotland during two days at Strathpeffer than in twenty years' wandering about the empty moors.

The first part of the road from Dingwall to Invershin goes alongside the Cromarty Firth. The country thereabout is the kind you have seen already—a fertile strip between the moors and the water. The road goes close to the firth for some miles so that you have a delightful aspect of the cornfields in the Black Isle across the still water. At Alness you must leave the firth and strike north across the moors. Now the hills that have been standing away from you since you left Inverness come near again; and when you get to Invershin you will find yourself beneath their dark shadows. You may go yet farther north, to Caithness and John o'Groats but that is unknown country to me, and I'd rather you committed yourself to the hills at once, along the road to Oykell Bridge and Ullapool.

How shall I describe this part of the way? It is a journey through desolation. There is nothing but hill and glen, moss hag and river, and everywhere the cold stone breaking through the miserable soil. Here and there you will see a herd's cottage, once or twice you will pass an inn, over towards the west there are crofter settlements, and that is all for miles and miles of waste inhospitable land. In some parts of the Highlands you see land that might be cultivated at great expense of money and labour and hope, but this Ross-shire country has a savage heart that looks beyond man's taming. Nothing grows there but heather and sour grasses that have little feeding in them and there are always outcrops of stone in witness to the land's unfruitful heart. As you go on through that country you feel yourself alien. You are dominated by the constantly changing, always more fantastic lines of the hills. When you get to Ledmore you find incredible mountains, worn into the shapes of a nightmare by the weathers of unimaginable time. These peaks, they say, are the oldest earth in Europe. They are old not by the ages of men but according to the aeons of the hills. If you could compare your life with theirs you might indeed be humble but there can be no comparison between things that have so much and things that have so little time. There is something horrible about that country-side. It denies all the warmth and fruitfulness of life; and even the shapes of the hills are so fantastic, so perverse, as to challenge reason. It is not a land for men to live in. It is a sanctuary made by nature for its own wildness, the howling place of the winds and the powers of destruction.

Then quite suddenly you come to Ullapool and the delectable shores of the west.

Surprise is one of the delights of travelling, so the first sight of Ullapool should delight you greatly. It is (or was) a fishing station, a row of white houses along the shore of Loch Broom. Nowadays the herring have deserted the loch and Ullapool depends on the visitors, so the hotels are the most important part of its life. It is just the sort of place you might wish to find at the end of a long day's journey in the waste—utterly peaceful, warmed by a generous sun and cooled by delicate airs; the sort of fishing town where old men sit on crumbling walls and swear at the seagulls that disturb their stories. Now and then a boat goes swiftly over the water; the shapes of the hills in the evening dissolve and re-form as if they were made of air; and at night the loch is a heaven of stars. You can sit on the pier, absorbed in the quiet, until you feel that you have been there before, a long time ago, in another life; and you may wonder if you have not found in the west that peace and wisdom that are the end of living. Then again Ullapool will offer you contrast, for it has at least one hotel of the modern kind that sells the strange drinks this age delights in. There you will find sophisticated people from London leaning on the bar with elbows tailored off Piccadilly and trying to forget they are so far from home. Thus you may go easily from one extreme to another, from the desolate wastes to the sophisticated tourists, and wonder if both have not attained by different ways, to sterility. There are times when progress seems to have gone right through civilization and come out at the other side.

As you travel south from Ullapool you tread the margin of the land and sea on which a few people maintain a thin existence. The road takes you up to the head of Loch Broom and you should stop when you come to a plantation

on the right-hand side, for the sake of a high waterfall and
a deep mysterious gorge. Then you turn the head of the
loch and go west by Dundonnell and little Loch Broom
over a various road between the water and the hills. By
and by you will run along Gruinard Bay, where the soft
beaches receive the calm Atlantic waves. You go on to
Gairloch, a charmed place on another wide bay, where
you will find simplicity and sophistication, a crofter town
and a big hotel.

There, too, you will see the islands of the west.

I have never been to the islands so I cannot tell you what
manner of people live in the swell of the great Atlantic.
I have only seen them from Gairloch where I lay by the
fire at the mouth of my tent and watched them lying like
shadows under the moonlight. They had an enchantment
then; and indeed they may be enchanted. Few people
that go to them return unchanged. They come back with
a magic in their spirits, a radiance in their minds, a lilt
in their speech, and a craving for Highland ancestors. Not
that they are wholly transmuted; they conduct their business much as usual; but now and then the influence comes
over them and they feel the magic calling them back to
the west. I don't know anything about it myself; I can
only tell you what I have seen; and I must warn you about
the possibility of sirens across the blue water.

I must put the journey to Invermoriston into a single
paragraph. It is always the same and always changing—
an alternation of moor and loch and mountain, a confusion
of the most gorgeous colour, of contorted mass and awesome
shadow. At one time you are down as it were at the
bottom of the world far under the light that touches the
golden peaks: at another time you are high on some
shoulder with an incomparable world of lochs and moors
below you. It is a country of moods that change upon
the minute and your own moods change with them, from
glory to despair. By the time you reach Invermoriston you

will likely feel that nature could do no more nor you abide it.

You will get respite at once, for the motor-road to Fort William is very civilized. It has a perfect surface and almost every house by the way offers eggs or milk or honey or camping ground or that dreadful perversion, the aerated water. You will find Ben Nevis by Fort William and it may be significant that the highest mountain in Britain has a passable road to the top. The Ben has also been undermined, for the fifteen-mile tunnel from Loch Treig to the Fort William Power Station passes underneath it and you can see the great pipes that issue from its sides. Fort William is quite a modern town, with its smart hotels and its fried fish suppers and, unlike most parts of the Highlands, it may have a future of considerable importance. Beyond it, and across the waters of the loch, you will see the Ballachulish slate quarries that have spread bleakness across the roofs of Scotland. There is wild country as you go towards Kinlochleven but men have laid their hands on it after the fashion of their kind. The village at Kinlochleven where aluminium is made by the power of water led through the hills might have been intended as a museum piece of the horrors of industry. Given a unique opportunity of designing a modern town from the very beginning, the builders have housed a miracle of engineering in a shoddy village. I doubt if you will ever see a finer example of ingenuity married to complete disregard for taste and set among the magnificent works of nature. But there may be some consolation when you reach Glencoe. The new motor-road is one of man's better works. On through the awful desolation of the glen it runs like an exercise in pure reason imposed upon chaos, so that motorists can express the irrational at eighty miles an hour. You may use it to reach Crianlarich in record time, and thus leave the grim austerities of the Highlands behind you.

And now I must tell you something about the other

Highlands—the problem that is so much with us to-day.

By the time you have reached the West Coast you will have got some idea of the problem. You may remember the so many people in England that have Highland names or claim a Highland ancestry. You may have heard of Gaelic-speaking colonies in Canada and men that keep sacred the memory of Lewis in the heart of Africa. Thus remembering, you may think that the Highlanders, like the Jews, can be found everywhere except at home. In all the vast area of the Highlands there is only one town—Inverness —of any size. The cause is not a wide diffusion of the people over the hinterland. The glens are empty. Even the inhabited shores cannot maintain the population they have. The people that remain will tell you of the good times there used to be—never of the good times there are, never of the plans for a glorious future. If you search the old records you will read about glens that once sent forty men to battle; if you look in those glens to-day you will be lucky if you find three shepherds. If the old songs of the people are true, the men that lived there were not savages; they had the arts of poetry and music and they could make rare pleasure with them at their feasts. You may think that the Highlanders were savages or you may think the Highlands enjoyed a Golden Age while the Lowlands were still uncivilized, that is an old argument that could go on for ever. But when you look at the empty glens and see the ruins of houses falling back into the waste again, you may be sure that a whole society is passing away from the Highlands of Scotland. It does not require a great imagination to foresee a day when there might be hardly a soul to the west of the Caledonian Canal. That, you will understand, is a considerable problem for those who regard the good of Scotland as a whole.

You might of course think it would be very easy to do something about the problem. We might discover what the Highlands are worth to us and then see that we made the most of them. Unfortunately the problem is not as easy as that. Some people will not admit there is any problem at all. And the rest find it so tied up with sentiment that they don't know what to do.

You might find Culloden Moor an easy approach to the question, because you will meet the ghost of Charles Edward Stewart there, and some people would have it that loyalty to Charles Edward was the ruin of the Highlands. All the evils that have befallen the Highlands since 1746 were part of an insurance by the Hanoverians and the English that the clans would never again be able to rise against them. Well, there were repressive measures after Culloden and Cumberland deserved to be nicknamed the Butcher; such things are inevitable in war. But I doubt if they were the cause of the decline of the Highlands. The glens were emptied by the same forces that defeated Charles Edward before he was born.

These powers may have won the decisive victory at the beheading of Charles I. Thereafter no matter who should be King in name the rule had passed away from the Crown to the wealthy merchants and the nobles. This new class kept Charles II poor, drove out his brother, James II, and then won to final power when they set the Hanoverian Georges on the throne. They did not have matters all their own way: there was still a party who swore by the Divine Right of Kings against the unhallowed power of trade. They, however, were only a few of the old families, a number of Highland chiefs and some of the common people who had always a sentimental fondness for the Stewarts. These composed the Jacobite Party against the conquering Whigs. These Jacobites made several attempts to overthrow the Hanoverians with help from France. Only two of these were of any importance—the Rebellion of 1715 and the Rebellion of 1745. Both were completely unsuccessful and the '45 was such a total failure as to end the story for ever.

The '15 was a poor mismanaged thing and ended as far as Scotland was concerned in the battle of Sheriffmuir near Stirling. The '45 began with success. Charles Edward went through Scotland in triumph and led his troops to Derby. At that time, some maintain, London was his for the taking; but he turned back. The delay gave the Government time to organize effective resistance and they sent the Duke of Cumberland against the invaders. As the mass of the Scottish people were not in favour of Charles Edward, he was forced to retreat before the Duke. The armies met at last on Culloden Moor and the Jacobites were beaten. The rest is an old and immortal story of a prince who wandered from one hiding to another yet was never given up, though the Government offered a reward of £30,000 for his head. Finally he escaped to a long exile on the Continent and the Jacobite cause was ruined for ever. The forces of change were too strong to be turned aside by one man's hand.

There is a nice comparison between Charles Edward and Mary Stewart. Both had many of the gifts that are supposed to adorn a throne without the power of decisive action that can maintain it. You may have some difficulty in making up your mind about Charles Edward. He has become a legend like Mary and it is not easy to see the man behind the legend. He had the art of charming. He had some attraction for women. But how much else ? Was he anything more than a French courtier born in an immoral time ? The good Whig historians say No. But then historians seldom see more than they wish to find. This can be said about him—he came to Scotland with little more than the prestige of a fallen house, raised an army in the Highlands, beat the Government's forces at Prestonpans, entered Edinburgh in triumph and then marched as far as Derby. The young man who could do as much must have been more than a courtier. Then he must have had some fortitude to endure outlawry with such a price on his head, and to inspire such devotion in the poor Highlanders that they did not betray him. Just as Mary was something more than a queen that married foolishly and too often, Charles Edward was more than a seductive prince that did not wait for marriage.

Legends collect a deal of foolishness in a century or two but every legend has a centre of truth. What can we say about Charles Edward ? He had courage and charm but he lacked wisdom. He could not or would not see the strength of circumstances. Fountains ran with wine for the return of Charles II because the people were tired of restrictions on their pleasure. No fountains would have played for Charles Edward because the people had no intolerable sense of oppression. He came at least a hundred years too late. Scotland as well as England was settling in to enjoy the wealth that came from trade. Highland chiefs might support the Old Cause and the old kingship in the hope of titheing the Lowlands; but the merchants of Edinburgh and Glasgow had too much to lose. A Hanoverian who respected their privileges in return for money to make a show on the Continent was better than a Stewart who might interfere at home. They remained loyal to the Government and their own interests. So Charles Edward came to Edinburgh, not as the guardian of ancient liberties, but as an invader backed by a horde of the plundering Highlanders that the Lowland men had always feared. It was a dangerous position; and when he advanced into England where sentiment for the Stewarts was even weaker, it became untenable. If as they say he could have taken London he could not have held it. Even if he had been able to take back the throne of his fathers he would soon have been reduced to the political insignificance of the Georges. In the end the success of the '45 would have meant the exchange of one puppet for another. But failure was inevitable; or, if not inevitable, of small account. So when you read the story of this adventure you see that Charles Edward had the qualities that inspire men but not the power to change the lives of nations. His, like Mary's, was a personal tragedy. He was born too late and could not see that his day was gone.

The battle of Culloden was not important in the history of these kingdoms, for the issue had been settled before. But there is something profoundly moving in the sight of the battlefield. There a defeated order made its last hopeless stand. There some hundreds of brave men died fighting against time, the commander that always wins. Loyalty and courage found a sorry bed under the green turf, and sorrow was the only reward of so many hopes. What else you see will depend on the kind of person you are. Perhaps Charles Edward the very soul of nobility, the spirit of all that was lovely and precious in the olden time, defying Cumberland, a gross vulgarian, the guinea-pig of the industrial age that was soon to destroy so much of good in Scotland. Perhaps the ruin of the Highlands, the empty glens and the English brewers slaughtering the grouse and the deer. Perhaps the criminal folly of princes that lead men to death for their royal vanity. Perhaps nothing at all but the empty moor and the road to Inverness. Maybe the last is the best : for the battle was fought a hundred and ninety years ago and far different powers face each other on more decisive battlefields to-day.

It is very rash to lay down the law about what might have happened in any set of circumstances ; but I risk a guess that the Highlands would have been as empty to-day even if Culloden had never been fought, even if there had never been a Union between Scotland and England.

First there were the Clearances. Towards the end of the eighteenth century the Highland landowners found that sheep farmers could pay better rents than the old tenants. So they cleared away the crofters, destroyed their houses, levelled their dykes and turned thousands of acres into a single sheep run. It is a revolting story of men and women driven by force of arms from the places where their people had lived for generations and shipped to Canada to make new homes in an alien and savage land. It was an offence against Heaven. The Government were to blame that could allow it; the landlords were to blame that could order it; but it may be that economics were most to blame, circumstances that neither the Government nor the landlords could control. The tragedy was that sheep paid better than men; and as long as that was so the sheep would have driven the men away. Landlords would have been tempted never to repair a croft but to let it fall into ruins when it would have been absorbed into a larger farm. The process would have been slower. There would not have been the needless misery. But the result might not have been very different to-day. I would like to believe that, if there had been no Union, a Scottish Parliament would have done things better, but there is no reason to think that Scottish ministers would have been wiser than British ones. After all, you can't blame Adam Smith on the Union; and look at the things that have been done in Adam's name. We have to admit that western Europe has been run on the principle that the maximum private profit is the maximum public good. We must also realize that the glens could have been kept populous only by sacrificing private profit to the idea that human life is valuable, the true wealth of nations. That is an opposition that could not be resolved: the stronger had to prevail: it did prevail and the sheep devoured the Highlands.

But the sheep were not left undisturbed in possession of the Highlands. Just as the crofts became sheep-runs so sheep-runs have become deer forests. The final degradation of the Highlands was reached when the waves of Victorian prosperity cast up wealthy sportsmen on the shores of the west and the people lived by flattering those that they privately despised. Deer paid better than the sheep and so the sheep had to go. Given an individualistic political economy, it is difficult to see any other possible result.

There is another reason why I think the glens must inevitably have lost a great number of their best young men and women. Earlier in this journey we saw that Glendevon lost the half of its population in a hundred years. Now Glendevon, being in the Lowlands, has a favoured position; and factors working against its prosperity must have been, and must still be, all the more devastating in the remoter Highlands. Any differences will have been differences in degree. So if we can infer, as I have inferred, that farming in Glendevon was subsistence farming; we can also infer that farming in the remote glens gave a low level of subsistence at the best of times. Now any district that has a low standard of living will lose its people to a district that has a higher standard. Therefore as soon as the growth of industry raised the standard of living in the Lowlands, it was inevitable that enterprising young men and women should go south to try their fortunes. The depopulation thus begun would have continued. It still continues and nothing on earth can stop it until the glens offer as high a standard of living as other places in Scotland. The Highlander may be sentimental; but he likes something more substantial than sentiment for his diet.

As I see it, there is no hope for the Highlands outside a planned economy. Individualism having ruined them, only the State can restore them. That holds good for every part of the world destroyed by the greed of the last two hundred years, whether the glens of Scotland or the towns of Lancashire or the prairies of America. Some part of the wealth that the sheep took from the hills must be returned to the hills. Some part of the rents taken from the glens must be returned to the glens. And not in the way that is done at present. The Government has been generous to the Highlands. It has treated them as a distressed area for generations. The standard for a grant to the Highlands is a nice round hundred per cent. There is nothing you can teach the descendants of the bards about the mysteries of public relief. But it is the wrong kind of generosity. The money is wasted in patching. Doles do not ruin the unemployed man : their fault is that they are not enough to save him from ruin. So with the grants made to the Highlands. They do not ruin the Highlander; but they do not save him from a lazy indigence and inevitable decay. Something more is needed. The whole of the area within the Highland Line should be taken over by a department of the State. A survey should be made of all its resources —its arable and grazing land, its sporting land, its fisheries and its water-power. These should be developed to their utmost so as to give the best possible living to the people employed. And of course the population would be discouraged from exceeding the resources. Perhaps that would not fill the glens. It might even mean fewer people in the Highlands. But surely we have learned by this time that mere numbers are nothing. It is only the quality of life the people live that matters.

There are many people who deplore the present state of the glens. They cannot bear that the place where their fathers lived for generations should be abandoned to the sheep and the deer and the casual tourist. They would like to see the glens filled with an industrious peasantry assured of a good living and the contentment that rises from honest labour. They argue, and they are right, that we should not have a quarter of our population in Glasgow and a quarter of our land uninhabited. But how are we to rearrange our population. How are we going to people the glens. We hear about a Homesick Highlander who would return to the land of his fathers if only he had the chance. But sometimes we fear he is an abstraction like the Economic Man. The Highlander does well when he gets out of the glen, away from the midges and the enervating air of the west. Is he really willing to go back to the croft ? Would he go back if he had a good house and a sure three pounds a week ? Some that are most concerned to make the opportunity for him would not themselves go back for less than five hundred a year and a motor-car. They prefer the amenities of the Lowlands. And so perhaps does the Homesick Highlander.

What chance is there for a bigger population in the glens ? There is crofting: but the amount of land that will give a decent return for reasonable labour is small. There is more hope in grazing, for Professor Stapledon has shown what can be done with upland pastures, and thousands of acres might be treated so as to carry more stock than they do. There is some hope from industry, for the Highlands have immense resources of water-power; and not every manufacturing town needs to be as grim as Kinlochleven. But the one thing the Highlands are pre-eminently suited for is tourism. There the inhabitants of these overcrowded islands could wander at their will without doing any harm and they would pay good money for the pleasure. That money would support a considerable native population in the style that we are now accustomed to. It would also encourage the country trades in the country places and ensure the survival of the Highland stock. Some people think it would be better that the Highlanders should die out than that they should be dependent on the tourists. But a great many of them are parasites on the shooting gentry already so they would not be any worse. They would in fact be better off. It is easier to maintain your self-respect if your living depends on a thousand people than if it depends on one. You do not need to be servile though you serve: the Edinburgh shopgirls have an hauteur that a Highland chief might be proud of, and the consummate bad manners of an ancient aristocracy. What difference is there between a crofter who sells his pig, whole, to the butcher and one who sells it in rashers to the tourist—except that the second makes the bigger profit. The Highlanders need money: the tourists have it. Once that money is circulating in the glens there will be work for craftsmen, gardeners, fishermen and farmers. Other industries may come along, attracted by cheap land and water-power. So people might be maintained on the west side of the Canal with a reasonable chance of comfort. They would have very different lives from the men and women of the fabulous Golden Age but, unfortunately, we cannot re-create the conditions of the ancient past. The state of the Highlands may be tragic, but we must accept that tragedy and then try to order things a little better in our own time. It is, alas, no use blaming those that are dead and gone beyond our censure.

We can't leave the Highlands without noticing the most curious fact of all. The Highlanders may be a beaten race, being driven to destruction by their conquerors, but as so often happens the conquered have got their revenge. The Romans took over the vices of the Greeks as well as their sovereignty. The Americans sentimentalize the Red Indians and dance to the music of the negroes. So the Lowland Scots have adopted the nostalgic songs and the decorative kilts of the Highlanders. There is something quite fantastic in the Highland cult. People that have never been farther into the Highlands than a day's sail up Loch Lomond will tell you with pride that their mother was a Macleod from the Isles, though they have forgotten that her husband, a good Lowland Scot, discovered a new way of putting sand into sugar. The kilt, the hideous bagpipe music, the pretty songs, the legends of loyalty and daring—Lowlanders have swallowed the lot. Now the English that come north to shoot the grouse and the deer go away with amazing homespuns and a wistful longing for the Islands of Everlasting Youth. The poor down-trodden Highlander has the last word. Probably a derisive laugh.

CHAPTER NINETEEN : GLASGOW AND THE SATURDAY AFTERNOON COUNTRY

THE next part of the journey lies between Crianlarich and Glasgow. There is only one road from Crianlarich to Ardlui, down Glen Falloch. Then you may hold on straight along the west side of Loch Lomond; or sail among the islands to Balloch; or you may go from Ardlui by the side of Loch Long and Gareloch to Helensburgh. Whichever way you go, you should make for Dumbarton. to see the castle on the rock and the traffic on the Clyde, The first is a symbol of the old Scotland; the second of the new Scotland; and together they may give you an unforgettable vision of changing time.

There is a choice of roads into Glasgow. If, after so long in the country, you wish a gradual breaking in before you commit yourself to a big town again, you should take the road by old Kilpatrick, through the suburbs. If you wish to enjoy yet more of the hills, and then have a swifter transition to the city, by way of contrast, you could hold north from Dumbarton to Drymen and then into Glasgow by the Stockiemuir. Your choice will depend on your ideas of the picturesque. If you choose the Drymen road you will pass through a delicious union of ploughland and pasture. If you choose the Old Kilpatrick road you will see the smoke cloud on Port Glasgow, the freighters weighing up the river with strange cargoes, and gantrys making fantastic patterns in the mist of the farther shore. Whichever way you go, you will find that Glasgow is all about you. Indeed, you might be wise to avoid the city altogether and study its people, on the Bonnie Banks of Loch Lomond.

I have a sentimental fondness for this part of the country. Like thousands of other unfortunate people I found it a blessed escape at the week-ends during the years I worked in Glasgow. But it was more than escape; I might almost say it was an essential part of Glasgow life—if you had money enough to enjoy it. Glasgow is not a beautiful city; much of it is sordid, most of it is dull, and its essays at the magnificent often end in a comic extravagance. Although it is lived in by very friendly people, and there are many ways in which a young man can find his pleasure, life would become intolerable if it were not for the country round about. Glasgow is unfortunate in the crowding together of its houses but there is a blessing in that misfortune. Within half an hour you can get right into some of the most beautiful country in these islands. The shores of the Clyde and the Banks of Loch Lomond are not something to be dreamed about for holidays—they are just another part of the city—the part that keeps you sane in spite of all the rest, if you have a shilling to spend on Sunday.

Now in the days when I was new to Glasgow and had not yet fallen in love with it, I began to look on the town as one of the world's great deserts. Then I fell in with a commercial traveller who introduced me to Loch Lomond and the Saturday afternoon Country.

Sandy was young, and had red hair, and a charming amiability. I doubt if there was ever such a man for making entertainment out of the humiliations of life. He was an impulsive creature. I have seen him buy a lobster on a Saturday night, because he liked its colour, and later present it to a strange young woman in a cocktail bar, because that colour matched her lips. Such gestures invited humiliation; and when they were introduced into what he called his passionate chapters, the results would

Down to the Irish Sea

Ardlui
Loch Lomond
STIRLINGSHIRE
Drymen
Row
Helensburgh
DUMBARTON
Gourock
Dumbarton
Pt Glasgow
GLASGOW
Renfrew
REN FREW
R. Clyde
Largs
Lanark
Ardrossan
Saltcoats
Irvine
LANARKSHIRE
Kilmarnock
Troon
AYR SHIRE
Prestwick
AYR
ISLAND
OF
ARRAN
ROBERT BURNS
FIRTH OF CLYDE
Girvan
Thornhill
DUMFRIES SHIRE
New Galloway
KIRKCUD- BRIGHT SHIRE
Dumfries
Newton Stewart
Castle Douglas
Stranraer
WIGTOWNSHIRE
Gatehouse of Fleet
Glenluce
Kirkcudbright
Port-patrick
Dundrennan Abbey
Luce Bay
Solway Firth
Port Logan
Drummore
Whithorn
Mull of Galloway

CWB

have devastated an ordinary young man. Sandy had a delightful way with them. He would come into the common-room of our lodgings, wearing either half of his pyjamas (but seldom both) and tell a long *conte* about a person called Simple Sandy who also had got himself into a fantastic situation with three women, a female relation and a toy dog. These tales of misadventure were comic enough in themselves, and they were adorned with the art of mispronunciation as learned from Mr. Polly. They had an effect on me after half an hour as if they had released all the fundamental insanity of the world.

I think Sandy invented himself to be a character for James Thurber and thus gave his simplest actions a touch of cosmic confusion. That would have been forced on him by circumstances. He was always in trouble. He attracted misfortune just as some people attract success. Though he was by-ordinary intelligent and accomplished, good at his business and a diverting companion, everything he did went slightly wrong. He was a first-rate motor driver, but his sudden irresistible touches of fantasy ended in more accidents than I could keep trace of. So with his games; so with his unlimited friendships; so with everything. He contrived to give his life the appearance of an uproarious comedy; but the source of the comedy lay in his own loneliness and bewilderment. He was acting all the time, externalizing his own worries, and there were moments when we were troubled by a kind of tragic pity at the thought of what would become of him. He died very soon, in lodgings, of a chill that he had not the strength to withstand. I had not seen him for two years, but when I heard I felt it an unbearable injustice that such a rare spirit should die while the legionaries of dullness lived on.

In some ways he was the very soul of Glasgow and may stand here as the type of its people. He loved the town, with its smoke, its fog, its great surge of business, its coffee rooms, bars and music-halls. He had all the friendliness

A Houseboat on the Leven beside Loch Lomond

of the Glasgow people, the need to give and take friendship and be comfortable in pleasure. And equally he loved the river and the hills. Just as Tom afterwards introduced me to a larger freedom, Sandy gave me freedom from the town. At two o'clock on every Saturday afternoon he brought round his little green car and drove me out by Loch Lomond, sometimes up to Crianlarich, sometimes far into the Argyllshire hills. He was a lively driver. As soon as he got into the country he sang extraordinary songs, doggerel of his own composition to the music of the Scottish psalms changed into rag-time. It was a very small motor-car, that did not hold the road very well, and there were times when it jumped about. That alarmed me; but Sandy always knew when the bumps were coming, and he leaped too, with shouts of ' Gone Away ' and ' Tally-ho '. Other motorists did not like that very much; it seemed to upset them; but it was divinely right. It was the proper mood for them that go out of Glasgow to the hills.

I wish you could have gone with us in that little motor-car at a rollicking 50 miles an hour, then you would have realized what Saturday afternoon and the hills mean to the people that work in Glasgow.

Even now, ten years later, so many pictures come into my mind, each one crowding upon its neighbour, that I can hardly find the words to make one stand still. I can only see us, young and foolish and a little gay, whirring through the country-side in that ridiculous car. We were among houses past which we caught the gleam of a white liner anchored in a pool of sunlight off the Tail o' the Bank. We were out in the open country going over the Stockiemuir in the full tide of song; then suddenly falling quiet, for Loch Lomond shone before us, under the hood of the ragged hills. We were climbing over a steep road from Balloch, a lost road among the trees, that sometimes swung into the world, showing us the grave waters of the loch behind us, then dipped out of the world and climbed again, till we reached the summit and looked down, amazed, upon the Clyde. We were up in the Campsie Hills on the incredible road from Lennoxtown, headed for the first primroses by Loch Tay, and at four o'clock that afternoon we were bucketting down Glen Falloch at 60 miles an hour slashed by the spring rain off ·Stobinian. And loveliest of all those precious hours were the nights when we had stayed late at some inn, eating, and drinking and making fantastic nonsense. It would have been dark when we set out for Glasgow again and we ran for a long way down a tunnel of light that closed mysteriously behind us. Then a new light shone from behind the mountains, as the young moon came up with her attendant clouds. There was a struggle between light and darkness, for some little time, then the moon swung clear into her glory. We took little notice until we had climbed the top of some steep brae. Then Sandy stopped the car and switched out the lights and we both sat very still, awed into silence; for, looking down from the heights, we saw the shining fingers of the ocean lie far back into the darkness of the hills. The dark earth, the calm water, the serene light of the moon, were three elements knit in such perfect union that thoughts and dreams and desires became for a moment irrelevant. Then, since we could not endure more than a little beauty, we jumped into the car again and roared down upon Glasgow, profaning the still night.

I made many excursions to that country-side with other companions on sweet Saturday afternoon. Sometimes we used to go from Helensburgh to Row, then take the ferry across to the inn where we drank bottled beer among the roses in the garden. Then there was an afternoon we spent at Kilcreggan, on the tongue of land between the Gairloch and Loch Long. As we had gone by paddle steamer from Craigendoran, we had refreshed ourselves in the saloon. When we arrived at Kilcreggan, our host, who knew the strain of a sea passage, met us at the pier with three bottles and a glass. An afternoon, so worthily begun, blossomed into rare beauty, as we played golf on the course at Cove, high over the Firth of Clyde. I doubt if there can be such another place in the whole world. If we looked north we saw the mountains, peak after peak embattled against the sky. If we looked south there were the river and the sea-lochs, and straight before us the Firth lying into the sun like a sea lane into eternity. There was an Anchor liner, the *Transylvania*, I think, at the Tail o' the Bank; a couple of big merchantmen were passing out to the open sea; a little cloud of yachts from Hunter's Quay, dipped and flashed like butterflies in the sunlight; and the paddle steamers sailed everywhere on charters of delight. I was in a mood of quick appreciation that afternoon; even so, I doubt if I have ever seen any landscape so full of light and graceful motion. Our laughter was as free, our wit as far above morality, as the August sun. Our host swung his golf clubs as sweetly as the little yachts gybed round the marks. Even the large striped bottoms of the lady golfers in front of us sailed across the fragrant turf with the ease and fullness of the great white clouds in heaven.

That day ended as it began. We missed the last steamer to Craigendoran, so we had to cross over the Firth in a motor-boat. The wind was blowing up very fresh; violent little waves went slapping against the pier; the motor-boat rocked incontinently when we embarked. I am not a sailor; I hate the sea; and I looked anxiously to Heaven while I tried to find a safe place in the bow. But, as I looked, the last red of the sunset died out of the sky; Heaven had denied my supplication. The engine started with a roar and the boat pushed off into a wet grey mist. Maybe that crossing wasn't as bad as I thought, for the youth who was in charge of the boat ate steadily through a fish supper between Kilcreggan and Greenock Pier.

But to me—we might as well have been going down the Styx with a following tide. Vicious cold waves slapped out of the mist and drenched us; sirens bellowed suddenly, like a dreadful menace; and once we passed so near a great dark hull that we might have been going to ram the *Transylvania*. Then we slid alongside Greenock Pier and I had become a hero to myself, for life. So ended one of the days that are saved from oblivion.

I doubt if there is any more surprising country than this. Each district had its own reputation—and though it may exceed reputation, it does not surprise it. Lincolnshire is said to be flat, and when we see it we do get a new idea of flatness, for it never shocks us with a spine of lofty mountains. Indeed, the only surprise that most districts can give us is their nearness to reputation, the shock of finding something true that we suspected to be false. But it is different when you go down the Clyde. This is the border of industrial Scotland, dominated by Glasgow and the shipyards along the river, so at the most we can hope to find only a country that once beautiful has now been destroyed. But there it is, mile after mile of river and sea-loch, pastureland and mountain, glorious in every season of the year, with the green of the summer, the warm red of autumn and the winter snow. It is a total surprise. You have been to Ross and found Highlands majestic but desolate. Here, within an hour of Glasgow, are the true romantical Highlands. The perfect setting for Charles Edward and melancholy songs and silent toasts drunk under the harvest moon. It is a land for the dear deceptions of Romance. Two lovers parting in Ross would be so overwhelmed by the immensity and desolation of life that they would drown themselves in the nearest loch; but on Lomond side when the moon is on the water and the windows of Luss are a cluster of stars on the shore, parting would become sweet enough sorrow. It is the sort of country that sets men thinking of a Golden Age; and then, if they look about them they will see the dark cloud that is Port Glasgow to the east, and the darker cloud of the city beyond it.

There are just two places where you should try to meet the Glasgow people—in their public-houses on Saturday night, and in their holiday towns along the Clyde.

Now, of course, there are many kinds of Glasgow people, but most of them will not interest you, because they can be found everywhere all over Britain. I mean the kind that are rising in the world, or just managing not to fall—the people that like to be thought the right people in their particular society. Glasgow has plenty of them—the young men that clip their vowels, know the names of six-teen cocktails, and believe with all the fervour of the true religious that Rugby football is a nobler game than the Association kind: the girls who maintain a precarious balance between chastity and gin; the people who despise everything native to them and run up to London for a week of musical comedies and farces every summer, just to keep in touch with civilization; the people that—in short all the characteristic snobs of this day and age are as common in Glasgow as anywhere else and just as little interesting.

But there is an essential Glasgow quality, something warm, generous, even reckless, that comes from the mixture of Lowland, Highland and Irish. Glasgow alone of all Scots towns gives you the feeling that something wonderful might come out of it. The people of the East Coast have hard clear minds: they could reduce anything to a system. But I doubt if they could invent an entirely new one. The people of Glasgow on the other hand could disorganize the nicest system that ever was, yet something new and very effective might emerge from that confusion. If I walk down Princes Street in Edinburgh, or Union Street in Aberdeen, I am stimulated to a clearer apprehension, I feel that I could reduce the world to first principles in an hour. But when I look down on Glasgow from Park Terrace, on the shapes of industry that grow out of smoke, my reason retires defeated, strange confused emotions come upon me, and I find myself waiting for the moment when something very rich and very wonderful will flower out of the chaos around me.

If you take away the temporary sophistications—the Rugby, the cocktails, the respectability, the nominal religion and the ballyhoo, there remains something generative in the temper of Glasgow people. Something less self-conscious, a little more reckless, more sympathetic, more kind in laughter and, in the last count, perhaps more truly alive. They are more definitely lower class than the people of any other town in Scotland.

I like to remember them best in their camp at Roseneath on the shores of Gareloch. As I was taking a little refreshment in the garden of the inn one July afternoon, I noticed some boats along the water-side. I went along to investigate and found they belonged to some people that had come over from Greenock and Port Glasgow for the week-end.

Now of course the Clyde is a famous place for yachts and cabin cruisers; but these were different. There was never a more curious fleet. I am quite ignorant about ships, but I would guess these crafts had been intended for life-boats and fishing yawls and anything except pleasure. They had been treated with love and care. Their hulls had been painted. They had been christened with famous names like *Mauretania*; they had been fitted with motor-engines and decked in to form a sleeping place. Some were even fitted with chimneys, like those that sprout on a greenhouse. The old hulks had been transformed into cabin cruisers.

About twenty of them were anchored in the little bay, while their owners and their families played on the shore. The men—engineers and the sort from Port Glasgow—lay

on the grass, asleep under the Sunday papers; the wives
sat in little companies, half undressed, gossiping in the sun;
and the children splashed, noisily, in the small green waves.
Pots of stew were bubbling on fires of driftwood and paling
posts; and on one boat a woman was hanging out baby
clothes to dry on a line between the chimney and the tiller.
The whole aspect of the expedition was unheedingly
domestic and comfortable. They quarrelled, laughed,
made bawdy jokes, played melodeons and sang about the
love that grows sweeter as your hair turns grey. It was all
very easy and delightful.

Then Sunday evening brought a touch of wonder.
When sunset came over the burning water, the fires were
drowned, the children were collected, the adventurers
returned to their boats. Women cried to each other
reporting fantastic calamities; babies girned, fractious with
too much sun; engines began to scatter their echoes through
the woods. Anchors came up glistening, and the little
boats rocked on the quiet waves. Slowly engine after
engine swung into a steady beat that filled the air with
drumming. There was a moment of expectation. Then
a flag, a sixpenny Lion Rampant, was broken on the mast
of the largest boat. The beat of the drumming quickened.
One by one the squadron weighed out across the water of
Gareloch and disappeared beyond the point into the first
shadows of the summer night. Last of all went the homely
craft with the baby linen signalling to all the world that
one Scotsman at least had done his duty. That to me
shall be for ever Glasgow.

The people of Clydeside have been gravely misrepre-
sented in the last twenty years. Because of the I.L.P.
and the gangs they have got a reputation for lawlessness.
Quiet respectable citizens in England have trembled at the
mention of Glasgow because Mr. James Maxton seemed
to be attacking the Constitution from the top while bands
of hooligans with razors were undermining it from below.

15

Those fears were a little exaggerated. The gangs existed: tragic young men that society had no use for and allowed to waste in idleness. They were significant of an ill-guided world; but they had very little effect on the life of Glasgow. To most of us they were only another problem in the news-papers—and some papers made the most of them.

The I.L.P. were—and are—as profoundly misunderstood by those who have a stake in the country. They are moved not by the principle of destruction but by an inconvenient sense of misery.

The conditions that produced the gangs have produced the I.L.P. It is easy to take a long view of Progress if you and your friends are all quite comfortable; not so easy if gradualness seems less inevitable than waste. If the I.L.P. seemed to have a lust for destruction, it may have been because they saw so much in Glasgow and in Scotland that was unworthy of preserving; because human lives were even more sacred than property. That is a very subversive doctrine in the ears of those who think property the substitute for life, or its only justification. Those who have no property are forced to value life all the higher because it is the only thing they have. Perhaps that is why Glasgow has such a subversive reputation. The wild revolutionaries are invincibly domestic. If you wish to have a symbol of Glasgow I would suggest neither the hammer and sickle nor the *Queen Mary,* but the working-class family. If you look around this romantical West of Scotland in Helensburgh and Rothesay and Dunoon you will find the family everywhere. Though the dreadful engineer may denounce Capital in terms that threaten the doom of law, order and the Four per Cents, he will also go paddling with the children, and even wash the baby when his wife is tired. If you believe in the Clydeside legend of a red dawn over Glasgow, I hope you will go to Dunoon on a Saturday afternoon, or walk down Argyle Street on a Saturday night. The contrast between the legend and the fact will amaze you. It is difficult to reconcile a passion for destruction with such a regard for family life. Perhaps it is just because those men care so much for their families that they dare to fight for what they think is justice. Their Socialism is not a manifestation of evil, but springs out of a true regard for human life. That is why the baby linen that fluttered over Gareloch shall for ever be Glasgow.

So far we have been meeting the Glaswegians out about, and looking at Glasgow from a distance. We might now venture into the cloud of smoke and look at the town itself.

There is just one tolerable way of entering Glasgow, and that is up the water on a boat. All the land roads pass through slums or modern homes of the more deplorable kind, and therefore you may wish to avoid them. The water road passes through no refreshing scenery either; but the shipyards, warehouses and granaries do have an element of the fantastic, where the suburbs and the slums are only depressing. As you go through slums and suburbs you cannot help thinking of the opportunities wasted. But, as you sail up the Clyde about sunrise, when the derricks on the bank take shape vaguely through the mist, with here the ribs of what will be a fine ship and there the lights that attend some mysterious industrial process, you can feel tremendous possibilities all round you, as if the divine forms of the future were in the throes of a monstrous birth.

There could not be a better way to the miracles that lie in the power of the amazing town than the river down which so many beautiful forms have passed. The launching of the *Queen Mary* was ruined by all kinds of false symbolism; the end of a fine bit of engineering and craftsmanship was debased into a stunt by the merchants of sensation. Let us forget it. But I would like to remember Glasgow and the Clyde on a Sunday morning when the *Empress of Britain* went down the water.

It was a serene day with a light mist before the sun. As

we stood at the top of a brae near Old Kilpatrick we could see a line of people waiting quietly along the river-side. Beyond them the dull water had a milky whiteness; and the distant banks faded into nothing. Then the great white ship came towards us out of the haze, all comely and innocent, like a child of the mist and the morning sun. Little tugs went before and after her, fussy and anxious, like mortal nursemaids tending an immortal child. She passed us very slowly, with just the thinnest trail of smoke from one of her stacks. I noticed then that a curious thing happened. As she came abreast of us, through the diffused and milky light of the morning, she gleamed in her whiteness as though she had not borrowed from the sun but possessed a radiance of her own. It was an illusion born out of sentiment perhaps; but the illusion was perfect. Nor would I have been the only person who thought he had seen a wonder. The people watched her go by not quite in silence but with a subdued and murmuring excitement that showed a deeper emotion than silence or cheers. So the lovely white ship, wrought in the unlovely town, passed down the river and out of our sight. You can hardly wonder that the Glasgow people are so proud of their ships. The pride may seem a little ridiculous at times —when people who have had no possible connexion with the ships speak of them as their own. Yet it may not be ridiculous at all, for good workmanship is always a thing to be proud of, and the people of Glasgow may surely be proud that they can produce work of unquestioned beauty. But one does regret that they keep so little of the beauty at home.

There are a few things you should look at in Glasgow —the University Buildings in Gilmorehill; the Art Galleries at Kelvingrove; the Municipal Buildings in George Square. There must be some beauty in them that eludes my taste; so I will not try to describe them in case I do an injustice. You must see them for yourself. If you admire them, say so, and the people will give you anything you ask. If you don't admire them, you may love them as I have learned to love. That people can go so utterly wrong, with the very best intentions, sinning out of an excessive goodwill, endears not only the sinners but the sin. That love, however, should be locked up fast in your own bosom: the people who own the buildings might not understand it.

If you like fine old buildings you might go to the Cathedral and also look in at the Provand's Lordship near-by. These preserve the best of what has remained from Old Glasgow. They are also beautiful, which is not always true of the antique. I can't think of anything else that must be seen in Glasgow. It is not a showplace but an old-fashioned workshop. Or, as somebody once said, ' Thank God for Glasgow's warm heart because it saves you thinking of her face.' And yet, if you look about you, it is surprising what graces you may find hidden under layers of obliterating soot.

What more is there to say about Glasgow ? A word about her trade perhaps, because Glasgow and trade have come to mean the same thing in Scotland. A few years ago it looked as if Glasgow was going to mean lack of trade. There was an uncomfortable feeling that good times would never return. Glasgow, and the towns behind her, depended too much on the heavy industries and let the new light industries go by them. So, when the depression came, and the heavy industries went on short time, or closed down, there were no prosperous light trades like electrical engineering and radio making to mitigate the suffering. But the West of Scotland has survived bad times before ; and there is an even chance of survival again. The wealthy market in London attracted manufacturers to Essex and the valley of the Thames, until people began to complain of the southward trend of industry. Now the certainty that London would be attacked from the air in case of another war is making people think of the greater safety of the north. There may be a northward trend of industry in the next few years; and if you get your living by manufactures, you had better take a good look at Glasgow, because you may have to live there soon.

You might also take a look at the Hillington Industrial Estate, where elegant accommodation is being prepared for you. It is a fascinating place, that can provide you with what the picturesque writers call food for thought. Look at the awful factory buildings left behind by the last few generations; and then look at the Hillington factories designed with more amenities than most housing schemes. That contrast at least will give you some reason to congratulate yourself that things are done better now. And Hillington is a sketch of the greater things that quite ordinary people could do if they only had the will to do them.

CHAPTER TWENTY: AYRSHIRE AND ROBERT BURNS

It is time to be going on the last stage of the journey from Glasgow along the South-West Coast by Gretna to Carlisle.

Once again there are alternative roads. You might, if your time is short, take the high road to Dumfries, and if you do so you will pass through some interesting Border country. Or you could go up the Clyde, and thence to the delightful town of Moffat, and so to England. But once more I would like you to choose the road that I know best, and follow the coast by the Firth of the Clyde and the Solway. That way you will pass through some interesting small towns and many beautiful reaches of land and sea. I would like you to take away some good impressions of Scotland, and if you go my road I think you will remember Scotland kindly all the rest of your days.

You might find it amusing to follow the water-side right from Glasgow. If so, you would go to Renfrew and then along through Port Glasgow, Greenock and Gourock, past shipyards and docks and engineering works right into the holiday world of the Clyde. I could draw a nice contrast between Clydeside as it was a hundred years ago and Clydeside as it is to-day, but that has been done before. Besides, the intelligent traveller knows all that for himself—how meadows become streets and innocent salmon rivers become sewers. So I will leave you to guess the past for yourselves. All we can get in one short tour is a series of broad impressions: too many details would only spoil the outlines; so we will look and then pass on.

From Gourock onwards you will be on the holiday shores. At Largs, for instance, you can watch the Glasgow people about their respectable diversions, and wonder again where are the wreckers of the constitution. Beyond Largs you will find more industrial towns—Ardrossan, Saltcoats and Irvine, where the coal from the Ayrshire coal-field is shipped overseas. Beyond them you will see the fine golf-courses at Gailes and Troon and Prestwick; and so you will come to the town of Ayr.

There is a better way to Ayr, by Fenwick and Kilmarnock, because it passes through farming country and is thus a proper introduction to the town where you will find so much about Robert Burns. It is not rich land (until you reach the wealthy belt along the coast), but it is a great dairy country and the fields support grand herds of Ayrshire cows. As you run down to Ayr I think you will get the impression of a land not particularly fertile by nature, where people make money by working hard. Dairying is the hardest, or the most exacting, of all farm labour, for the cows must be fed and milked on Sunday as well as Saturday, and that makes a seven-day week for fifty-two weeks in the year. People accustomed to eight-hour days and five-day weeks will find something fantastic about life in the dairy farms of the south-west.

Once a farmer from Aberdeenshire (a place where farm people know something about hard work) wished to interview an Ayrshire dairyman. Knowing that the Ayrshire farmer had business that took him away from home early in the morning, the Aberdeenshire man made sure of catching him, and called at his farm at six o'clock when it was still dark. But he did not find his man.

'O what a pity you're so late, he's away,' they told him.

'Late?' the Aberdeenshire man was just able to say.

'O yes,' they replied. 'You see, the master left *in the morning*.'

As the hard-working Aberdeenshire man went back to his hotel he could only think 'What a life, when six in the morning is late in the day.'

It is a life that has retained the rigours of the olden time right down to the present day, and the people of Ayrshire can thole it because the tradition is in their bones. Try to imagine that life as it is to-day: then try to think back two hundred years; and you may guess at the life into which Robert Burns was born.

There is not, I think, a great deal to detain you in Ayr. It is a country town with the characteristic life of a provincial capital—in the banks, lawyers' offices, auction marts and hotels. It is also a seaside resort for Glasgow people, and a dormitory for those that can afford to travel every day. It has a racecourse, where the Scottish gentry display themselves, and the hopeful try to make some money by cheating fate. Though the town is hardly beautiful it has a marvellous situation on the Firth of Clyde, with Ailsa Craig rising like the peak of a submarine mountain out of the blue water. If you have a taste for the real (not the imaginary) life of country towns, a taste for idiosyncrasies and local humours, you may spend an agreeable time in Ayr. But mind you, it needs the meticulous eye and the subtle ear to catch those local characters.

Ayr is a town for the connoisseur: Alloway has a more common appeal, because there you will find the cottage sacred to Robert Burns. This simple house has now become a place of international pilgrimage. Many relics of the poet have been collected within it, and if you go there, as you must, you will be able not only to have remote communion with a genius, but also to moralize on the fate of genius in this curious world.

The history of Robert Burns was quite simple. He was the son of a small farmer near Ayr and was brought up to farm labour. At the same time he showed a very good intelligence and got the kind of education Scotland is still proud of, though no longer with reason. He began to write verses; and, since they were amusing, he got a considerable reputation as a wit in the country-side. He had other accomplishments, and found considerable favour with women. Too much favour; for one of them, Jean Armour, bore him twins. Though he wished to marry the girl, her parents would not allow the marriage. Disgusted with his circumstances, Burns planned to emigrate. Before doing so, he had a collection of his verses published in Kilmarnock. These had such an immediate and financial success that Burns decided to remain in Scotland. In a short time he was called to Edinburgh, where he became the lion of the salons, the pot-companion of the wits and the adored of the women.

Edinburgh made a great fuss—and then betrayed him. Those were the days of comfortable sinecures, and surely a place could have been found for such a lively wit. But no. After showing him a life of ease and accomplishment, his patrons allowed him, encouraged him, to start farming in Dumfries. It pleased them to think of the farmer poet. It pleased the men of feeling who were getting ready for a literary return to nature, but it was disastrous for Burns who had not the qualities that make a farmer. His farming did not pay; so he eked it with a post in the Excise. His duties as a gauger took him so much away that he neglected the farm. Inevitably he lost the farm and had to rely on the Excise. During his last years he lived in the town of Dumfries, always harassed for money, always failing in health, and always less regarded by the fine gentlemen who had once acclaimed him. He died, still young, in poverty, and then became immortal. Women and drink, the virtuous said, were the cause of his undoing. Women and drink, some others feel, were the cause of his after-glory. In the last hundred years he has been condemned as a satyr: hailed as a sublime pagan, denounced, whitewashed, explained away. Now, in spite of some criticisms from the eternal opposition, he has attained divinity and his worship has become a religion.

The best of his work can be divided into two classes—lyrics and satires. The lyrics are true lyrics: they sing themselves, or, to put it another way, the tune seems to be implicit in the words. We owe most of them to a very fortunate circumstance. One Thomson, an acquaintance of the poet, was making a collection of the old Scots songs, but found that the words were often too naïve, or too utterly indelicate, to offer a refined public. So, by a very good chance, he invited Burns to help him. It was work that suited Burns perfectly: he had a naturally good ear, he was a poet, and he loved the old songs. As a result he provided innumerable old songs with genuine lyrics, or touched the old words with genius. Thus while others have produced a song or two, Burns has a whole minstrelsy to his name—a body of living songs, still known to the common people. Indeed his influence has been so great that almost any old song is popularly ascribed to him, just as traditional wisdom is ascribed to Shakespeare, Dickens and the Bible in England.

The Satires are among the best ever written in these islands. Of course since they are written in the Ayrshire dialect, English readers seem to find them unreadable, though they can be amused by the equally idiosyncratic Yorkshire tongue. That is a pity because, although there are satires with more finish, there are certainly none with greater force. Burns had the power of seizing a character, holding it up to a searching light, and then displaying its fundamental weakness in a single line. The result is not elegant, but ruthless. Remember that Burns was the product of the Ayrshire land where the business of living has always been a matter of hard realities. Remember that Burns was a farmer's son, and that farmers have a terse way of expressing themselves about the things they understand. Take a sense of realities and a terseness of peasant speech,

fuse them with a blazing imagination, and you have the
satires of Burns. There is a kind of satire, like Pope's,
that is malicious and sly. There is the satire, like Swift's,
that comes from the darker side of life. The satire of Burns
is like neither. It is the expression of a mind on fire against
the meanness, cruelty, cold lust and creeping hatred that
deny the divinity in a man. There is the kind of satire
that is directed against good and bad alike for trivial ends;
there is another that turns good and bad to nothing; but
the satire of Burns strikes only at those who deny the
Kingdom of God within themselves.

The Scotland of his day was filled with the roarings of
righteousness, but many of those who cried hardest were
the greatest sinners. There was a great deal of institutional
religion and very little Christian charity; a deal of Church
Law and little Christ; much talk of sin in which love
had been forgotten. Burns was caught in that society.
He was a man of warm feelings and generative passions.
He was a man in whom impulse led the way and prudence
came breathless, far behind. He was just the man born
to be the victim of such a gang. They caught him. They
denounced him as a fornicator and a drunkard. He turned
on them, stripped them of their decent blacks, and showed
the miserable hearts within. He destroyed the men who
would have sat upon his case as the arbiters of God's judgement, but he never denounced God or tried to reduce the
whole world to a resounding hypocrisy. He was a man
in chains to mortal weakness on whom society would have
loaded other chains of its own making; and conscious of
some divinity within himself he demanded to be free, so
that he could deal with his mortal weakness, shaping his
life to glory or damnation as best he could. For there are
two moralities in the world: one that is of time, and one
that is of eternity; one that is the convention of a particular
time and place, the other that concerns the Kingdom of
God within. It was the misfortune of Burns—as it is the

misfortune of all people who are truly alive—to be continually annoyed by the lesser morality when he himself was concerned with the greater. Burns slept with women and got children on them and was horrified thinking of the sorrow he had made, and got drunk to forget that sorrow. These acts were questions for the higher morality, and Burns alone could judge of them and give the sentence on himself. But at the same time he had to suffer the damnations of the godly, the judgements of Kirk Sessions and all the little tricks by which society punish those that overslip the bounds of decorum. It is one of this poet's glories that when the godly attacked him he replied by inviting them to inspect their own lives; that he reduced convention to the quite admirable but unimportant thing it is, and left man alone with the higher morality, the eternal conflict between love and pain, between the ideal and the reality. At the centre of his best work there is always the sense of pity that things begun so well can end in sorrow, and always the plea that moral judgements should be left to heaven:

> Had we never loved sae kindly,
> Had we never loved sae blindly,
> Never met or never parted,
> We had ne'er been broken-hearted.

or again:

> Then gently scan your brother man
> Still gentler sister woman.
> Tho' they may gang a-kennin wrang
> To step aside is human.

You may be surprised that such a man should have become a hero, even a god, in a country where respectability, and the official kind of religion, are, or have been, so strong. Yet there is no denying the Burns Cult. You will find Burns Clubs everywhere in Scotland, everywhere that Scotsmen settle. Each of those clubs holds a dinner on the twenty-fifth of January, the birthday of the poet. Haggis is served, whisky is drunk, and speeches of laudation are made. There cannot be a single public figure in Scotland who has not made a Burns oration at some time or other; and some have earned an excellent dinner once a year for a generation with the same address on 'Burns the friend of Man', 'Burns the true Democrat', 'Burns in Song and Story', 'Burns the Great Lover', and 'The Religion of Robert Burns'. These pious occasions have been condemned in recent years as a great hypocrisy. It is argued against them that the members have no knowledge of the poet's works, and would be the first to turn against him if he were alive to-day. It is alleged that the clubs are at best an excuse for a dinner and at the worst an excuse for the nauseous form of self-congratulation bodies of Scotsmen delight in. These are very grave charges, and I am afraid they are wholly true.

Yet the Burns Clubs are a guide to the genius of the poet. There are only two writers in English that have inspired a devotion among all kinds of people, a devotion greater than their work would seem to justify. They are Robert Burns and Charles Dickens. These are the only two men that have created a legend—whose words have passed into the life and thought of the common people and have earned there an increase of fame that no longer depends on the words themselves, but is securely rooted in some emotions common to men. Dickens has almost become a synonym for the English Christmas, for goodwill and Christian charity, and love ye one another. If all his books were forgotten, lost utterly off the face of the earth, his legend would survive, until he became St. Dickens, a figure coeval with Santa Claus; and it would survive as long as people had the impulse to be merry and foolish about the Christmas time. So with Burns: he too is the legend of all those impulses that are too big for the arbitrary

bounds we put on conduct. He is the legend of a man
born to be free who finds himself in chains of circumstance. If all his works were lost, the legend would survive,
because all men in some degree are conscious of their chains,
and, however furtively, of warm impulses that prudence
must restrain. Is that a mark of the greatest genius?
Perhaps the question is irrelevant, for you can't grade genius
like eggs for the market. It is the legend that is important.
You cannot say that Shakespeare has the same kind of
legend. His genius was too diffused, too various. He has
a legend, but there is something impersonal in it. The
man is somehow unimportant to the work, just as a field
is unimportant after the crop has grown. It is otherwise
with Burns and Dickens. The men always rise up even
more significant than their works till they stand for something vital in man that every man can feel.

   If you like to be sure that your poets are great before you
waste your time on them, then I can assure you that Burns
has a fame beyond question. His satires and his lyrics, at
their best, have the high seriousness that is one mark of
great poetry. They are not for one age or another but for
all the years of the human race. Words like ' great ' and
' greater ' and ' greatest ' are ridiculous applied to literature :
let us use rather the term enduring. Well, these lyrics and
satires are enduring. Apart from the question of obsolete
words they require no annotations. Their effect is still
immediate, because they deal with love and death and folly,
the three enduring realities. That must be a sign of virtue.
There are vast works that enjoy a great fame, then gradually
retire into a place of unregarded stateliness, while other,
judged more lightly in their day, gather an enduring reputation because of their immediate power. Who reads
Paradise Lost to-day ? That great work has subsided under
the mass of religious and other frivolities that the poet
mistook for life. But Marvell's invocation ' To His Coy
Mistress ' has not aged by a single year and will not age

as long as young men are eager and young women cautious. It would be a nice exercise to prove that Marvell's little poem is far greater than Milton's big one—but like most literary exercises it would be a waste of time. It is enough to say that Burns and Marvell have something in common, something that will keep their verses alive when Milton's Cosmogony and Scott's old trumpets and Barrie's whimsies have ceased even to yield theses for the Honours Schools. The lyrics and satires of Burns will retain their immediate power. So far then Burns is of the Immortals.

Just one thing more, and another comparison with Dickens. If you care to play the old game of representative men, I'd offer you these two as Representative Englishman and Representative Scot. Dickens had, as I see him, more than any other writer, the qualities that belong to the commonalty of Englishmen—a vast intellectual laziness and a considerable power of emotion, an infinite capacity for self-deception, a genius for doing the right thing for the wrong reasons and the wrong thing with the very best intentions. He was a true man of the precarious middle class, invincibly respectable, emotional and cosy, to which the majority of the English belong. So Burns represents something essentially Scottish. I have set, at the front of this book, the ploughman I once knew in Aberdeenshire to be a symbol of Scotland. Burns was just such a man in whom intense powers had won to freer expression. If you can generalize about nations, you might say the Scots have more vigour than the English, more turbulent passions, more active minds. You will find that in the common people, among the revolutionaries who talk about destruction because they value human life, among the farmers and ploughmen who have never allowed official moralities to interfere too much with their natural pleasures. I would say that, on the whole, the Scots are more adventurous in life than the English, less inclined to the safe middle way, more inclined to extreme courses of intellect and passion.

There is more anger in Scotland because there is more love. Burns is the man whose work most shows the working of that love and anger. Therefore he may stand as the representative Scotsman.

CHAPTER TWENTY-ONE: DOWN THE IRISH ROAD

As you journey south from Ayr, I would like you to keep Glasgow and all the ugly towns of the world at the back of your mind. Because, for friendliness, I would like you to see this part of the world as I discovered it, having gone out from Glasgow on a September morning. All my ideas of the south-west are so bound up with that delicious adventure that I cannot treat this part of the country other than in the most personal way.

In those days before I retired from labour, I had just one month of freedom in twelve; thirty (or, if I was fortunate, thirty-one) days out of 365 in which I could do as I pleased without any thought of yesterday or to-morrow. There was no hour to be wasted. We did our work at night, preparing sensation for breakfast tables, so my holiday began at half-past one in the morning. Other people, I believe, went home and enjoyed a good night's sleep on such occasions; rising to begin their vacations in a leisurely style. I couldn't do that. Partly because I would not have slept, being always so excited at the thought of going places, but even more because every minute slept in town was a minute lost to freedom. So my holidays always began in those bleary trains that leave with the newspapers at four in the morning. I spent the first hours of freedom asleep, lulled by the wheels that were carrying me away from town; and even though I could only lie back in a painful doze, there was, more dear than sleep, the thought of freedom. And when I really awoke again I was standing in some country station, among the empty churns and the boxes of bananas, while the quaint, incomprehensible dialects of English enchanted my ears, and the six tall poplars soared towards an English heaven. There was no compromised industrial waste between. I looked on Glasgow, I shut my eyes; hey presto: I opened my eyes again and I found myself in a different world. So I discovered the south-west of Scotland by going from Glasgow on a dreadful train that steamed (giving off clouds that fell in a little rain of clammy soot) into the morning's darkness and bumped away towards Ayr, with an uncertainty that became almost maudlin about dawn. I shut my eyes, lay back in my corner, and tried to forget it. There was a very painful hour; that awful hour of a journey when householders are full of misgiving about the gas and the water. I had no house to worry about; but a piece of news I had trimmed that night began to obsess me. It was not an interesting piece of news, and I had dealt with it in a very casual way; now it had its revenge. It rose up before me, out of a mass of print, full of dreadful misprints, that make the journalist feel weak, even to think on them. For maybe half an hour I felt a kind of panic. Then I fell asleep.

When I awakened again the porters were playing handball with the churns in Girvan Station. I let down the window, looked out on the morning, and forgot everything except that I had fifteen days of freedom in my hands. For a keen wind stung my face; the sun on the waves dazzled my eyes; and the salty freshness of the air blew the smoke and the miseries of the town out of me. I had slept through a wall of blackness into a world of light and space—dazzling light and empty space. Between the resounding dunts of the churns and the shouts of the porters I could hear the sough of the waves running gently down the shore, and peewits crying as they wheeled across the pasture. I stood at the window entranced, like a child seeing in his first pantomime all the wonders he had ever dreamed on. The engine whistled; the guard waved his flag; the porters slipped comically among the churns; the fireman put his thumb to his nose comprehensively at Girvan. We moved off into wonderland. I returned to my seat, in peace.

I have never had an adventure so well begun; first wonderland, then the fantastic. As I lay back in my seat, with a look of beatitude, a very ripe voice said:

'Aye, me boy, it's good to be going home.'

A lively man at the other end of the compartment was moving over towards me, with the lust for conversation manifest in his face. I knew at once he was a liar and I was glad.

'But I'm not going home,' I said.

He started back about six inches too far. 'Well now. And would ye be tellin' me ye're not going home to Ireland?'

He sounded close to tears.

'Never a step farther than Portpatrick Pier.'

He made a gesture, as if to hit his own cheek. 'Ach, and when ye was snorin' there so pretty, didn't I say to myself there's a lad from County Mayo, or maybe from County Clare. I can tell by the sound of him.' Then he looked at me appealing. 'Ye wouldn't be having it in your mind to cheat me?'

'Not a bit,' I said, 'there's nothing Irish in me except my snoring.' He nodded, partly to himself, as much to say 'Danny, ye damned fool, ye've put your foot in't again.'

Then a smile leapt over his face and he hodged towards me again.

'But ye're a good lad,' he said, 'and friendly.' I can see it in your eye. If I was a girl now you wouldn't be lettin' all this weary waste o' cushion lie empty atween us.'

'You aren't though,' I replied. But of course he had won my friendship for the rest of the journey. Who can resist that insinuation about the girls, and the success it implies.

He looked at me, questioning like, then laughed and

settled himself in the corner opposite me. 'If I had a cigarette I'd be offering you it,' he said, and I felt somehow that he would also have given me the moon and the stars.

I did what was expected. As he blew out smoke he laughed again and settled himself down for conversation.

He was one of the world's great talkers, for he had the art of giving a moment's intense life to supremely uninteresting affairs. His mind roved freely over his life, annihilating time. He did not remember the past; he relived it. This is the way it happened. He leaned back in his corner, a thin shrunken man lost in a dirty waterproof; his eyes sombre under his bonnet. Then he gave a laugh that began privately, far away inside him, and came nearer, growing stronger, till it reached the present riotously as he sprang forward into life and slapped his knee.

'Be God,' he said, his eyes winking with delight, 'if that doesn't mind me o' the postman's daughter.' Then he told me the story of that compromising affair; mimed it vivaciously, now coy, now eager, now melting, now winning, now won, now the sorrowing daughter, the outraged father, the neighbours, the priest and the midwife divining the shadow of an event still eight months off. His eyes changed with every emotion; his expression changed like faces in a dream; his fingers, stained with tobacco and rimmed with dirt, played on the air like it had been an Irish harp. As he leaped to the climax of his story, the carriage was filled with a shouting crowd of postmen, daughters, neighbours, midwives and priests. The affair grew mad and madder until I, and the train, and the cows that rushed past us, seemed to be all caught up in a tremendous drama. Then, suddenly, he fell silent, holding us up on the tremendous peak of the crisis. He held us all there, for a second, during which not only the train but even the Earth was still, then he slapped his knee and said, 'I skipped it in the mornin' train.'

The illusion collapsed. So did the magician. He shrank again, back into his corner, back into his waterproof. His eyes fell sombre again and there was no sound but the clickety-click of the wheels in all the exhausted world. It has never been my good fortune to make another so remarkable journey. At one moment we were passing over the moors, or down into the farm lands about Dunragit: a minute later we were in a fight in County Mayo, or a temple in Hong-Kong, or somewhere in the bloody future when Belfast had been restored to the faith and to Hell with King Billy. There was something enlarging about that conversation. We were undoubtedly on an ordinary train, travelling towards a predestined end, but my companion made me feel the deserts of vast eternity all about me, deserts peopled by bedouins, camels, postmasters' daughters and all the mirages of the unexpected. It was just the thing to slacken the grip of routine, to enlarge the horizons of the world. When I had said goodbye to the Irishman in a public-house near the station, I went on to Portpatrick, ready for any diversion that chance might offer me. I had come very, very far from Glasgow.

I had expected something rich and original in Portpatrick, for the small town lies away at one of the extremities of Scotland, and such places often retain a very individual life through their remoteness. Portpatrick came very near to expectation.

A pelting rain blew up from the Irish Sea, as we crossed the moor, and I could see little from the carriage window except a dark blue that was the moor, with lighter patches where the ripe corn bent heavy under the storm. All kindliness had gone out of the day and when I left the railway station I felt, right to my bones, that I had stepped into winter. Portpatrick was as wet and grey as a body fished up from the sea. Cold houses, crowded together along narrow precipitous streets, seemed to be turning away from

the assault of the rain and the wind that came whistling up
from the interminable grey leagues of ocean. Instead of
something rich and original left over from a Golden Age,
I might have come into the last outpost of the inhabited
world.

Nothing happened to correct that impression. The
parlour of my lodging was full of chairs and sofas that
looked as if they had been made out of old American
organs, with padding where the body wouldn't notice it,
and there were three stuffed birds that witty visitors had
tried to feed with biscuits. A little slate fire was discouraged by the steady draught that blew down the chimney.
The serving-maid was very annoyed because she had not
been given the afternoon to go to Stranraer, annoyed with
every one, but most of all with me. It was all a trifle
cheerless in the sitting-room; and when I looked out
between the chill lace curtains I could see the grey waves
coming, line upon line, from the dreadful ocean. Altogether I would have done as well on Tristan d'Acunha.

Yet we can find some sort of pleasure even in the most
cheerless places. After tea I walked along the cliffs to the
south of the town, growing always colder and more miserable, till I came to an ancient ruined castle that looked
over the sea. That castle seemed utterly right in such a
place on such a day. It was a square tower, with broken
windows and an air of gaunt dilapidation that would have
drawn a cloud before a summer noon. But posed on its
windy headland, as gaunt and cheerless as the day, it might
have been the ancestral home of the storms. It was the
little more that made the too much bearable. It localized
all the misery of the afternoon, gave form to the formless,
was the intelligible shape of so much unintelligible fury.
I made my way somehow into the ruin, and then found
relief from the afternoon by dramatizing the elements without and the stench of antiquity within. It was a very
picturesque story that I made up, out of the storm, and my

recollections of the films and my memories of Scott. It contained a beautiful girl married to a beastly baron whose only friend was an ourang-outang that slept in his bed-room. The girl's life was pure Hell in the lonely keep, as she lay in her cold bed, listening to her husband singing bawdy songs to the ape. I can't remember how the action developed, but I do remember the climax—the ape got drunk one night and threw its master over the cliffs while the heroine ran off with a bold young smuggler from the Isle of Man. Having thus expressed the mood of such a place and such a day, I returned to my lodging as quickly as I could.

The evening passed as even the worst evenings do. Supper consisted of that basic substance called food that is supplied in bulk to hotels and seasoned according to the menu. By eating a great deal of it and drinking half a dozen bottles of stout, I induced a state of melancholy contentment in which nothing mattered at all, not even pain, as I sat over the slate fire in the illusion of warmth. Of course I might have gone into a bar parlour, and enjoyed the rich society that is said to frequent such places, but I am usually unfortunate in strange bars and seldom get anything there except a headache through desperate lonely drinking. So I sent out for two bottles of stout and a gill of whisky; mixed them into a nauseating drink with boiling water; and ran up to bed while there was yet time. The potion worked. Though the bed seemed to be lined with sheets of ice, there was such a heat inside me that I felt warm for the first time since I left Stranraer. Then, too, I began to like the sounds of the wind and rain, mad sopranos rising over the bass of the sea. Because I was at last comfortable in Portpatrick, I began to be fond of the little town set on the rocky coast above the unceasing waves. I saw it then as a brave little outpost of my country, a place of simple faith and plain cooking and homely ways. I rather think I wept a little, because my emotions were so quickened by the picture. Then everything grew vague, the house rocked as the wind grew louder and I fell asleep in the impression that Portpatrick had become a ship and had put out to sea with an ourang-outang as master.

The town looked very different in the morning. The storm had blown over: the sea had gone down: the sun filled the untroubled sky. Then Portpatrick was indeed a quaint and charming place. It was once, they told me, a busy town, doing a big trade with Ireland; but that trade is gone and there is little business now except the visitors. It was, as I saw it then, an ideal place for quiet holidays, for it had moors to walk on, sandy beaches for bathing, and the sea for them that like to play at boats. There was also a golf-course, which caused some excitement that morning, because Mr. P. G. Wodehouse was coming down from his hotel to play a round. We gathered on the edge of the course, hoping for a good laugh. Unfortunately his golf was not quite as funny as his books; but our time was not wasted for we had got the thrill from seeing the great in the unofficial, or off, moments.

Then the day blossomed out in all the rich beatitude of autumn. The grey town was softened by the warm light; the drowned corn-fields began to rustle again as the full ears dried on the wind; the moors glowed, wine-red up to the blue horizon; all to the west the sea lay calm and shining like a silver dish. There was a perfect hour about three o'clock, one of those autumn hours when you can feel that the year has come to its full achievement. As I looked across from the cliffs, the town and the fields and the moor and the sea were as quiet and composed as a picture in a frame. It was utterly beautiful, utterly satisfying. No doubt if I had gone into the town at that moment I would have found abuses and miseries enough to put Heaven in a rage; supposing Heaven can feel emotion any longer. Yet they did not seem to matter. It was an hour and a scene composed by some great power for itself, and the troubles made by men for each other seemed to have no importance for that power and no relevance to that beauty. It is not often that the greater powers are all in harmony, nor do they remain so for long. At the end of an hour I knew I would never see that place more beautiful, so I collected my things and took my road for the south. That was eight years ago, yet to-day I can see the desolate ruin in the storm and the beatitude of the town between the harvest and the sea. There are moments time cannot take away. Indeed yes, you should go to Portpatrick in September by the Irish road, and as you go you should look about you. Things most worth seeing come unexpectedly and do not stay for long.

CHAPTER TWENTY-TWO : FORGOTTEN VILLAGES

THERE are many stages between the fullness of life and the emptiness of death, and most of existence is passed about the half-way state, in a mean that is hardly golden. But there are occasions when we reach something that is like the fullness of life, when our perceptions are so keen that every sense devours the world with pleasure. The days that I spent in Galloway were such a time. The Irishman had set me free from the ridiculous inhibitions of my ordinary life; the storm had brought me enough of the physical misery that can be a wonderful solvent for boredom; and the afternoon's beatitude had raised my new freedom and delight to an unaccustomed harmony. I was ready to find pleasure in everything, and everything delighted me as I walked up the road towards Stranraer; the startling clearness of the earth's colour after the storm; the tang of the sea wind that played among the corn; the brambles that hung, luscious and black, under the dark green leaves; the primitive music of the hidden birds in the autumnal trees; and even the menial business of walking, like a snail, with my household on my back. I think I sang a little, the first lines of popular choruses (because that is the most I ever know) on the easy grades, changing into the dirge for 'the Bonnie Earl o' Moray', when the road grew steep before me. I could have gone on that way for a long time, in spite of the pitying looks given me by the country people who do not understand walking for pleasure, except in the madness of courting, when it has a definite object. I could have gone on that way, in a kind of rapture, till the dreadful moment when the rapture turns to utter boredom; but I was saved while my spirit was still keen, for a bus came along and carried me to Drummore, on the long finger of land that ends in the Mull of Galloway.

There have been many times that the face of Scotland has surprised me; and never more than on my journey to the Mull. This finger of land has the Irish Channel on one side, Luce Bay on the other and points towards the Irish Sea. Therefore I had expected a bleak and windswept land, a barrier of rock and poor soil against the encroaching sea. But the reality was a little different. There were indeed plenty of rocks and the soil may have been poor enough; but generations of farmers and improvers had been at work: there were trees and gardens and fields of corn along the moors; and Drummore in autumn was the kind of village you might dream on.

The village stood, as I remember it, in a slight fold of the land that gave it a sheltered air. It had little more than two streets, one facing the water and the other at right angles to it. There were farms beyond the houses and I have no doubt that the dark red moors lay up towards the skyline. I found a night's lodging in a house on the waterfront, and, as I unpacked my things in a little attic room, I looked out on a scene that was traditional beyond belief. There was a stretch of land between the houses and the bay, a grassy place, where a few hens of the cross-bred sort chased flies upon the air and a string of white ducks came up from the water in a comic solemn procession, led by a handsome young drake with a virile curl in his tail. A short distance along there was a small harbour where a sailing boat was discharging coal. That was evidently something of an event, for at least a dozen men had gathered round and settled themselves comfortably on the wharf while a squad loaded the coal on to a lorry drawn by a sleepy mare. There may have been some lively conversation earlier in the afternoon, when the seafarers told the latest news from

Whitehaven, the latest scandals out of Cumberland; but the party had now settled down, some to an easy rhythm of labour, and some to an easier contemplation of that rhythm. Beyond them the water stretched out to the east, an empty plain without an island or ship or lighthouse, a flat sea reaching to a low green shore under a level unclouded sky; these three making a world so devoid of life or motion as to be less a world than a state of cosmic idleness.

Eyes could find nothing to rest on at first, then they were slowly drawn by the figures of the men unloading the barque, till those figures gave the landscape its peculiar significance. For I could guess that there had been years of promise in Drummore. Men had built the harbour for a trade that might have no bounds. The men who owned shops and land in the tiny village may have dreamed of a time when Drummore would grow as big as Stranraer, as big as Leith, as big as London; of a time when an acre of land would be worth £10,000, and the blue sky be gloriously obscured by the smoke of commerce. But that time never came. The little trade of the hopeful years had grown steadily less: the sky was still unobscured; and the men could unload the barque as if they had all eternity for their stevedoring. The figures of the horse, the men, and the gently swaying ship were reduced to infinite smallness under the tranquil sky that stretched across the empty sea, and, thus reduced, their lives seemed to have a charming simplicity, idyllic and serene. No doubt they were poor, but perhaps they were the less troubled by the delusions of Progress, that inflict their poverty on the greater world. Thus the scene had a slightly incredible air; as if I had found the original of a picture that I had always thought to be a painter's dream of an imagined world. And was it real? I hardly dare to say. The landscape seemed to be always rearranging itself into the conventional attitudes of popular art. As I went to bed that night, a round moon hung over the placid sea and the barque swung at her moorings, the one black cloud in all the silver world. When I looked from my window again, in the morning, the sea had retreated far beyond the horizon, leaving reach upon reach of dark sand, and the little barque lay on her side at the bottom of the harbour where the ducks gobbled for worms in the mud round her keel.   It was all incredible, that there should be one place so untouched by our peculiar madness that life was still lived by the old rhythm of the sun and the tides and the seasons, and that men should be able to sit by the water's edge, not through lack of work, but for contempt of it.

That night I visited the Mull.   It is difficult to say what attraction there could be in a head of rock sticking into the sea.   Perhaps it was the Scottish fondness for driving things to their logical conclusion that made me want to stand on the extreme point of Scotland.   I did go, under a windy sky, and I did stand upon the last bare cliff, and I did look out across the water hoping to see the Isle of Man in the gathering dark.   I even waited there in the cold, till the lighthouse began to wheel great rays of light across the evening.   Then I walked back to Drummore again with a sense of having accomplished something.   But I'm damned if I can give a name to my accomplishment.   Of course I can always say I've seen the Mull of Galloway, and I have in my mind a fading picture of a lighthouse set on a high rock over the waves, and I don't ever need to bother about the Mull of Galloway again.   By so much I suppose I am richer.   Perhaps some trick of memory will give the visit some startling significance after fifty years.   At least I hope so, about that and many other occasions, else how many hours of travel and sightseeing will have been wasted.

It is not wise to stay in a place where, for a little time, you have found the perfection of a mood, so I left Drummore and walked across to Port Logan.   So far the Irish- man's luck had gone with me, making ordinary things both strange and wonderful, but I felt I had gone beyond his spell at last when I came into Port Logan. I'm afraid that the shape of the village has gone out of my mind, leaving only a vague impression of scattered houses along the shores of a bay, where a little fishing boat with a brown sail tacked and veered in the light wind. Port Logan, like Drummore, must have had a future in some distant time; there may once have been commerce from Ireland in its harbour; but that was long ago and the village had settled down into that state of suspended animation where communities survive more by force of habit than by any conscious will. It certainly did not promise any diversion.

But the Irishman's luck still held.

' Is there anything to see in Port Logan ? ' I asked an old man sitting on a rock.

' Nothing but fish that come when you whistle on them,' he replied.

' Mermaids ? ' I asked in the way that trippers do.

' No. Honest respectable fish—across there.' He pointed to a house along the shore.

When I had knocked at the door, a dignified old lady said, ' Wait till I get my key.'

Then she led me into a rocky place with a quiet pool of water in the middle of it. It was mysterious green water, very still, where shadowy figures moved, as you might say, just beyond the range of vision.

' Call them up,' the old lady said.

But I did not know any words to charm the heart of a fish, so I just stared into the green water, like the village idiot at the village pond. There was a queer vacancy in my mind.

Then the old lady called them herself. She bent down, rippled her fingers through the water and said, ' Tommy, Tommy,' in a quiet musical way.

The fish came up from the depth of the pool, as cows over the pasture when the dairyman calls them. Twenty, thirty, forty of them rose up to the old lady's hand and rubbed their cold noses against her fingers and shouldered each other away from her caresses. I can't tell you what kind of fish they were; some were quite small and might have been sea trout; others were big as cod and saithe; but all of them would normally have been the wildest, the least approachable, of creatures. It was quite fantastic to see them thus domesticated; as if the old lady had been some one out of a fairy tale and they her charmed familiars. It was so fantastic as to be quite credible; and they took pieces of bread from her hands in a perfectly natural way. But when she invited me to stroke one old fish, the boldest of the company, I was a little disturbed by the strangeness of the idea; and when I did touch the cold body with a tentative finger, I drew away, repelled by the feeling of that cold inhuman life. The fish, however, was not so dainty, but poked up his greedy mouth, waiting to be fed. I gave him crumbs, marvelling at such intercourse between the creatures.

'I suppose it is generations of captivity that makes them so tame,' I said to the lady.

But 'No,' she replied. 'We don't keep them here very long. The fishermen catch them out there and bring them to me and they get tame quite soon.'

I'm not sure that tame is the word. Familiarity and kindness had bred a certain trust in them. But they were not tame in a way that a dog or a horse is tame. They rose to the surface, to the point where a man and a fish can meet, drawn by one thing common to all nature—desire of food —but even in the act of feeding they would be suddenly taken with one of these mass emotions common to so many creatures, and would dive back, as if in panic, to the safety of the deep water. Then, communally reassured, or communally in hunger, they would return to the surface and poke up their greedy mouths, out of their own world into the strange world of men.

' Oh yes,' the old lady said, ' it's queer how you can get fond of them.'

It was certainly queer. Man is not so far from the birds and the beasts, for they live in his own element; but the fish is a stranger, living in an alien element, and to hold some little commerce with a fish on the margin of the water was like making some contact with the unknown through a wicket gate at the edge of the human world. I left Port Logan very conscious of wonders everywhere about me. The Irishman's spirit ran like the wind before me over the sunny land.

So I came again into Stranraer when the waters of Loch Ryan were blue and still and the Irish boat lay off the pier. I could feel an invitation in the air, to sail out across that blue water into the afternoon, but there was no invitation to remain in Stranraer. It seemed a pleasant enough little town, as Scots towns go, but most of the pleasure came from the very beautiful situation, for the houses might have been built on a misty day, which alone could charitably account for the total disregard of natural beauty. No doubt I could have found entertainment in Stranraer: I'm sure it's a place where you can spend an amusing night with a ten-shilling note in your pocket; it has probably got a very individual civic life, for I discovered the uniforms of the local band housed in an ancient tower; but, like so many other Scots towns, it was only a convenience, a place to feed in and then be gone from, as soon as possible, to the blue loch and the harvest fields and the dark red moors. I ate and drank and went on my way through the autumn afternoon.

So many things happened to me in those last few days that when I remember them I feel as if they must have happened to some other man in a distant land.

I was making towards Glenluce, through one of those kindly plains between the sea and the hills. They had cut a good harvest there, and now that the wind had dried the

17

sheaves, carts were out in the fields for the leading home. Once again the Irishman's spell of unreality had fallen over the country-side. The harvest scene was too like the ideal we feel could never have happened just so.

There was, as I remember, a low plain stretching over to the Bay of Luce, without majesty, a humble plain sinking gently into a long expanse of earthy sand that passed imperceptibly under the level water. Earth, sand and sea were all a continuous low plain, without any feature of pride to affront the magnificent arch of the sky, and there was such a great distance between that plain and the sky that you'd have thought the infinite dwelt between them in a misty light. Sweet savours came up on the delicate airs —the sweet smell of salt water, and the sand flats, and the herbs along the shore with, partly sound and partly savour, the rustle of the dried ears of corn.

In the fields at either side of the road, cottar women were forking the sheaves on to the carts. Their bright print dresses and the red handkerchiefs tied round their heads, their free movements as they drove the forks into the sheaves and lifted them up with a sweeping gesture, were at the same time both primitive and disciplined, idyllically right for a harvest scene. Then out on the road I met the carts going to the stackyards with their loads, the horse stepping out with a kind of pleasure in its strength, the ploughman walking at its head, without pleasure or anything but habit, and now and then a broken head of corn that fell in the dust to be snapped by the angry birds. That was a pleasant convoy for a little way, then it turned into the stackyard where oldish men were building ricks with a skill made perfect in so many harvests. That easy labour continued all afternoon, the forking, the carting, the building, in the sweet air and the hot sun; with a grateful rest for a can of tea under the shade of a beech and a draw at the pipe to keep away the midges. It was almost too perfect, as if the best that poets and artists had ever imagined about the harvest had been gathered into that country-side. I have assisted with a harvest or two and I cannot remember an afternoon that was not flawed by some anxiety. But all the people I talked to along that road felt the same easy pleasure that I felt who had no concern in the harvest. It was too perfect; and once or twice I expected to hear the Irishman say, ' But I skipped it in the morning train,' and see the calm illusion blasted with reality. But the illusion remained till night came, and I walked under the stars by the water of Luce.

So many things happened that should not happen, except in a story.

I came to a handsome gate certainly leading to some great house. I thought it would be pleasant to go a little way into the grounds, so I opened the gate and went quietly in. Then an old lady came out of the lodge and asked me, very kindly, if I had a card of permission.

I confessed I had not.

Then she was sorry she could not allow me to pass.

But how could I get a card ? By going to the steward's house some distance away.

Would she show me how to get there ?

She did show me, with that wealth of geographical, historical and personal detail all Scots, except the upper classes, put at the service of a stranger.

But that was a considerable distance away, and couldn't she just make an exception——?

No. I might pick flowers, or make fires, or disturb the pheasants or carve my sweetheart's name on a tree.

I said no, because I hadn't a sweetheart.

Then that was a pity because a young man like me needed a girl to keep him in good humour.

And then I knew that no card of admission would be required.

Ten minutes later she allowed me to go a little way into the grounds, after which she blessed me and returned **to** the lodge shaking her head at the loneliness of my condition.

When I had gone through the wood to the edge of a cleared space, and had sat down there lest I should disturb the owner of the house, or his pheasants, about their lawful occasions, the afternoon took on a yet greater perfection. That gentleman's estate could have been painted on the air by some courtly master for Louis le Soleil. There was an old house set nicely among the trees with terraces dropping down to a green lawn. Then a lake began at the foot of the lawn and swept away into the woods, with islands so covered with trees that the branches seemed to float on the shining water. A little stream came out of the woods to the east of the house, twined through the green lawn and tumbled into the lake by a waterfall. All these were very charming, the perfection of good taste; and there was one thing more that knit the scene together, gave it the final touch of art and subtly coloured it with illusion. A bridge crossed the stream, midway through the lawn, an elegant bridge that leapt from lawn to lawn, like a young deer. Whichever way I looked my eyes came back to that dainty creature carved out of shapeless stone and my wonder increased at the beauty that could be raised out of heavy earth. I stayed there only a short time at the edge of the wood, for if I had remained a hundred years I could have seen no more than I saw in the first amazing glance. It was all as perfect, as unreal, as the scene on a willow pattern plate. There was nothing to do but look and come away, as you leave an argument when the last word had been spoken.

There may have been a word or two more to say. When I had gone a mile farther along the road, I overtook a small company that were part of the harvest scene, though they could find us no hospitable place in it. They were a man and wife and two small children, homeless tramps, among everything that was rich and domestic. The man would have been about fifty and looked as if he had always been accustomed to a labouring life. Though he took no great pleasure in the open road and the harvest day, he was ready to speak about anything and we kept in step together agreeably for a mile.

He was a casual labourer, and he had been accustomed for many years to work in town during the winter and turn to the land in summer. But there was no longer any work, either in town or country. That summer he and his family had sought work all over the north of Ireland without any success: they had come over on a coasting steamer the night before, and were making for the north of England.

A hard life, I said.

Not for himself, he replied, because he was tough, but the wife took ill with it and the children got tired.

He looked behind with a face from which habit had almost taken the pity.

I, who was not accustomed, could hardly bear to look for shame.

The woman had not been intended for the roads. She would have been gone forty, and showed all the signs of malnutrition—bad teeth, bad feet, a shambling walk. To these there was added the dreadful resignation seen on the faces of those who have resigned themselves to shameful poverty and homelessness because they have lost all strength and hope. She was not a woman but the figure of a woman in rags, shuffling wearily from one dykeside to another through the hot September day, indifferent even to the children she dragged beside her.

They, a boy and a girl, were horrible in their likeness to their mother, with broken mouths and rickety legs, in a woeful decrepitude at five years old. The boy who might have been five, and the girl who could not have been three, hung trailing at their mother's skirts and whined continuously, despairing misshapen creatures crying on a mother as tired of life as they. If she did not listen, it was no great wonder; for her husband told me what could easily be seen, that she was carrying another child. I asked him when and he replied in three months' time. It was hard on her, he added, for women like to be in their own houses at such a time, but he might be able to find some place for her in a casual ward if she were taken suddenly on the road.

It was a fascinating story, because, the Irishman's spell being on me, it was only a story. There was no anger in the man's voice, no pity, no whining; he spoke evenly and without personal feeling as if it had all happened long ago and in another country. So, when I wished to be going on, I gave him half a crown and wished him luck, and marched away in a generous glow. It was not till long afterwards when the Irishman's spell had worn off, and I was able to think of that little company as they really were, that the thought of the half-crown came back to me with an intolerable sense of meanness. If I ever get to Purgatory I expect the half-crown will be waiting for me there.

But no thought could trouble me on that afternoon when everything was arranged to give me pleasure.

As I walked towards Glenluce and began to feel a little wearied of the road, I was overtaken by a farmer in a high dog-cart drawn by a fat grey pony. Would I like a lift as far as Glenluce? he asked me. I accepted gladly, and so we drove on at a steady five miles an hour while the shadows grew long on the fields and the carts went home with their last full loads. Once more my fortune was almost too good to believe in. The farmer could have driven his cart and pony right into a story-book. Though he was not old he did not look as if he had ever been young. I could imagine him as a serious middle-aged baby who had not aged a single day in fifty years. He was big and broad; his face was brown and never smiled; but he had an inexhaustible curiosity. He asked me a hundred questions—whence I had come, whither I was going and why.

They were not frivolous questions and he did not treat my answers lightly. He considered everything I said with a gentle surprise, like a man amazed at the diversity of God's creatures, yet not angry that they differed from himself. There would, I imagine, have been no end to his questions, if I had not questioned him in turn. He was as pleased to answer as to ask. He told me, in some detail, the story of his harvest, his views about the Milk Pool and his theories on making cheese. He also gave me short, slightly malicious sketches of his neighbours. It was all done in the easiest possible way, and when he could not find a word, he looked over the harvest fields, as if his inspiration dwelt there. At no time did he raise his rather husky voice above the tone of easy conversation, except when he swore at the pony which had the trick of dropping insensibly from its five miles an hour to a walking slumber. I drove with him for maybe half an hour, eight years ago, and I have never seen him again, yet when some one speaks of the ideal farmer I remember him, that big sunburned man, with the old check bonnet and the briar pipe, leaning a little forward on the high seat of the dog-cart to look round and down at me, with a look of quiet wonder he must have learned from his own cows. I have known a lot of farmers in my time, and most of them were quite unlike the ideal, being troubled with ambitions, colics and fierce irrational angers. The man from Galloway had neither ambition nor anger, only the peace that comes from health and a quiet mind. When I got down at his roadside I watched him drive away across the plain under the falling sun and I believed for quite ten minutes that there might have been a golden age, perhaps no earlier than that afternoon.

I could not swear an oath about the nature of Glenluce, for I was not in my ordinary cautious mind that night. All I can say is that I remember it as the perfect end to my journey. There was a stone bridge to cross over a dark stream, then a village street with two inns about the middle of it. I chose the more modest inn, received a kinder welcome than I had expected, and ate a good supper daringly compounded of trout and cold ham.

It was just under nightfall when I went out again, and walked by the fields and woods now cool with the dew, to the ruined abbey on the banks of the Luce. It was then the humblest of ruins, much fallen from its original estate and so overgrown that it seemed to be on the point of sinking back under the ground.

It moved me profoundly, not for itself, because stones have no use for pity, but with a personal sadness that the things we value so dearly may be so little valued after we are dead. One part of the abbey, on which there was still a roof, had been used as a cattle shed: the house that had once been so beautiful was now a draughty shell with a few sticks nailed across the door. Much pride, much care and craftsmanship, some holiness had gone to the making, and the builders may have thought they were building for all eternity. But cattle now stood in their places, and in time there would only be a few mounds of grass as their memorial. That time is not yet, for the remains of the abbey have been preserved; but I could not foresee the preservation and I went back to Glenluce in the dusk, enjoying a pleasant melancholy that soon passed into sleep.

CHAPTER TWENTY-THREE : OVER THE MOORS

THE next day was just about the worst I have ever lived through. The morning was dull when I set out in a bus for Whithorn, and rain grew steadily heavier until Whithorn seemed to be deep under the waves. So I had better not tell you what happened there in case I put you against it. Whithorn is a very historical place, I am told, and I certainly went in a gale to look at the chapel nearby the site of the tiny cell in which they say St. Ninian dwelt.

This saint was one of the earliest missionaries in Scotland, an almost legendary figure, about whom there are the usual quarrels among historians.

These are of little account, but it might be interesting to start from Ninian and trace the dissensions in the Scottish Churches. Any one who comes new to Scotland must be puzzled by our religions, or the many sects of one religion. These are due to the Scottish weakness for what might be called logic. The English seldom draw out any argument to its logical conclusion and therefore they find it easier to compromise. The Scots love to get down to the first principles and defend them to the last of bitter eloquence. Perhaps that difference is a reason why the English and the Scots should work in partnership. For instance the Scots have been wonderful Empire Builders by reason of their tenacity and method, but it is the English contempt for principles and genius for compromise that has kept the Empire together. If the Empire had been a wholly Scottish State the constitutions of both Scotland and the Colonies would have been so inflexibly fixed on what seemed to be first principles that there would have been continual wars of independence. It is only the Englishman's lovely confusion of mind that has kept the Empire together.

And it is the Scotsman's inveterate lust for principles that has given us such a heritage of Churches. These are not only the results of schism but sometimes the fruit of union, for if some minorities set up establishments of their own after a schism, there have been other minorities that refused to participate in the Unions. Some of the smaller sects are old, some are recent, but they have one thing in common—they were founded on some principle though that principle may be almost forgotten. These are the truly Scottish Churches. The other small sects are, in some way common to all nations, caused by a sudden upsurge of evangelism or a peculiar revelation of the Light. They have a vivid life until the Light grows dim, then they as suddenly pass away. The native institutions, founded on principle, remain.

I cannot really help you through the maze. The major bodies are Presbyterian and Catholic, the Church of Scotland and the Church of Rome. The Church of Scotland, the Official Church, has survived since the Reformation, with many vicissitudes. There were schisms, especially in 1843, over the evil system of patronage. As a result of those schisms there were, among others, the United Presbyterian Church and the Free Church. These united at the beginning of the present century into the United Free Church, but a minority of the Free Church stayed out of the Union, making the present Free Church of Scotland. A few years ago the Church of Scotland and the United Free Church united, and this time a minority of the United Free Church formed the United Free Church (Continuing). There are others. Then the Episcopal Church in Scotland, a small and very select body, continues the Episcopalian form of religion, and

Hills and Towns of the Border

C.W.B.

claims a considerable age and authority. Though it resembles the Church of England it is a completely independent body with traditions of its own, and its members are insulted by any suggestion that it is a branch of the English Church.

I had better not say anything about the place of religion in Scottish life. It is not a matter that concerns me at all, and besides, there is not, as far as I can see, much difference in this respect between one country and another. I prefer to meditate over the cell of Ninian, wondering what the Saint would have thought if he had known what a crop of dissension was to grow out of the seed he had cast upon Scotland, and whether, if he had had a true prophetic vision, he might not have left the Scots to their native superstitions. Ninian had not the prophetic vision, only faith; but faith alone, one fears, is not enough, when it could not prevent a vast aggregation of material things that nobody wants very much in a world bankrupt of delight and at last empty even of faith itself. I'm not sure which was more melancholy—Luce Abbey crumbling back into the earth or the Whithorn cell preserved by the Office of Works for people that value the stone and lime because they have lost the spirit. Almost I could have wished that every sanctuary of all the old religions had been allowed to perish out of sight and out of mind, for what can we do now for our salvation but go back, far beyond the saints and start all over again?

I rode to Newton Stewart in a country bus, through the wind and the rain. If I had been able to see the countryside I am sure I would have liked it, and a warm sun would disclose familiar pastoral beauty. All this south-west is dairy country, supplying industrial Scotland with milk and retaining in an occasional farm-house the art of making cheese. Newton Stewart is the sort of small town you would expect as the centre of such a district. It is

Afternoon in the South–West

typically Scots, grey, a little cold on a wet afternoon, almost charming on a fine one. It has the usual hotels and banks, and a weaving mill where visitors may buy tweeds and whatnot designed with a true regard for beauty. It was in this small town that I met something that has endured a long time in the Scottish character.

While taking a walk along the street after my supper, I met a man that I had known casually for some years. We stopped to speak, more from curiosity than friendship, as one does on such occasions. After we had made an exchange of ' I am fine, and how are you ? ' he told me he was living in the town.

' Then you can give me the lowdown on it,' I said.

' It's pretty good,' he replied. Then he came nearer, dropped his voice an octave, and gave me the benefit of his experiences, as man to man.

There were, he said, at least four young ladies of the companionable sort in the town, and if I wished for society no formal introduction would be required.

I, knowing something of small Scottish towns, must have been just a little sceptical, so he led proof, in the terms that easy lovers use, his hands and his eyes and his husky voice all pleading belief.

This subject of universal interest drew us close together, and warmed us against the cold grey smirr coming off the moors, and we felt ourselves to be very devils for the space of maybe ten minutes. Then my acquaintance said, ' I must be going,' gave me an expressive wink, and made to depart, leaving me to wonder at and envy his success with women. My envy and wonder were so great that I called him back. ' Tell me,' I said, ' how long have you been here ? '

Before he had time to think he said, ' I came this morning.'

We parted ; he, straight home to his own cold bed and I to mine, as young men go.

The Scots have most fertile imaginations.

The next day was one of the happiest I can remember. The rain had passed off in the night, leaving a white mist that grew always more luminous till it dissolved before the sun. I intended to sleep in Kirkcudbright that evening, so I took a train to Gatehouse of Fleet Station. That part of the journey was pure magic. When the train passed over viaducts and high embankments the luminous mist so enclosed us that we might have been flying through clouds of milky light. Now and again the mist parted and we could see the dairy cows in pasture or the bright gleam of the sun on Wigton Bay. Then the train climbed up on to the moors, where the sun and wind scattered the mist, and the wine-red country lay clear about us, with only a few white ghosts retreating towards the summits. I stepped out into a world that might have been born that very hour, and looked about for Gatehouse of Fleet.

A stranger might have thought that the world was so new that the builder had not had time to make a village, but I had some experience of rural amenities and I was not altogether surprised to find a station serving only an empty moor, through which a narrow white road wound along into the south.

When the station-master took my ticket I asked him how far to Gatehouse.

He looked, as all sane men did, pityingly at my knapsack, and replied, ' Some say five miles and some say six, but (waving his hand at the weary-looking road) it's a damned long way whatever ye call it.'

Probably; and yet I can't remember any tale of miles that seemed so few. The air was so clear after the rain that every hill had an immediate quality; it was no longer a vague mass on the horizon but something alive with a thousand features of line and contour, light and shadow, like expression on a human face. Then, between those gallant hills, the moor rolled down to Gatehouse in a rich variety of colour as the slopes lay against or towards the

sun. Lively winds blew every way still fresh from the
drench of rain. I wandered on, singing a little, telling
myself stories and thinking of beer at half-past seven. I
did not think of food, for great ripe brambles hung, shining
black and luscious, by the side of the road. I gathered
them as I went along, squashing them into my mouth
until my hands and face were dyed black with their juice.
I would have spent two—three hours on that road in a
very rare enjoyment of freedom. I seemed to have got away
from the duller habits of an aspiring existence into a life
of immediate sensation. I was not, as we must be, one
man playing a definite part, which is the discipline of
society, but all sorts of men, according to the impulse of
the moment—now the adventurer alone on the dangerous
moors; now the lover sighing for his lady by a green
waterfall; now a greedy boy surfeiting on brambles; the
poet, the artist, the practical man, with an eye to water-
power, till you might have said a hundred men had been
born along that road, each for an instant's sake, and had
died, leaving a hundred ghosts of pleasure in my mind.
And sometimes I was just a body that walked to an easy
rhythm, careless of fatigue.

I could not stay in Gatehouse in case I might break the
rhythm of the day, but I have such a memory of that
adorable village on the Fleet that I would like to go back
there and discover its quiet secrets. These might be other
than you would expect, for Gatehouse has been frequented
by writers and artists. Though it looked open and fair
enough in the autumn sun I felt it had a mystery, set there
by a dark river among the hills.

I passed on to the moors again. Now the afternoon
became very warm, for the winds had failed and I began
to desire the ease of cool water. When I came to a burn
running down out of the moor through the corn-fields it
had such a promise of delight under its shady banks that
I found a private place and bathed there. It was not deep,

but deep enough that I could sit in a pool with the ripples breaking at my cheek, and its brown peat water had an ampleness that somehow comforted me. I sat there for a long time while the sun came down through a wild rose in flowers of light upon the water. Or again, I allowed myself to float upon the current of the stream. Then I swear that my body—even mine—was like a god's in a legend, beautiful, so dark golden brown in the peaty water, half unseen. It was the moment of completest magic: the most deceiving moment of all that amazing time.

Drenched by the sun, cooled by the water, enchanted by the wind, I held on south between the harvest fields. It was four o'clock as I passed through Borgue and children came running out of school, like joy released from darkness. I have never walked as I walked that afternoon, feeling my life so light a burden, nor I think, have I ever been so near to absolute contentment. I had everything I wished for, the sight and smell of the harvest fields, that always move me; odd tunes and scraps of poetry that came into my head; memories of the smugglers that used to make their landfalls in Galloway coves; and, for contrast, stray recollections of misadventures that had befallen my friends going after women in the heat of their youth.

So I came to a long arm of the sea and walked by it, between the beech trees and the water, until I found Kirkcudbright, a grey old town, so coral red, lapped upon by the waves of sunset. As I first saw the town it appeared to me utterly beautiful: a place where one might live nicely poised between drunk and sober all the days of an harmonious life, thus attaining to the great wisdom in which one makes one's soul and prepares without remorse to die. Looking at Kirkcudbright among the trees across the still water I thought I had found the perfect unflawed beauty. I stood there for a little time, maybe half a minute, wrapt in wonder, then, as one does, I longed for cold salmon and a bottle of wine. It was the measure of Kirkcud-

bright's perfection that it gave me both. The salmon is
a tasteless fish, unless it has been canned, but that salmon
had, as the fish can have in its diviner moments, a subtle
flavour, a reminiscence of all richness. As for the wine—
I am not learned in these matters, so I can't tell its name
or the year of its birth, nor can I make an elegant phrase
about its soul. But this I can say—when I had eaten that
fish and drunk that wine, I made a promenade through
the town and found it yet more beautiful, though the sun
had gone down and all the colours, except grey and darkness, were lost to the earth.

Next morning I went on, again through a misty light,
towards Castle Douglas, by the coast. At Dundrennan
I stepped aside to see the ruined abbey, and walked, for
a little time, piously above the graves of lords and abbots.
Not alone, for an old man from the village walked along
with me and we talked agreeably about them that lay
beneath us. There never yet was a true Scot that did not
like a corpse, or find some rare melancholy pleasure in
attending the burial of a friend. The Scots have a curious
independent attitude to death. They make jokes about it:
indeed, nothing delights a Scottish audience more than a
crack of wit about a funeral (unless it is some nasty piece
about the Church). I don't know why it should be so,
unless the Scots, more than all others, realize the awful
majesty of death. So there we were, the old man and I,
speculating about the lives of them that lay under the turf.
They were dead, and the worms had had their fill of them
and we who were still to die might have feared the thing
that was to come to us. But for me, and perhaps for the
old man, the bones beneath us made our own life more
pleasurable; just as an old friend at another's funeral says,
' Puir Jamie's dead and here am I still living.' We stepped
gently over the turf, as if the dead bell were still ringing
in the trees. ' Aye, they were warm men in their time,'
the old man said; and I thought to myself, what may

18

happen to me before this day's done, for I am still alive ?

That night I lay in Castle Douglas, at a good inn, where the locals drank beer and whisky time about and argued against the Pope. I went to the pictures for half an hour and listened to American voices mechanically distorted, talking about love in an apartment house, had my hand most emotionally pressed, but only for too short a moment, by a young woman who mistook me for her neighbour on the other side, and then I returned to the inn where the locals were still denouncing the Scarlet Woman that sits upon the Seven Hills. I went, or was assisted, to bed about the time when, God having saved the King, the youth of Castle Douglas went home, uttering a thoroughly Scottish passion in the accents of the Middle West. Some speak of Alexander, I said to myself, and some of Tennessee. Then, praise God, I fell asleep. It was perhaps not inappropriate that my three enchanted days ended on such a note.

CHAPTER TWENTY-FOUR : FAREWELL ON THE BORDER

WHAT more can I say in praise of Scotland ?

The road goes straight before you from Castle Douglas through Dumfries to the Border and Carlisle. It is fine country all that way, pasture land, bearing grand herds of dairy cows. If you have time you should go up to new Galloway and St. John's Town of Dalry, among the hills and the great moors. There, in the most primitive and desolate places you may come on the dams and the power-houses that are the most modern part of Scotland. So to Dumfries. That is a town I have never learned to love, but it has a very ancient history and memories of Robert Burns, and who am I to say what you may not find there ?

But if you go a little way out of the town you will discover Sweetheart Abbey, one of the loveliest of ruins. It is a quiet place set among the trees, with a few houses at its gate. As you pass through the village you will per-haps see an old man or an old woman sitting at the door in the sun, or a few children playing in the dusty road. You may enter the grounds of the abbey and walk, in all humility of spirit, through the ruined aisles. Then, if peace descend on you, will you, for friendship's sake, bide there, thinking about the things you have seen in Scotland ? There, in one of our oldest and loveliest places, think kindly of all the things you have seen that are neither old nor beautiful. We have made too many mistakes in the last three hundred years : we have made deserts and called them progress : we have been proud, contentious, greedy and stupid : we have behaved like every other people. These are not matters for blame or excuse. We who live in Scotland and have quite an irrational love for some small part of it, hope you have seen us with the eyes of men and women that have, in your own country, some small beauty that you love; then you will have known how to separate the evils that are common to all the world from the few humours that are peculiar to ourselves. And, perhaps, as you go from Sweetheart towards your own place, you may take away some memories of pleasure and good-will for the strange people that live on our side of the Tweed.

But I, that have been so disrespectful about ancient monuments, can't say good-bye to you in a ruin. Besides, there remains one part of Scotland that may serve as a microcosm of the rest. I mean the Border, and I would have you go out of Scotland that way, so that you may take with you a fine picture of this land. For you will find in the Border the closest synthesis of the manufacturing and farming between which the life of Scotland is divided: and you will find the two of them side by side in a very beautiful country where legends of the olden time grow like wild flowers under every hedge.

There is the usual choice of roads to Galashiels, but I would go by Moffat. This road runs from Dumfries to Lockerbie across the dairy farms, then up to Moffat, a delightful small town among the hills. It then goes easterly, along the side of Moffat Water. Half-way up the valley you will find the Grey Mare's Tail on the left-hand side. This is a fantastic waterfall, that comes sheer down out of the hills, so straight and so delicately that you might think it the tail of a mare ridden by some god in the pagan times. If you climb by the side of the waterfall to the high land above you will come on such a desolation as strong men have feared in winter-time when heavy clouds came out of the east. Even in summer that wild place can make you feel powers that are utterly indifferent if not hostile, to life, that prise you away from the securities with which we surround our lives, and make you afraid, because you have come, alone and helpless, into an old and terrifying world.

When the road has crossed the summit you will find the Loch o' the Lowes lying between the hills like a drop of water in a crinkled leaf. Beyond it there is St. Mary's Loch, and, on a narrow space between them, Tibbie Shiels Inn offers refreshment for man and beast. It also offers memories, for a naïve statue of James Hogg, the shepherd and poet, some distance away, looks over towards the place where he enjoyed many convivial nights with Scott and other intellectual drinkers. Away beyond the Loch o' the Lowes you will come into Yarrow, and so, running between the hills, with a small river at your hand, you will come to Selkirk and Galashiels. Then you should look at the peel tower in Darnick on your way to Melrose, carry on down the majestic Tweed to Kelso, turn back from Kelso to Jedburgh, then take the south road by Ferniehirst Castle over Carter Bar and into England again.

Let me try to sum up the qualities of this Border Country.

It is a very beautiful land. As you turn towards Beattock and Moffat you reach the sheep country where round green hills rise steep out of the valleys and go rolling away towards every horizon, like a green sea frozen in the act of gentle motion. These green hills are divided into sheep farms that are themselves divided into hirsels, and a great value of mutton and wool goes off them every year into the Lowlands.

They are lonely hills given over to solitude, with here and there a quiet farm-house, and some miles beyond it a shepherd's cottage and farther away a square ruined tower at the end of the world. Then as you go down Yarrow you reach more sheltered country. There are fine trees at the road-side with a stream beyond them, tumbling over the rocks. Then the lovely Tweed and mansion houses —Abbotsford and Philiphaugh—and the great ruined abbeys. The Tweed valley from Galashiels to Kelso is a delicious place in the height of summer. Its slopes are high banks of foliage: the cottages are knee-deep in flowers, and you can taste fruitfulness upon the air.

There are beautiful meadows along that river and shady brakes where you can sleep all day in the peaceful shade. You can bathe in the river, as I once bathed on a hot Sunday in July. The road to Kelso was very long and very dusty: I was very hot and very dry. The Tweed beneath Dryburgh sang like joy's fulfilment. I left my clothes in a brake at the edge of a meadow, and lay down in the cool water. I have not the words to say what peace I felt as I lay there, conscious only of the river, and the warm sun, and the birds and the cows that came down to look at me with kind inquisitive eyes. Nor equally have I the words to express my horror when, coming out of the water, I found that one of the cows was eating the left leg of my only trousers, while my small change dribbled into the long grass.

The river, the trees, the esuriant cows are not peculiar to the Tweed, but the valley hereabouts does have its proper magic, for the Eildon Hills stand above it, a trinity marking the gates of fairyland. These hills are, according to legend, enchanted. Michael Scott, the wizard, cleft the hills into their three blue peaks, and since then they have about them the air of another world. That is not a literary fancy. The Eildons stand up so blue under the summer sky, and such curious shadows lie on them at evening, that they have a beauty struck with wonder. If there had been no fairies in the world, then even the Romans, if they had camped by those hills for a twelve-month, would have invented a little people to live in their shadows. I think that a man who looked at them for a day would go to bed speaking in a ballad metre; and a man who looked at them all night under the stars would come back singing, if he came back at all.

It was on their slopes something happened to me that has never happened again, and maybe could not happen in another place. I was lying under a broom bush away from the sun, and thinking upon Thomas the Rhymer who was stolen away into Fairyland, when a sweet noise came from the wood behind me. At first it seemed nothing more than the wind. Then it grew upon the air familiar and sweeter with a human sound. I turned to look. There a band of girls came through the wood, their print frocks dappled with the light falling through the leaves; and as they swung their bare brown arms in unison, they sang ' En passant par la Lorraine ', in their clear childish voices. I held my breath, astounded, uncertain if they were mortal girls, or the creatures of Fairyland come to lead me away down under the Eildon Hills. It could not have happened in any other place.

There is magic by the Eildons, and magnificence by the gates of Kelso, where the Tweed and the Teviot meet. I have seen few things more beautiful under sunset than the swans upon the quiet water above Kelso Bridge, with Floors Castle filling the middle distance, and, at the right hand, the thousand candles on the chestnut tree that stands like an altar before the abbey door. That is more than picturesque; seen at the moment of complete beauty it is an experience that can never be forgotten. Beyond Kelso you will find the summing up of the Scottish country-side —the rich fields along the river banks: the hard scarps of the rising ground; and then the hills, mile after mile of windbent grasses, till you stand on the border at Carter Bar, looking down upon England in the summer mist. This Border country has many kinds of beauty living together, from the domestic through the faëry to the sublime. It is, in a way, the epitome of Scotland.

It is very beautiful, and it is also very romantic. If you

were fanciful you might think its woods in autumn were dyed with all the blood shed in the Border wars. English and Scots fought in these dales for centuries, sometimes in pitched battle, sometimes in swift maurading forays. Like all debateable land, it encouraged the independent leaders that owned neither one king nor another, but plundered in the shadows between them. And since great families have undying hatreds many blood feuds disturbed the peace of the dales. These events have left a great body of tradition in songs and tales and customs. Some of the finest ballads were taken down from the lips of old men and women in the dales; there is hardly a mile of ground that does not have its own fantastic story, handed from generation to generation; and the towns still have there Common Ridings in memory of the wars with England. I have sat on a dry-stone dyke in Yarrow and listened for hours to a young man telling over, as if they had been something that happened thirty years ago, stories that were the very stuff of the ballads. The romantical part of the Borders is not dead. It is a part of Border life. The great ruined abbeys at Melrose, Jedburgh, Dryburgh and Kelso; the square peel towers deserted on the moors; the memories of battles and killings; and the songs that ordinary men have made about these things, retain a moving power, and still influence the lives of those who have inherited them. So again the Borders are an epitome of Scotland; for in Scotland we are much concerned with the past. But, while our interest in the past is usually an excuse for doing nothing about the future, in the Borders it is still something of a live tradition; not an escape but an inspiring force.

Besides a very lovely country and a live tradition, there are some towns in the Borders; and these are the most exciting part, for they make just the sounder balance between urban and rural life that is so necessary to-day.

Galashiels, Selkirk, Hawick and Jedburgh are manu-facturing towns. Galashiels and Selkirk along with

Earlston, Langholm and Walkerburn make the fine cloth called tweed; Hawick specializes in knitted garments; and Jedburgh has an artificial silk factory employing over a thousand hands. With the exception of the artificial silk their industries are long established and still prosperous. They grew up naturally out of the resources of the country-side—the wool off the hills and the water-power off the rivers; and they have still survived though they no longer depend exclusively on the local wool or power. They have had their vicissitudes. Great fortunes were made before the War, and a great deal of money has been lost since, but there is still plenty of enterprise in the Border towns, and there is no immediate danger that the Scottish woollen industry will go the way of cotton—to the north of England.

There are difficulties, of course. The Border manu-facturers have lost many of the foreign markets in which they used to make very desirable profits, but they lost these markets because of tariffs, and when the tariffs are lowered they may recover the markets again. Then the Borders stand by quality, and there is a danger that the appreciation of quality will become a lost art. These are just the accidents of this foolish world.

The really significant thing is that the Border towns are the chief centres of a very important industry and yet are pleasant towns to live in. They are hardly beautiful, though they have their charming moments; they are still some way from having all the amenities of a civilized existence; they may even have an occasional house that falls below the best standard of public health—they are ordinary enough small towns. But they have an intensely individual life, and the industries to support it; they are big enough to provide some variety of experience but not so big that the individual is lost; and though industrialized they fit into the country-side without destroying it. There-fore I, at least, find them exciting, not because they are perfect, but as showing how efficient industries can be spread about the country, without losing their efficiency or spoiling their surroundings. Life in properly organized towns (which we have not, yet) will always be preferable to country life, but there is a size beyond which a town will begin to lose its amenities. That best size will have to be discovered. It may be a population of 20,000 or 50,000 or 100,000. Less than 20,000 might be too small, because you need a fair number to give you freedom from your neighbours; more than 100,000 would certainly be too large. The ideal may be somewhere between these extremes; and the Border towns show that the idea is possible. None of them have a population of 20,000, Hawick having 17,000; Galashiels, 13,000; and Peebles and Selkirk just under 6,000. They are not perfect; but they do show the way. They have an industry producing goods of a very high standard: they have a tradition of fine workmanship: they have a Technical College (at Galashiels) for the development of their art: and they retain close contact with the country round about them. Each of them is a market town: the farm people are an essential part of their economy; and town and country meet in their streets, and in their social occasions. People who care about the future of Britain are anxious to plan that future. Perhaps these towns that have grown up naturally, developed slowly, and maintained their place in the world, may suggest a plan for saner Britain.

The Border people are a good race. They are grand farmers. Kelso Ram Sales are a high occasion in the agricultural year, when £500 may be paid for a single sheep. They also breed a good class of horses and cattle. The shepherds are—as always—splendid men; and it may be the responsibility of their job that makes them superior to the ploughmen, who, I am told, are very much under the thumbs of their women—at least on the Borders. As for the spinners and weavers they seem to retain something of the old Border spirit. They play Rugby in a way that still shows the primitive ardours of the game. Rugby, of course, has become rather polite in recent times, debased by the Englishman's idea of everything being cricket, so that its natural brutalities have been restricted to a little sly hacking and punching. I'm told they used to play a heartier game along the Borders, the motto being ' Get your man down and make sure he can't get up again.' The Border teams still produce a hearty type of forward, valuable for stiffening the Scottish teams. If ever an artist wishes a model of the old Borderers leading a fray against the Percys of Northumberland he should watch Jock Beattie with the Scottish forwards round him at Twickenham or Murrayfield. It is a glimpse of the more furious pleasures of an older world.

When you have passed Ferniehirst, that grand Border castle, and have won to Carter Bar, you will take farewell of the Borders and of Scotland. Then, if I have pleasured you, will you pleasure me by taking away this last impression of Scotland—the windy hills, the sheltered valleys, the small towns, the good craftsmanship and the living traditions out of which the future must grow ? We have made our mistakes and we have great problems. We have Glasgow, and the ruined industrial counties—Lanarkshire and West Fife. But, though these are so very urgent, they are temporary ; and I have deliberately given them less than their place, because I doubt if they are essential to Scotland. It may be that Scotland has reached a crisis, that ruin or prosperity depend on our actions now. Therefore I have tried to write about those qualities and resources that may bring prosperity—the essential Scottish qualities. They are, I think, a capacity to work hard, a tradition of high farming and fine workmanship, and, in spite of all our sophistications and respectabilities, a passion for life. When you think of Scotland, you will remember Glasgow and the empty Highlands ; but please remember also the Lothians, and the Carse of Stirling, and Angus, and the small farms of Aberdeenshire, and the road to Glenluce, and the little towns of the Borders in their pleasant valleys. If we have disappointed you, remember our misfortunes— the long struggle with England, the selfishness of the great nobles, the century wasted on religious fury, the disaster of wealth that came suddenly and uncontrolled. You will see the effect of those misfortunes—but it is more important to notice what has flourished in spite of them. And, as you go into England, I'd ask you one last thing—to remember us not as Scots, as aliens belonging to a comic race, but as children of those fields and valleys and towns, who must decide now on a future of unimaginable glory—or disaster.

Printed in Great Britain by
Butler & Tanner Ltd.,
Frome and London